# Inter-Act:
## Using Interpersonal
## Communication Skills

Kathleen S. Verderber
Rudolph F. Verderber
*University of Cincinnati*

*Wadsworth Publishing Company, Inc., Belmont, California*

*To Allison*

Communication Editor: Rebecca Hayden
Designer: Dare Porter
Copy Editor: Ellen Seacat
Illustrator: Dean Vietor

Printed in the United States of America
1 2 3 4 5 6 7 8 9 10—81 80 79 78 77

**Library of Congress Cataloging in Publication Data**

Verderber, Kathleen S    Date
    Inter-act: using interpersonal communication skills.

    Includes bibliographies and index.
    1.  Interpersonal communication.   I. Verderber, Rudolph F., joint author.   II.   Title.
BF637.C45V47      158'.2      76-40280
ISBN 0-534-00507-1

**Preface**

Countless hours of your life will be spent interacting with others, a process involving face-to-face transactions and sharing equally in the roles of sender and receiver. Some of this interaction will be to develop relationships with other persons—a great deal of it will be for making your way in life: giving and receiving information and trying to exert influence on your own actions, the actions of others, and on your environment. Regardless of what your goals in life may be or what roles in society you will take, your skill in communication will be an important aspect of your life as well as an important determinant in how effective you will be. Gaining confidence in the use of communication skills that you may need is what this book is all about.

Our principal goal is to help you achieve what Bochner and Kelly have defined as "interpersonal competence," the ability "to interact effectively with other people."[1] As you might expect, there is less than universal agreement on how to achieve that goal. One type of textbook in the field proceeds from the assumption that a student can best learn to practice appropriate skills by understanding the basic theory of interpersonal communication. A recent study by Tortoriello and Phelps suggests that the assumption of such books (that first a person understands theory, then he internalizes the theory, and finally he

---

[1] Arthur P. Bochner and Clifford W. Kelly, "Interpersonal Competence: Rationale, Philosophy, and Implementation of a Conceptual Framework," *Speech Teacher*, Vol. 23 (November 1974), p. 288.

applies the theory to behavior) may be faulty.[2] Our experience with books of this kind supports the notion that knowing theory does not necessarily lead to application.

A second type of book proceeds from the assumption that interpersonal communication is a way of life and that by presenting the writings of humanistic psychologists and philosophers and by stimulating you with the value of an "interpersonal" quality, you will be motivated to change your personality. Out of such a change in personality, the authors assume, knowledge and ability to apply skills will naturally follow. Although we do not doubt the potential for personality change in any individual, we doubt the ability of teachers of basic communication courses to cope with the kind of growth-group atmosphere these books call for. Moreover, we believe the place for personality change is in a clinical psychology program and not in a basic communication course.

We believe the book for a basic interpersonal communication course should provide a discussion of communication skills. The book should include enough theory to support the skills and, further, should offer some opportunity for experiential learning. We believe a textbook works best when the major emphasis is on presentation and practice of skills. This textbook has been written to meet these criteria.

Does the mastery of communication skills guarantee effective interpersonal communication? Not necessarily—no more than mastery of typing skills, filing skills, and shorthand skills guarantees that a person will be a good secretary. Other variables may intervene. Nevertheless, just as without the mastery of clerical skills a person *cannot* function well as a secretary, *without mastery of certain interpersonal skills a person cannot expect to communicate effectively.*

*Inter-Act* is organized to facilitate the learning and application of skills. Part A defines basic terms of interpersonal communication and explores the important concept of perception—a concept that affects the total interpersonal communication process.

Part B presents basic interpersonal skills in a four-chapter unit. In the presentation of each skill, we define the skill, show its importance, consider procedures for implementation, and guide practice. At first, you may be self-conscious about trying some of the skills that seem foreign to you; but if you practice seriously, you will soon see how these skills can make a difference in your communication. When you come to a skill that you think you already have mastered, do not skip over it. You may be surprised to discover that even a skill that "seems like common sense" and that "everyone can do" is not really so easy to do well or consistently.

In Part C we apply skills you have learned to coping with common communication problems that result from various barriers to free and effective flow of communication.

---

[2]Thomas R. Tortoriello and Lynn A. Phelps, "Can Students Apply Interpersonal Theory?" *Today's Speech,* Vol. 23 (Fall 1975), p. 48.

In the final unit, Part D, we look at specific communication settings and discuss the variables that are important to interpersonal success within each setting. One chapter discusses the interview. Since decisions that may well affect your entire life can occur during an interview, you should learn to apply interpersonal skills to that setting. In another chapter we discuss group communication. Since so many important decisions come from groups, committees, and "blue ribbon" panels, you need to learn to apply interpersonal skills to this setting as well. The final chapter of this book applies communication skills to the most important goal of developing and maintaining good interpersonal relationships.

Perhaps one of the features that you will most appreciate in this book is the Appendix. The Appendix consists of a glossary of the interpersonal skills and the most common communication problems. In an easy-to-use, quick-review form, we have included the skill, its importance, the procedure for putting it into practice, an example of its use, and the pages in the text where the skill is discussed in detail; for the problems, we have included each problem, its potential harm, the kinds of skills that are most likely to reduce or to alleviate it, and the pages where each problem is discussed.

In the text, we have attempted to provide both a means of practicing the skills and an opportunity for experiential learning of the skills. These goals are accomplished in the Communication Sessions that follow major sections of each chapter. The Sessions are positioned within rather than at the end of each chapter to encourage you to work with each concept or skill *at the time you encounter it*. Each Session has two or three kinds of activities: Reflections, Actualizations, and Discussions. *Reflections* are primarily to stimulate thought. Although you may not want to write down your thoughts, our goal in writing them is to get you to weigh and consider your own experience. The *actualizations* provide you with an opportunity to put into practice what you have learned. In some instances, the actualization calls for pencil and paper practice that you can do on your own; in other instances, the actualizations call for you to practice orally. The *discussions* provide you with an opportunity to share your thoughts, ideas, and feelings with other members of the class. Most of the discussions are intended for small groups of from three to six persons. Although it is unlikely that you would have the time to complete every Session, if you are intent upon learning the skills and concepts presented, you will find it essential to put in a reasonable amount of practice time. For your convenience, at the end of each chapter we have included a list of Payoffs—summary statements of what you should have learned and what you should now be able to do as a result of reading and working with the Sessions in the chapter. We have also included a short list of additional readings at the end of each chapter.

We hope that as a result of working with this textbook you find that we have met our goal in helping you learn the kinds of skills that will help you function more effectively in your day-to-day interactions.

We give our thanks to the following professors who read the manuscript at one or more stages and offered encouragement and helpful criticism: Thomas L. Attaway, North Carolina State University; Brenda H. Burchett, Northern Virginia Community College; Rex M. Fuller, Madison College; Ruth L. Goldfarb, Nassau Community College; Jo-Ann C. Graham, Bronx Community College; Dan Pyle Millar, Central Michigan University; Larry D. Miller, Indiana University; Jack V. Phipps, American River College; Patrick M. Schwerdtfeger; and Paul A. Walwick, East Tennessee State University. Most of all, we thank Rebecca Hayden of Wadsworth for the combination of prodding and praise that is so necessary in getting authors to meet deadlines.

# Contents

**Inter-Act:**
**Using Interpersonal**
**Communication Skills**

**Part A: Orientation**

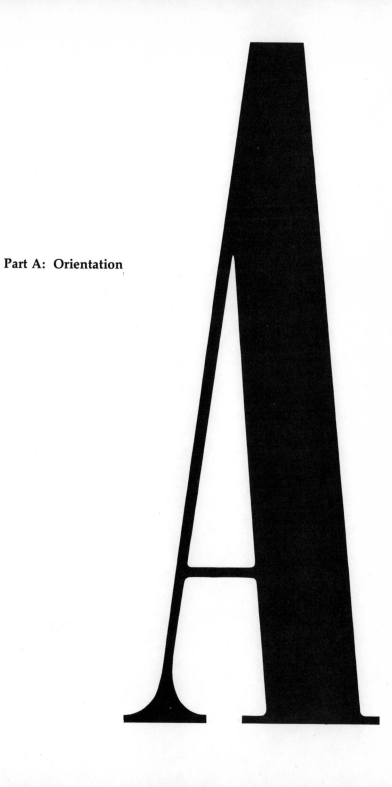

**Chapter One:**
**The Interpersonal Communication**
**Process**

"Communication." How many times this week has the word "communication" popped up in your conversation? You have probably encountered statements like "That painting just doesn't communicate"; "She seems to communicate so many different things at the same time"; "Her house communicates such a feeling of warmth"; or "I think we're having a communication problem."

From these examples you can see that the word "communication" has many different uses. The idea that ties all these various uses of the word together is *meaning*. If you get meaning from a person, an idea, an action, a painting, a building, a room, or whatever you are dealing with, then it communicated. By definition then, communication is the process of sharing meaning through the intentional or unintentional sending and receiving of messages. In this book, we will focus our discussion on that facet of communication that is called interpersonal.

Dean Barnlund defined interpersonal communication as "relatively informal social situations in which persons in face-to-face encounters maintain a focused interaction through the reciprocal exchange of verbal and nonverbal cues."[1] Although we subscribe to the essentials of the definition, we prefer to interpret "face-to-face" as including telephonic communication. Thus, a chat with your roommate about the problems of registration, a "heavy" talk with your boy friend or girl friend about the nature of your relationship, as well as a telephone call to your mother when you are lonely are all *interpersonal communication*. In the rest of this chapter, we will preview the realm of interpersonal communication, looking at its variables, its purposes, and its settings.

---

[1]Dean C. Barnlund, *Interpersonal Communication: Survey and Studies* (Boston: Houghton Mifflin Company, 1968), p. 10.

## Variables of the Process

In the first part of our definition we said that communication is a dynamic process. By "process" we mean that communication is ongoing and continuous and as such has no beginning or ending, yet there are various distinct events and actions that make up this process. Envision yourself at a party. You join three or four people who are conversing. After ten or fifteen minutes you leave the group to fix yourself a sandwich and get a drink. Communication was going on when you joined the group and it continued after you left. Eventually the entire group will disperse, but communication will continue.

Let us freeze this dynamic communication process for a moment as it is occurring interpersonally between two people. By freezing it, we can isolate the variables that blend to form the total process. What is happening with this one portion of a conversation that we have frozen may be described as follows: The *source*, one person, sends a *message* encoded into symbols through a *channel* to a *receiver*, another person, who decodes the message and responds by *feedback*. If all the variables operate as they should and if *noise* does not interfere too much, successful communication takes place: The one person shares meaning with the other. Let us take a closer look then at these six major variables of communication: source, message, channel, receiver, feedback, and noise.

### The Source

The *source* is the originator of the communication message. In our two-person conversation described above, the source was one individual; however, it could be a committee, a company, or even a national government.

As the authors of this book, we are the source of the communication you are reading. During various portions of this book, you will be the source as you participate in exercises and assignments.

The source has a variety of experiences, feelings, ideas, and moods that overlap and

*Sources encode, receivers decode (sometimes).*

interact to affect his or her communication. Thus what you say or write is related to or affected by your past experiences, moods, feelings, attitudes, beliefs, values, upbringing, sex, occupation, religion, and even the climate you live in and the weather you are experiencing today. Later we will discuss how the source's field of experience affects the message he intends to communicate.

### The Message

The *message* is the idea or feeling that the source communicates. For purposes of analysis we see messages as having three components: meaning, symbols used to express meaning, and form or organization of the message.

Meaning is not some static concept that can be moved in total from one mind to another. Meanings are within people. You know what it feels like for you to be hungry, to be tired, to be in love; you know the nature of the ideas within you. Communication of meaning involves sharing your ideas and feelings with others so that they might understand your experience in light of their own. Perhaps eventually we will develop our ESP powers sufficiently to allow us to experience another's meaning directly. But for now, we must turn our ideas and feelings into symbols, the words or actions that stand for or represent meanings. This second component, the process of turning ideas and feelings into symbols, is called *encoding*. Now, you have

been communicating for so long that it is unlikely that you consciously think about the encoding process. Your eyes grow bleary and you say, "I'm tired." You don't think, "I wonder what symbols I can utilize that will best express the feeling I am now experiencing." Most of us are aware of the encoding process only at those times when we must grope for words, when we have an idea but stutter and stammer to find the word that "is on the tip of the tongue" and that best expresses the idea.

In this encoding process, we select symbols to stand for or represent meaning. As we speak, the mind selects words to convey the messages; however, at the same time, facial expressions, gestures, and tone of voice—all nonverbal cues—accompany the words and affect the meaning of the message. Moreover, as we stated in our definition, communication may be intentional or unintentional. By "intentional" we mean that the source makes a conscious effort to select the symbols used in the communication—the message he or she sends has a purpose. Yet, at the same time, the source may be sending the same or conflicting messages unintentionally by means of another channel. For instance, if you ask someone how things are going and get the reply "Great!" your interpretation of the message received is different depending upon whether "Great!" is accompanied by a smile or a growl and whether the tone of voice was pleasant or sarcastic. Regardless of what the speaker intended to communicate, you may interpret the message differently. For now, let's say that both intentional and unintentional messages are important in sharing meaning.

Because an idea or feeling may have many facets, a third component of the process of communicating meaning is the determination of a form or organization for the message we wish to send. Again, part of this organization is conscious and part is subconscious. Your background of cultural experience as well as trial and error influence how you will shape, form, or organize your ideas.

## The Channel

The *channel* is the means used to convey the symbols. Words are transmitted from one person to another by air waves; facial expressions, gestures, and movement are transmitted by light waves. Usually, the more channels that can be utilized to carry a message, the more likely the success of the communication. Although human communication is basically two-channeled (light and sound), people can and do communicate by any of the sensory channels—a fragrant scent and a firm handshake are both forms of communication.

## The Receiver

The *receiver* is the destination of the message. Like the source, it may be a person or a group of persons. The message is received in the form of symbols by means of sound waves and light waves. The receiver then turns these

symbols back into meaning. This process of turning symbols back into meaning is called *decoding*. Did you ever send a boxtop from your favorite cereal along with just ten cents (or was it half a dollar) to get your "super decoder" so that you could be in on the secret messages of the star appearing on your favorite television program or cereal box? In the

*The meaning may not be the same.*

case of most communication, your decoder is your own brain.

Just as the source of a message is affected by his or her entire field of experience, so is the receiver. As a result, the meaning that is stimulated in the receiver may not be the same as or even analogous to that of the source. Much depends upon how the receiver's field of experience affects the decoding process. Most of the time, people just are not aware of the complexity of the decoding process or the potential for misunderstanding. Someone says, "It's raining," and you have an instant mental picture of the meaning that is being communicated. Again, you do not think: "Let's see, 'it' is a word that represents something indefinite, 'is' means 'the same as'— OK—'raining' is a word representing precipitation falling to the ground—OK—now I can go back to 'it', which must mean 'what is happening outside.'" Moreover, you do not worry too much about whether your mental picture of "raining" is necessarily the same as that of the source. It might be drizzling or it might be pouring. Considering the complexity of the encoding-decoding process, you can see that you are very lucky to be able to communicate at all.

At this stage of the process, some analysts might say that communication between our two persons is complete. Early communication theories were based on the SMCR model—that is, a source (S) sends a message (M), by means of one or more channels (C), to a receiver (R). Such a model depicts communication as linear—one-directional. Modern analysts have probed the dynamic nature of the communication process and argue that the variable of feedback is also fundamental to this process.

## Feedback

Whether a receiver decodes a message or not, he has some mental or physical response

to that message, and it is the response of the receiver that enables others to determine whether communication has really taken place. This response, if properly received, is called *feedback*, tells the source whether his message was heard, seen, or understood. If feedback indicates that the communication was not received or was received incorrectly or was misinterpreted, the source can send the message again, perhaps in a different way, so that the meaning he intends to share is the same meaning received by his listener.

Different kinds of communication situations provide for different amounts of feedback. A zero-feedback situation is said to exist when it is virtually impossible for the sender to be aware of a receiver's response. Suppose that right now we stated in this book: "Stop what you are doing and draw a rectangle resting on one of its sides." We would have no way of knowing whether you understood what we were talking about, whether you actually drew the rectangle, or, if you drew it, whether you drew it correctly. As the source of that message—as well as the other messages in this textbook—we cannot know for sure whether we are really communicating. The lack of direct feedback is one of the weaknesses of any of the forms of mass communication such as books, radio, or television. The source has little or no immediate opportunity to test the impact of his message.

Suppose, however, that instead of being the authors of a book, we are your instructors in a class of fifty students. Now suppose that we asked you to draw a rectangle resting on one of its sides. Even if you said nothing, our presence would enable us to monitor your nonverbal feedback directly. If you drew the rectangle, we could see it; if you refused, we would know; in some cases we could see exactly what you were drawing. This physical presence is a partial feedback system. Now suppose that in this classroom, as we asked you to draw the rectangle, you were free to ask us any direct questions and we were free and willing to respond. The free flow of interacting communication that would take place represents the highest level of feedback, a complete interaction system.

How important is feedback to effective communication? Leavitt and Mueller conducted an experiment similar to the one described above.[2] They reported that communication improved markedly as the situation moved from zero feedback to complete interaction. In your communication, you want to stimulate as much feedback as the situation will allow.

As we will see later, feedback can be used as more than just a test of the understanding of the message; it also can be used to help you gain insight into yourself as a person, to stimulate personal growth, and to verify or validate your perceptions.

---

[2]Harold J. Leavitt and Ronald A. H. Mueller, "Some Effects of Feedback on Communication," *Human Relations*, Vol. 4 (1951), p. 403.

## Noise

An analysis of the communication process is incomplete without consideration of one additional variable, noise. Communication involves the sharing of meaning. Yet a person's capabilities for interpreting, understanding, or responding to symbols is often inhibited by the amount of noise accompanying the communication. It might be nice if all communication occurred in a vacuum—for example, with nothing happening in your world right now except your reading of this message. Actually, however, there are also thousands of other sensory stimuli competing for your attention. If these other stimuli distract you from receiving this message, they are considered noise.

We define *noise* as both the *external* factors in the channels and the *internal* perceptions and experiences that affect communication. Much of your success as a communicator will depend on how you will avoid, lessen, or otherwise deal with noise. Coping with noise will be discussed more in Chapter 7 on barriers to communication. For now, let's explore what we mean by external and internal noise.

*External noise* refers to sights, sounds, and other stimuli that cause us to be attentive to them rather than to the messages being sent. For instance, if while one of us is giving the verbal instructions for drawing a rectangle, a lawn mower is being operated outside the window of our classroom, you would not hear the message because of the physical noise; and communication could not take place until

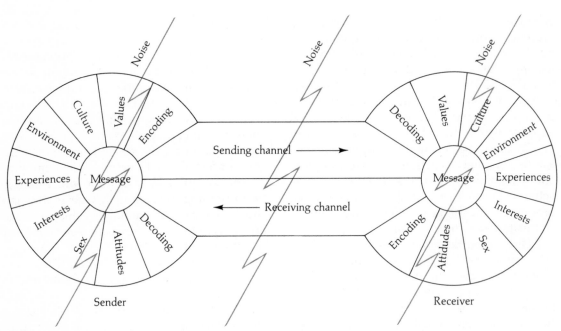

**Figure 1-1**

the noise was eliminated. Or if, while giving the directions, one of us exhibits certain annoying mannerisms or speaks with a severe speech impediment, these noise factors could intrude enough so that communication could not take place unless the one giving the directions could lessen the noise or you, as the receiver, could determine not to let the noise bother you. In each of these instances, actual physical noise would be clogging the channels of communication.

Often, the noise that provides a barrier to communication is not external or physical but an *internal or semantic noise* that grows from your perceptions and experiences—and semantic noises may cause you to misinterpret or misunderstand without your even knowing it. For instance, suppose Sam asked you to meet him at the green house. You may think of a "green house" as a place where plants are grown under glass; if Sam is thinking of a house that is painted green, you might never meet. Or, suppose in a conversation a professor told you that she would read a paper at the convention. If you thought reading a paper was something most people did when they wanted to find out the news of the day instead of the honor of being asked to give an oral report on the research that a professor has been conducting, you might be unable to understand her enthusiasm. Because all of us view language in terms of our own experiences, the semantic noise factor can be an important barrier to the communication process.

Now let us look at these six variables in model form. Through a pictorial representation you may be able to see how these variables interrelate. Figure 1-1 represents the communication process in a basic dyadic, or two-person, setting. Could you trace the variables of a simple interpersonal encounter?

Let's review the communication process through an analysis of a specific example:

*Joe says to Gloria, "What do you say we go out to dinner tonight?" Gloria frowns and says, "I don't know that I want a hamburger . . ." "Not a hamburger," Joe interrupts with a lilt in his voice, "I meant let's go to the Chalet!" Gloria gasps, "The Chalet—wow—you have a deal!"*

Joe is the sender. He encodes his thought into the words "What do you say we go out to dinner tonight." Gloria is the receiver. She decodes his words, gets a meaning she perceives as accurate, and she feeds back a frown and a verbal "I don't know that I want a hamburger." Joe sees that his message was not decoded accurately, so he attempts to correct the faulty interpretation. Nonverbally he gets a lilt in his voice and verbally he says, "I meant let's go to the Chalet." Now Gloria feeds back a nonverbal gasp and says verbally, "The Chalet—wow—you have a deal." Meaning shared—communication complete. On the first sending of the message Gloria's incorrect decoding was a function of some semantic noise associated with understanding of kinds of restaurants Joe frequents.

## Communication Session

*Reflection*

Consider the last oral communication encounter you had before reading this section. Focus on a single segment of that encounter. Can you identify the six communication variables in that stop-action segment?

*Actualization*

1. See whether you can write out an analysis (like the one in the review of the process above) of the following encounter: With a look of great anticipation Rita says, "That's a beautiful dress—can I I have it?" Ted frowns, shrugs his shoulders and says hesitantly, "Well . . . yes . . . I guess so . . ." Rita continues "and it's only thirty dollars!" Ted brightens and says, "Yes, it is a beautiful dress—go ahead and buy it."

2. Your instructor will ask for a volunteer to describe a diagram to the class.

   a. The volunteer will stand with his or her back to the class. You may not ask the describer any questions, but you must try to draw exactly what he or she is describing.

   b. The same volunteer will now describe a second diagram to the class. He or she will now face you and you may stop the describer at any time to get clarification on how to draw the second diagram.

When both are finished, check to see how much of the first diagram you got correct versus how much of the second.

*Discussion*

1. In groups of three to six, discuss the differences between the first and the second situation. List as many differences as you can.

2. Discuss why the two situations differ.

3. Record your list on paper.

4. At the end of discussion time, pass paper to the front of the room to allow the whole class to view it. Be prepared to defend your list.

## Functions of Interpersonal Communication

It is unlikely that any other behavior is as important to you as your communication. Every day you communicate for social and decision-making purposes that touch and affect every aspect of your life.

### Social Function

It has often been noted that human beings are social animals. Without interaction with others we would be psychologically and emotionally deprived. Of course we have heard of the hermits who deliberately live and function alone; but people like hermits are the exception. Most of us need and want to interact, to show feelings, to be wanted, to care.

On one social level people communicate for the sheer pleasure of interaction. At such times, the subject of the conversation really is unimportant. Two people may sit for hours interacting about apparently inconsequential matters. When they part they may have exchanged little real information, but they may carry away from the interaction a truly good feeling caused solely by the experience of talking with another human being.

On a second social level, people communicate to demonstrate their ties with other people. Why do you say "How you doing?" to a fellow you sat next to in class last quarter but haven't seen since? You may get pleasure out of the interaction—you may also see it as meeting a social need. When you see persons you know you overtly recognize them so that they will continue to recognize you. By say-ing, "Hi, Skip, how's it going" you conform with our societal norms—you acknowledge a person you recognize with one of the many statements you have learned to use under these circumstances. Failure to communicate is seen as a slight—the person may think you are stuck up. Recognition efforts serve to demonstrate your ties with people.

On a third social level, people communicate to *build* and to *maintain* relationships. When you do not know a person at all, you may communicate with that person to try out the relationship. If you find that you have things in common, the relationship may grow. Depending upon the results of the interaction, you may be content with an acquaintance relationship or a school-friend relationship, or you may seek a deeper, more intimate relationship. Some conversation is conducted for purposes of moving the relationship to higher levels of intimacy; some, for reinforcing the satisfactory nature of the relationship that has been achieved. Few relationships stay the same—especially during college years. You may find yourself moving in and out of a variety of relationships even within a single term. This is part of living—and it is an important purpose of interpersonal communication.

### Decision-making Function

Just as human beings are social animals, they are also decision makers. Starting with whether you were ready to get up and get going this morning, through what you had for breakfast, to whether or not to go to class, you have made countless decisions already today. Some of these decisions you made alone; others you made in consultation with one or more persons. Even more important, every one of the decisions involved some kind of language usage. There are several purposes for communication during the decision-making process.

One important purpose of communication is information exchange. It is impossible to function in our society without data. Some of these data you get through observation, some through reading, some through television, and a great deal through interpersonal communication. Jeff runs out to get the morning paper. As he comes through the door hurriedly, Tom asks, "What's it like out there this morning?" Jeff replies, "Wow, it's cold—it couldn't be more than twenty degrees." Tom says, "I was going to wear my jacket, but I guess I'd better break out the old winter coat." Such a conversation is typical of countless exchanges that involve sending and receiving information. Since decisions generally are better when they are based on information, anything that you can do to improve the accuracy of your information exchange is to your benefit in decision making.

A second important purpose of communication is to change attitudes and behaviors. After making a decision, you must be able to implement it. Implementation often requires that you effectively influence others. You try to get your friends to go to a particular movie;

you try to win the commitment of an acquaintance to vote for you; you try to persuade your father to let you use the car this weekend; or you try to get an instructor to change your course grade. These are but a few examples of attempts to influence people in order to make or implement decisions. Some theorists argue that the purpose of all communication is to influence behavior of others.

Just as there is a direct relationship between communication and human relations, so is there a direct relationship between communication and decision making. The better understanding you have of the means of processing information, sharing information, and persuasion, the better your decisions will be. Likewise, the more understanding you have of the problem-solving method, the more likely you are to cope with your problems systematically and to arrive at the best decisions possible in the particular circumstances.

For any decision, it is important that you go through the various steps of problem awareness, problem analysis, possible solutions, and selection of the best solution. Unless the decision was a spontaneous emotional reaction, it involves processing information, sharing information, and in many instances persuasion.

## Payoffs

If you understand the material in this chapter, you should now be able to

1. Define interpersonal communication.

2. Define and show the relationships among source, message, channel, receiver, feedback, and noise.

3. Identify the variables in a segment of a communication encounter.

4. Draw a model of the communication process.

5. Explain the functions of interpersonal communication.

## Suggested Readings

If you would like to learn more about communications as process and about model building, you may want to consult the following:

**Dean C. Barnlund (Ed.).** *Interpersonal Communication: Survey and Studies.* Boston: Houghton Mifflin Company, 1968. See particularly pages 3–29 for a good discussion of interpersonal communication goals and an interesting analysis of the evolution of models.

**David K. Berlo.** *The Process of Communication.* New York: Holt, Rinehart and Winston, 1960. Berlo discusses the interaction process in detail.

**C. David Mortensen.** *Communication: The Study of Human Interaction.* New York: McGraw-Hill Book Company, 1972. See particularly Chapter 2, pages 29–64, for a good survey of models, their functions and their limitations.

**Chapter Two:
Perception, Self-concept, and
Your Communication**

A young man rushes through the door of the interpersonal communication class, shouts something to the teacher, takes the teacher's arm, and the two scurry from the classroom, the teacher slightly ahead of the young man. The head of the department, whose office is next door, comes to the class to investigate when he hears what seems to be classroom chaos. When he asks three members of the class what happened, he gets the following reports: one says a man with a knife yelled at the teacher and dragged him forcibly from the class; the second says a man shouted in a pleading voice and the teacher turned pale and ran from the room; and the third says a man, his hands clenched, threatened the teacher, the teacher froze, but the man pushed him out of the room.

How can the stories be so much different? All three witnessed the same scene, yet each person reported not what actually happened, but what he perceived to have happened. You may not realize, but much of what you think, feel, and eventually say depends upon your perception. In this chapter we will consider the phenomenon of perception, the effect of perception on self-concept, and finally its effect on interpersonal communication.

## Perception

Simply defined, *perception* is the process of interpreting sensory input. In slightly more technical language, Kimble and Garmezy say perception is the "mechanism by which physical events are transformed into neural or mental events."[1]

Light waves impinge on the retinas of your eyes; sound waves bounce off the tympanic membranes in your ears; the nerve endings in your skin, the taste buds, and the olfactory glands send messages to your brain;

and you assume that what you see, hear, feel, taste, and smell are reality. You are likely to say, "Of course that's the way it is—I saw it happen!" However, as our opening example illustrated, even simple staged events show that when two or more people see the same event happen, their reportings of the event can differ significantly. Why? Because you don't see reality; you know reality only through your perceptions. That is the way your brain interprets the sensory input it receives from your senses. This interpretation involves various physiological and psychological factors that affect both the selection and the organization of the sensory data received. We can depict the perception process in model form, as shown in Figure 2-1. Because selection and organization are so important in the determination of what we see,[2] we need to look at each very closely.

### Selection

Every second you are bombarded by millions of sensory stimuli. If you had to interpret every sensory stimulus that impinges on your sense organs, you could go mad. We learn to cope with this complexity by focusing attention on only relatively few of these stimuli.

---

[1]Gregory A. Kimble and Norman Garmezy, *Principles of General Psychology*, 3rd ed. (New York: Ronald Press Company, 1968), p. 151.

[2]Throughout this section, emphasis is on visual perception. Of course, what is true of vision is also true of auditory and the other senses. We focus on visual perception both because many of our communication decisions are based on it and because we can best illustrate points visually.

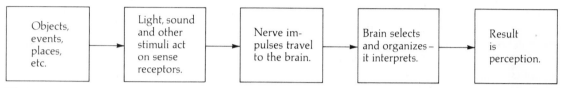

| Objects, events, places, etc. | → | Light, sound and other stimuli act on sense receptors. | → | Nerve impulses travel to the brain. | → | Brain selects and organizes – it interprets. | → | Result is perception. |
|---|---|---|---|---|---|---|---|---|

**Figure 2-1**

Right now you are reading this book, so your attention should be focused on making sense out of the visual data you are receiving from this page. Stop for a minute and look around— try to become aware of all the visual and audio input you might be focusing on right now. If you have ever had difficulty reading in a noisy room, you can appreciate the need to be selective in the sensory data you choose to attend to. Once you focus on a particular set of stimuli, the rest of the sights and sounds blend into an indefinite background. In the language of visual experience, what you focus on is called the *figure* and the rest of what you see is the *ground*.

The interesting fact is that you can focus on only one part of the total at any given instant. The scope of the focus may vary (you can use a wide lens or a narrow lens—a close-up or a distance shot), but the focus is still limited. For instance, in a televised football game, an instant replay reveals much detail that you missed the first time around. The isolated replay permits focus on actions that you may have missed entirely as the play originally unfolded. The experienced eye can enlarge the focus—the football commentator may see more than you did in the play the first

time around, but even he generally misses more than he sees.

Since the focal point of any given scene may be at any of an infinite number of places, ten persons viewing the same scene may have ten different perceptions, depending upon what each selects as the focal point. Let us exemplify the importance of focal points with a drawing that is often used to illustrate the figure-ground concept. Look steadily at Figure 2-2. What do you see?

At first you will probably see either the goblet or the faces. You will never see them both at exactly the same time. As you stare at the picture, notice that each comes in and out

**Figure 2-2**

of focus—although you may have the impression that sometimes you see them both at once, actually you are focusing briefly on first one, then the other. When two actions occur simultaneously, you can see only one of them; when two persons are talking to you at the same time you can listen to only one of them. Sometimes you can switch focus rapidly to give yourself the impression you are seeing or listening to both—but you can *focus* on only one at a time.

Why do you select as you do? Some of the selection is physiological, and you have little or no control over it. For instance, we know that human eyes perceive only certain rays on the color spectrum—you do not see the infrared or ultraviolet ends of the spectrum; likewise, human ears do not hear many of the sounds that come to them—they are limited basically to a range between 20 and 20,000 cycles per second. Most of your selection, however, is psychological and is based upon perceiving what you (1) expect to perceive and what you (2) want to perceive.

**Expectation** Spectators expect college basketball teams to have uniforms with the same colors and designs; they expect the numbers on the players' backs to be different—but not other parts of the uniform. At a recent basketball game, we saw that one of the starting players had a blue bobcat sewn on the pants of his uniform when all the other players had white bobcats sewn on theirs. When we told the couple sitting next to us, it took awhile for

the fact to register—it defied their expectation; once they perceived the difference, it was as disconcerting to them as it had been to us.

Expectation is determined largely by what your experience has shown you to be true: athletic teams' uniforms are supposed to be *uniform*. When experience does not conform with expectation, expectation sometimes wins out. On a day that bus drivers are on strike you may still believe you "saw" buses running; if your friend shows up with a new hair style you may still "see" the old one.

Observing accurately is a learned activity. It takes mental exertion to become receptive to more than what you expect to perceive; it takes mental exertion to override your expectations. Yet, you must be conscious of your perceptions if you are to avoid perceptual errors that may result in poor communication.

**Selective Attention** The second psychological element that affects selection is the tendency to see only what you want to see. This is called *selective attention*. The small child sees a man with a red suit, a white beard, and a pillow under his belt and perceives him as Santa Claus. When fooling yourself is a pleasurable activity with no harm to anyone, perhaps it's not so bad—after all, only a Grinch goes around stealing Christmases. But when you want to see only the bad or evil in a person, a place, or an event, faulty perception is harmful to you and to your communication.

Interest (or personal investment) is probably the major determinant of what you want to see. An architectural student may see the beauty (or ugliness) of the buildings on campus; a paraplegic is keenly aware of steps and curbings he has to negotiate to get from building to building; a naturalist focuses on the species of trees that grace the campus (or on the lack of plant life). You may have had the experience of acquiring a new car, then suddenly seeing that make and model of car

*Selection affects perception.*

wherever you looked. Ownership creates interest in the size, shape, and appearance of an object, and with interest comes awareness.

How does selection affect your communication? If you perceive only what you expect to perceive or only what you want to perceive, you can create a world of illusion and call it

reality. If you want to perceive blacks only as lazy, whites only as racist, women only as sex objects, men only as "male chauvinists," or objects, places, and experiences as either all good or all bad, your entire communication system will be based on and will reflect those faulty perceptions. You need to reason and draw conclusions from sensory input, but if your perception is not based upon *all* the pertinent data, or at least enough data, or if the nature of your perception is determined fully or in part before the experience—before the data are processed—then your conclusions will be faulty and your communication will be distorted.

## Organization

Data are received from the senses by the brain. The brain selects certain stimuli, and then it must try to sort the data into some intelligible order. This process of *organization* is the other major element of perception. The brain organizes sensory input by grouping similar stimuli in three ways: by patterns, by proximity, and by good form.

Let us consider organizing by *patterns*. Look at the three sets in Figure 2-3. In Figure 2-3a, the dots and circles may seem to separate into two groups because of the similarities of the dots and circles. In Figure 2-3b, you may see four columns of figures rather than sixteen individual figures. In Figure 2-3c, you may perceive an X surrounded by small circles. Similarly, when you consider a group

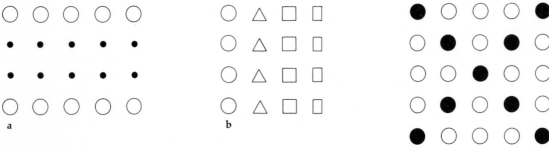

Figure 2-3

of people, depending upon your organizational frame of reference, you may perceive the group in terms of subgroups. Instead of perceiving a number of individual human beings, you may think of them as males and females or marrieds and singles or young, middle-aged, and elderly.

A second way of grouping is by *proximity*. We tend to group those things that are close together. Look at Figure 2-4. What do you see? Figure 2-4a probably appears as three pairs of parallel lines rather than as six individual parallel lines. Figure 2-4b probably appears as four sets of circles rather than as sixteen individual circles or as horizontal rows or vertical columns of circles. In a classroom, if you see a

group of five students sitting apart from the rest of the class, you may well think that they have something in common.

A third element of grouping has been called the *law of Pragnanz*. This law, which says people tend to perceive a stimulus as a "good" form, has two ramifications for visual perception: (1) If a figure approximates a geometric form, you will probably see it as that form; and (2) if the figure has a gap in it, you are likely to see it as a closed figure. Look at Figure 2-5. Because of this tendency to modify what you see, you probably perceived Figure 2-5a as a triangle, 5b as an oval, 5c as a circle, and 5d as a square. This same tendency explains why you may read a neon sign correctly when a portion is burned out and why you may finish a sentence correctly when a speaker leaves out a word.

How does organization of stimuli affect your communication? Instead of seeing things as they really are, you are likely to see them conforming to organizations for which your mind has a picture. If your perception is distorted, your communication related to the

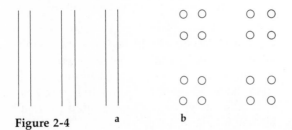

Figure 2-4

a          b          c          d

**Figure 2-5**

perception is likely to be distorted as well. Examine Figure 2-6 for a minute. Then take time to describe the woman you see in the picture. Consider her age, her features (how attractive she is), what she is wearing, and what you believe she is thinking.

If you saw her as a young woman, your communication about her differed considerably from communication based upon a

**Figure 2-6**

perception of her as an old woman. Which did you see? Keep looking at the picture until you have seen both possible perceptions. "Ah," you say, "but this is just a trick. No real-life situation could possibly fool me like this one." Don't believe it. People are fooled every day. You have probably been momentarily fearful of a threatening person or animal only to discover that what you saw was a shadow or reflection that *suggested* the feared creature. Are flying saucers real? Who knows? Many people have seen things that they have thought were UFO's only to find out they were flocks of flying geese or weather balloons or cloud formations or the like. What about communication based upon such misperceptions? Was it accurate?

So, you can be fooled by what you select and how you organize it. Let us now look at a few guidelines that you can use to improve your perception (or at least to keep you from relying on perceptions that may be inaccurate):

1. *Remember that in a complex setting, you are able to focus on only one aspect at a time.* The more complicated the "picture," the more focuses you will need in order to extract full meaning

from the "picture." To cross a street you must focus on the color of the light, the walk signal, the presence of autos either coming through the light or turning a corner, and the people coming toward you from the other side.

2. *Remember that perception is interpretation and not necessarily reality.* How you interpret depends upon selection and organization based upon such things as interest, frame of mind, moods, emotions, and attitudes. Snow is beautiful to the person who sees a white cover over the dirt of the city; it is irritating to the person trying to drive up a steep hill; and it is treacherous to the pilot trying to make a visual landing. Before you communicate perceptions that may have serious effects on you or those around you, you should check out the accuracy of your perceptions. It is often useful to change your angle, point of view, or attitude.

3. *Remember that the more ambiguous the input, the more likely that your perception will be distorted.* Most people have on occasion mistakenly "recognized" strangers as persons they know because they saw what seemed to them a familiar coat or hair style or gesture. Perhaps you have on an occasion been startled by something you viewed from "the corner of your eye" only to discover that what you thought you saw was far different from what was actually there.

Communication is based upon perception, and if perception is distorted, so is communication.

## Communication Session

*Reflection*

**Examine each of the pictures below. What do you see? Analyze your perception. Was it based upon selection? Organization?**

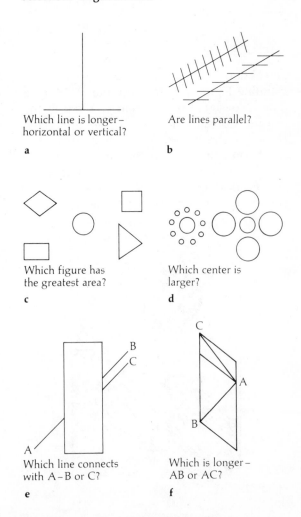

Which line is longer— horizontal or vertical?

**a**

Are lines parallel?

**b**

Which figure has the greatest area?

**c**

Which center is larger?

**d**

Which line connects with A–B or C?

**e**

Which is longer— AB or AC?

**f**

*Actualization*

**Your instructor will ask for three volunteers who will be sequestered outside the classroom. One at a time they will enter the room and describe to the class a picture that the instructor has given them. Based upon their descriptions alone, you are to try to visualize the picture exactly. When the three have finished, your instructor will show you the picture.**

*Discussion*

**What differences existed between the three descriptions? How did your image differ from the actual picture? How can you account for this?**

*152,805*

## Perception and Self-concept

A study of perception is important to a student of communication for many reasons, several of which we have already considered. Perhaps its greatest importance is in the formation of a person's self-concept. What is your self-concept? It is a collection of perceptions that relate to every facet of your being: your attractiveness, physical capabilities,

*Self-concept is partially formed through perceptions of one's self.*

vocational potential, sexual capabilities, size, strength, and so on. Your self-concept is formed through (1) the perceptions you have about yourself, (2) other persons' perceptions of you that they have shared with you, and (3) the roles you play.

The perceptions you have about yourself are based in part on your perceptions of your experiences. Your experiences have taught you what you are good at, what kinds of things you like, under what circumstances you excel, and so forth. However, remember that the conclusions you draw about your experiences are subjective ones based upon your perceptions. For instance, if you made a decision to spend the money you were given for your birthday to buy a new watch, you are likely to reflect upon whether that decision was good, bad, or indifferent. If you are satisfied with the decision, you may say to yourself, "I really make pretty sound decisions." Whatever the real worth of your decision, you perceived it as good. Now, one good and satisfying experience may not be enough to give you a positive perception of your decision-making ability, but if you perceive many or all your decisions as good, then your perception of yourself as a decision maker becomes quite positive. The more positive experiences you have in a variety of fields (decision maker, cook, lover, student, typist, and so forth), the more positive your total self-concept becomes.

A second determinant of your self-concept is your perception of feedback from others. Suppose that during a group discussion someone says to you, "You are a very convincing speaker." It may not take many such comments to cause you to develop a perception of yourself as persuasive or influential. Of course, the more highly you respect the person giving the feedback, the more important that statement will be in forming your perception. You use the data that others supply to talk to yourself about who and what you are. Much of what you are, do, or say is evaluated by others, and you pick up their reactions and use them to validate or reinforce your perception of who and what you are. The more positive feedback you get (as decision maker, cook, lover, student, typist, and so forth), the more positive your total self-concept becomes.

A third way you define yourself is through your perception of the roles you choose or are forced to play. Role definitions are often products of the value systems of society or of a group; some are determined by the individual value system of a person. For instance, you may find that society has certain role expectations for you. In this era of Women's Liberation, we hope that sex-role expectations are changing. Nevertheless, in many families, little girls are still expected to play with dolls and other homemaking toys to prepare them for roles of wife, mother, and housewife; little boys learn that it is unmanly to cry, and they are encouraged to play aggressively in rough and tough sports and to play with mechanical toys—all in preparation for their roles in society of he-man husband, father, and breadwinner. If a child in such a family is caught playing with "inappropriate toys" a boy is called "sissy," a girl is called "tomboy"—both are derogatory terms and can be injurious to self-concepts.

In addition to values of society, the value system of a specific group may also determine your role. Your family, your social organizations, your service organizations—every group you belong to approves or disapproves of things you do or say and of what you are. They "let" you be a certain kind of person in their presence, and you soon come to see yourself as that kind of person. For instance, if you are the oldest child in a large family, your parents may cast you in the role of model child, disciplinarian, or brothers' and sisters' keeper depending upon how they see family relationships. Your peers may look upon you as a "joker"; and you may accommodate them by playing your role: laughing and joking when you are really hurt and want to cry.

Other roles are products of your own value system. "Happy-go-lucky," "*Vogue* model," "sincere student," "doll," and "dude," are just a few examples of the roles you may adopt either to fit your perception of experience and feedback or to reflect a role you have chosen to play.

Each of us has a number of on-stage and off-stage roles—roles we play in public may differ from the roles we play in private. Although you may not be Superman hiding your real identity in Clark Kent, you do often show yourself as different from what you perceive yourself to be. In each new encounter, you may test a role you have been playing or you may decide to play a new role. If you perceive the role as meeting some need, you may alter your self-concept on the basis of that particular role.

So perception of experience, perception of feedback from others, and perception of roles work in total to create a self-concept that may be anywhere on the continuum from very negative to very positive. How real or accurate are your self-estimates? The answer depends upon the accuracy of your perceptions! All of us experience both successes and failures at things we do. If in determining your self-concept you select mostly successful experiences, your perception of self will be positive and your self-concept will probably be high. If, on the other hand, you select mostly negative experiences, your perception of self will be negative and your self-concept will probably be low. Whether you really are "successful" is not as important as your *perception* of success.

Of course, very few persons have a completely high or a completely low self-concept. Most of us see ourselves as quite good at some things, average at many things, and fair to poor at some. For instance, your experience and feedback may give you the perception of being good as a cook and in relating to others, average as an athlete, and fair to poor as a mathematician. If, however, you see yourself negatively in many aspects, this emphasis on the negative is likely to result in a generally low self-concept. A low self-concept then affects both your production and your communication.

As you develop your self-concept, you use it to predict what will happen in the future: the higher your self-concept, the more likely you are to predict positive experiences; the lower your self-concept, the more likely you are to predict negative experiences. Soon your self-concept begins to shape reality— you become the beneficiary or the victim of what are called self-fulfilling prophecies, which work something like this. Clifford says, "I'm very good at taking tests, so I'm sure I'll do well if I study." Then as a result of a good self-concept, he stays relaxed, studies, confidently takes the test in a good frame of mind, and does well. Pamela, who has a low self-concept, says, "I never do well at tests even when I study," then because she fears tests, her study is interrupted by negative thoughts, she goes into the test with a bad attitude, and just as she predicted, she does poorly.

How are self-fulfilling prophecies derived? By and large, your self-fulfilling prophecies, manifested in decisions you reach and experiences you have, are products of the kind of language pattern that dominates your thinking and in turn determines your behavior. Now, these language patterns need not be oral—they may very well be those that mill around in your head without ever surfacing as speech. For instance, this morning when you woke up, the "voices in your head" might have gone something like this: "There goes that damned alarm. I'm so tired—maybe if I just lie here a few more minutes. Hold on—if I don't get up, I'll go back to sleep. Oh, who cares—it feels so good. Let's see, what's the latest time I can get up and still be ready on time? Aw, it's already later than I like to get up. Oh, well, here goes."

The language patterns you hear (and eventually use in your speech) are roughly of three different kinds. By replaying and then analyzing exactly what went through your mind, you can learn to identify the kinds of voices and work for change in response to

them if you are not satisfied with which kind of voice has dominance over your thinking and eventually over your communication behavior. **The language patterns that you are trying to identify are those that are critical-evaluative, those that are emotional reaction, and those that are rational analysis.**

Suppose a person in a position of authority (perhaps your boss at work, your teacher, or the leader of a group you belong to) says to you, "I'd like you to be in charge of the new program on . . ." As you receive this statement, you may hear various voices in your head saying:

*"You know you can't do that kind of job."*

*"What will this mean to me personally?"*

*"Won't people ever leave me alone?"*

*"Another request for work—I think I'm going to scream!"*

*"Great—you know the botch you make of this kind of thing."*

*"How much time will this really take?"*

*"I'm never going to get out from under what I have to do now."*

Now let's group the statements by type: critical-evaluative, emotional reactions, and rational analyses.

1. These are critical-evaluative statements:

*"You know you can't do that kind of job."*

*"You know you make a botch of this kind of thing."*

2. These are emotional or "gut" reactions—such reactions can be positive as well as negative:

*"Won't people ever leave me alone?"*

*"Another request for work—I think I'm going to scream."*

*"I'm never going to get out from under what I have to do now."*

3. These are rational analysis statements—they are attempts to analytically weigh and consider:

*"What will this mean to me personally? to my career?"*

*"How much time will this really take to complete?"*

Hearing such conflicting inner voices is common. Which voices do you listen to and what kind of statements do you then actually make as a result? Eric Berne developed a system of analysis based upon the identification of these three kinds of voices. He called his system transactional analysis (TA).[3] Thomas Harris's book *I'm OK—You're OK*,[4] a best

seller, is a quite readable popular treatment of Eric Berne's theories.

While we do not view transactional analysis as the sole means of understanding communication behavior, our students in the past have found some of its concepts to be helpful in understanding or identifying certain communication events. For instance, the TA labels of *Parent* (which includes critical-evaluative statements or the voice of conscience), *Child* (which includes emotional reaction), and *Adult* (which includes statements of rational analysis) are easy to remember and to identify.[5]

Regardless of how you choose to label the types of language patterns you use, when you determine that a disproportionate number of your decisions and too much of your communication behavior are a result of paying too much attention to either the critical-evaluative voices or the emotional-reaction voices, you may want to reassess your method of decision making, for heeding these voices may well be affecting your self-concept and leading you to the formation of negative self-fulfilling prophecies.

We are not advocating that only rational analysis should ever determine decisions or communication behavior. Without emotional reaction, life would be dull. Much of your

---

[3]See Eric Berne, *Games People Play: The Psychology of Human Relationships* (New York: Grove Press, 1964).

[4]Thomas A. Harris, *I'm OK—You're OK: A Practical Guide to Transactional Analysis* (New York: Harper & Row, 1967).

[5]For a particularly good view of transactional analysis that discusses its strengths and weaknesses, its uses and abuses, see Gerald M. Goldhaber and Marylynn B. Goldhaber, *Transactional Analysis: Principles and Applications* (Boston: Allyn and Bacon, 1976).

happiness in life is a result of emotional reaction—love is impossible to understand outside of an emotional context. Likewise, your critical-evaluative self (your voice of conscience) often has good advice for you and is the guardian of your value system. An ideal situation is one in which critical-evaluative statements and emotional responses are mediated by rational analysis. As you examine what you *think*, what you *decide*, and what you actually *communicate*, try to determine whether rational analysis is playing its rightful part.

## A Program for Communication Change

In the remainder of this book you will study effective interpersonal communication skills. As you read, you may well determine that your present communication behavior is inappropriate and in conflict with newly learned skills. Now, at the start of this course (or very shortly thereafter), is the time to take a self-inventory to determine which communication behavior you are most concerned with and most committed to changing and to write a contract for change.

This contract should include (1) a statement of your goal, (2) a description of the present problem, (3) a step-by-step action plan to reach the goal, and (4) a method of determining when the goal has been reached. Why a contract? Because we believe in the truth of the old adage: "The road to hell is paved with good intentions." It is all too

easy to say something like, "I'm going to listen better in the future," but it is also all too easy to ignore the directive. Without a clearly drawn plan and a written commitment, you are less likely to follow through.

Let's look at the procedure for writing a contract:

1. *Statement of goal:* Perhaps right now, before reading another word of this book, you may have your major communication goal in mind. On the other hand, you may need to do some reading and some thinking before you are able to verbalize your principal need. As a help in self-analysis turn to the Appendix. Read through the communication skills listed there. Is there one that seems particularly important to you that you are not now practicing? Then read the communication problems listed in the second part. Perhaps you will discover that some communication behavior of yours is creating a problem. When you have determined a specific change you feel a need to make, write your goal specifically. *Example:* "Goal: To increase my listening efficiency with my parents—especially with my mother."

2. *Description of the problem:* Here you describe to the best of your ability the specific nature of that communication problem. *Example:* "Problem: Currently when my mother tries to say something to me, I find myself day dreaming or rehearsing my replies. Consequently, I sometimes miss important points or misinterpret what she is telling me."

3. *A step-by-step action plan:* By reading the procedures in the Appendix for implementing a skill or coping with a problem or by referring to the pages in the text where the skill or problem is discussed, you can gain insight into the various elements you may wish to include in your plan. When you have a plan in mind, write it out in sufficient detail. *Example:* "Step-by-Step Action Plan: (1) I will consciously attempt to 'clear my mind' when my mother is speaking. (2) I will learn to employ the skill of paraphrasing in order to check the accuracy of what I've heard."

4. *A method of determining when the goal has been reached:* Here you will write the minimum requirements for having achieved your goal. *Example:* "Test of Achieving Goal: This goal will be considered achieved (1) when I have completed two weeks of listening during which my mother never has to repeat something for me to get it; (2) when I have internalized paraphrasing to the extent that I remember to do it and do it well."

After completing the contract you should sign it. We would further suggest that you have another person in class witness the contract. (Perhaps you can witness his or her contract in return.) At the end of the term, you can meet with the witness to determine whether or not your contracts have been fulfilled.

## Communication Session

*Reflection*
**Think of the various roles you take in your everyday interaction. How do those roles affect your self-concept?**

*Actualization*
1. **Examine three of the decisions you have made during the past few days. Write out the conversations that went on in your head as you made these decisions. Try to replay the actual dialogue. When the decisions were made, what kind of statements had controlled your behavior? Did either critical-evaluative or emotional-reaction statements dominate all three decisions?**

2. **Write a communication improvement contract. Use the form in Figure 2-7 (page 32).**

**Figure 2-7**

**Communication Contract**

**1.**

Goal:

**2.**

Statement of the problem:

**3.**

Step-by-step action plan:

**4.**

Method of determining when the goal has been reached:

Signed: _____

Date: _____

Witnessed by: _____

## Payoffs

If you have accurately perceived the elements of this chapter, you should now be able to

1. Define perception.

2. Describe the process of selection and organization.

3. Explain the relationship between perception and communication.

4. Discuss the ways to improve perceptions.

5. Explain the relationship between perception and self-concept.

6. Define self-concept and discuss the ways it is formed.

7. Identify the kinds of voices that control decisions.

8. Write a communication contract.

## Suggested Readings

**Gerald M. Goldhaber** and **Marylynn B. Goldhaber.** *Transactional Analysis: Principles and Applications.* Boston: Allyn and Bacon, 1976. A good contribution to the theory of transactional analysis that combines the Goldhabers' explanations with a representative selection of readings.

**Jess Lair.** *I Ain't Much Baby—But I'm All I Got.* New York: Doubleday and Company, 1972. This popular paperback gives insight into the formation and importance of self-concept.

**Robert E. Silverman.** *Psychology,* 2nd ed. New York: Appleton-Century-Crofts, 1974. See especially pages 149–190. We recommend this as representative of a number of recent psychology textbooks that discuss perception.

Part B: Basic Communication Skills

**Chapter Three:**
**Skills That Establish a Positive**
**Communication Climate**

Do you recall those times when in the midst of an interpersonal encounter you thought to yourself, "Something's wrong—I can feel the tension in the air." If you later analyzed the situation, you may have decided the tension was the result of something that was said or something that was done, or perhaps the *way* something was said or done. Perhaps you were bewildered by why things went wrong this time when things went so smoothly at other times. Perhaps you felt a victim of circumstances beyond your control. In reality, you—and the others involved—have the potential for control over the kind of climate that will prevail in any communication setting.

Communication encounters take place within an interpersonal climate—an atmosphere comprised of the tones, the moods, and the attitudes of those communicating. Your effectiveness as a communicator may well depend on the type of interpersonal climate you help create. The more positive the climate, the more likely that the participants will have satisfactory outcomes.

Most communication scholars would submit that the communication climate you create is a product both of the attitudes you hold and of your actual behavior in interpersonal situations. We heartily agree with this analysis. If you are to be a truly effective communicator, your attitudes toward communicating and your communication behavior must coincide. If, for example, Bruce holds the attitude that "small talk" is a waste of time, then he will probably never develop the skills necessary for engaging in chit-chat. Thus, those he is forced to interact with at this level may perceive him as a "cold fish" or unfriendly.

Even if you hold attitudes that are conducive to good interpersonal communication, your communication behavior may cause you to create negative interpersonal communication climates. Although Paula may hold the attitude that good communication requires openness (an attitude that is a step in the right direction), she may have trouble with

behaviors that demonstrate or are consistent with this attitude.

In this unit we want to present you with many different communication skills—behaviors that may help you to improve your interpersonal communication. In this chapter we will consider those skills that seem most conducive to establishing a positive climate. In the next three chapters we will focus on skills that seem specifically sender oriented, receiver oriented, or nonverbally oriented.

A positive communication climate begins with positive attitudes and is signaled with behaviors that connote empathy, descriptiveness, provisionality, equality, and openness.

## Empathy

In discussion of their inclusion of empathic communication as a fundamental interpersonal skill, Bochner and Kelly say that empathy is the essence of all successful communication.[1] We agree with this assessment, especially as it affects the development of a positive interpersonal climate. By definition, we see empathy as having two aspects. The first is the recognition aspect: A person who has empathy for another has the "ability to detect and identify the immediate affective

---

[1]Arthur P. Bochner and Clifford W. Kelly, "Interpersonal Competence: Rationale, Philosophy, and Implementation of a Conceptual Framework," *Speech Teacher*, Vol. 23 (November 1974), p. 289.

Chapter Three:
Skills That
Establish a
Positive
Communication
Climate

39

state of another."[2] In this aspect, empathy is a perception skill. The second aspect of empathy involves sensitivity of response, the way a person shows the degree of empathy he has. **In total, empathizing is being able to detect and identify the immediate affective state of another and responding in an appropriate manner.** Let us examine the two aspects of empathy, recognition and response.

A person who has recognition empathy understands the other's feelings based on his or her own experience in a similar situation or his or her fantasized reaction to that situation. When Joe says, "And out of the blue he slugged me right on the jaw," and Maxie feels what it is like to be hit on the jaw, he is empathizing; if Joan says, "I failed the test," and Muriel can fantasize the feeling of despair she might have under the same circumstances, Muriel is empathizing. Empathizing puts a person in a state of mind in which he or she can be of help to the other person.

Whereas one aspect of empathy is recognition, the other aspect is action. A person with empathy first perceives information about the other person and acts accordingly. For instance, if Karen is criticizing Jim's term paper and she senses that Jim is becoming very uncomfortable, we say she is empathizing with Jim's feelings. If she then eases up

on the criticism, or says something to acknowledge Jim's uncomfortable feelings, we say she is being sensitive, she is responding empathically. If, on the other hand, she continues piling up the criticism until Jim stomps out of the room in a huff or punches her in the nose, we say that she has been insensitive to Jim's feelings.

Each of us has a certain level of sensitivity. Although it is doubtful that there is such a thing as a totally insensitive person, some people are considerably less sensitive than others. But even a person with highly developed empathic recognition can be relatively insensitive at times, depending upon what is going on in his or her world or how he or she is feeling at the moment. It is difficult to be sensitive to others when you are experiencing a trauma in your own life. Thus, if Karen's father had died recently, her insensitivity to Jim's feelings might be due to her grief rather than to her lack of sensitivity. Moreover, at certain times, you can be less effective and less sensitive because of your own anger, pity, shame, joy, or excitement. Some people, for example, become very short-tempered and insensitive when they are hungry. Once the hunger need is fulfilled, that person may be able to regain a former level of sensitivity.

Thus, empathy has two clearly definable aspects—the recognition, the perception skill, and the response, a communication skill. Our communication session in this chapter attempts to help you analyze your perception skill—the recognition aspect of empathy.

---

[2]Robert J. Campbell, Norman Kagan, and David R. Krathwohl, "The Development and Validation of a Scale to Measure Affective Sensitivity (Empathy)," *Journal of Counseling Psychology*, Vol. 18 (1971), p. 407.

What can you do to increase your skill at empathizing? You have already started by becoming aware of your potential for being more perceptive. The following are three guidelines for implementation:

1. *Analyze the basis for your perceptions.* The relative inaccuracy of your perceptions may well be based upon drawing conclusions from too few clues. In Chapter 2, we spoke of some of the consequences of selective perception. Perhaps you are selecting too narrowly or perhaps you are seeing only what you want to see. Furthermore, you may be basing your perceptions on verbal clues alone. Try to take into account both the verbal and the nonverbal clues people are sending. Your reading of Chapter 6 on nonverbal communication should help you considerably in sharpening your recognition of the nonverbal elements. Pay special attention to the skill of perception checking, a means of testing the perceptual inferences you draw.

2. *Analyze the methods of others.* If you will observe the behavior of your friends and acquaintances, you will notice that some are particularly skillful in accurate recognition of others' states of mind. Observe skilled persons closely. What are they doing to help themselves to be more perceptive? Through careful observation of apparently empathic persons, you may pick up some helpful clues.

3. *Practice.* Part of improving your skill depends upon your making a conscious effort. As you come in contact with another person it is well worth a few moments to ask yourself, "What state of mind do I believe the person is in right now?" and "What are the clues the person is giving that I am using to draw this conclusion?" Asking these questions will help you focus at least some of your attention on others, instead of keeping your thoughts mostly on yourself. As you gain skill in making these assessments quickly, you may find yourself much more in tune with the moods, feelings, and attitudes of those with whom you wish to communicate. As a result of such practice, you may be able to maintain or even to create a more positive communication climate.

What of the second aspect of empathic communication, sensitive response? In Chapter 4, we will be exploring several specific response skills that are manifestations of empathy. In that chapter you will learn to listen empathically, to paraphrase, and to give helpful feedback.

**Chapter Three:**
**Skills That**
**Establish a**
**Positive**
**Communication**
**Climate**

**41**

## Communication Session

*Reflection*

Think of the last time you fully empathized with another person. Did you both recognize and respond? What was the outcome?

*Actualization*

Consider how much you empathize with a person close to you.[3]

*1.* Choose your spouse, your brother or sister, or a close friend to complete this exercise with you.

*2.* Select a personality trait like self-confidence, leadership ability, or sense of humor.

*3.* Circle a number from 1 (low) to 5 (high) to rate each statement. You complete A, B, C, and D; your partner completes E, F, G, and H.

**Partner 1: On the personality trait of _____ :**

*A.* I rate myself          1  2  3  4  5

*B.* I rate my partner      1  2  3  4  5

*C.* I think my partner would
rate herself/himself        1  2  3  4  5

*D.* I think my partner would
rate me                     1  2  3  4  5

**Partner 2: On the same personality trait of _____ :**

*E.* I rate myself          1  2  3  4 5

*F.* I rate my partner      1  2  3  4 5

*G.* I think my partner would
rate himself/herself        1  2  3  4 5

*H.* My partner would rate me   1  2  3  4 5

The measure of your empathic ability is determined by calculating how closely your predictions of your partner's ratings (C and D) correspond with your partner's actual ratings (E and F); and, of course, your partner's empathic ability is determined by calculating how closely his or her predictions of your ratings (G and H) correspond with your actual ratings (A and B).

Try this test with three or four other people whom you consider close to you. Do you empathize more with some than with others?

---

[3]This self–other rating is adapted from a test developed by Rosalind F. Dymond, "A Scale for the Measurement of Empathic Ability," *Journal of Consulting Psychology,* Vol. 13 (April 1949), pp. 127–133.

## Descriptiveness

A second skill that is instrumental in maintenance or development of a positive communication climate is descriptiveness. In almost any interpersonal encounter, whether it involves strangers, acquaintances, or friends, the first few interchanges are likely to have tremendous influence on the nature of the communication that follows. These first few interchanges often establish the climate for that particular encounter. Yet very often people inadvertently get things started wrong by beginning with judgmental, evaluative statements.

Skillful use of descriptiveness should replace judgment in producing the positive communication climate.[4] **Descriptiveness means putting into words the behaviors you have observed or the feelings you have.** Human beings seem particularly inclined to see ideas, actions, attitudes, and the like as "stupid," "ridiculous," "great," "crummy," "fantastic," and other similar judgmental terms. Although some people may like to have their words praised, the anticipation of judgment, good or bad, can destroy a positive communication climate.[5]

Why? When you set forth an idea or state attitudes or feelings, you are setting forth a bit of yourself, putting a bit of your ego out on the line. Since your ideas represent a part of

you, you tend to be very protective of them. Thus, when you believe that any idea, attitude, or feeling is subject to judgment, you are likely to think more of protecting yourself than of communicating. When either party in communication is bent upon self-protection either by withdrawal or by striking out at the other person, the positive communication climate crumbles.

When you make an evaluation (when, for example, you say that something is "stupid") you are *expressing* a judgmental reaction, you are not *describing* the feeling you have. You should ask yourself what feelings or behaviors triggered your judgmental statement. Communicating those feelings or those behaviors would be descriptive. Let us make a comparison between judgmental and descriptive statements. Consider the following two situations.

1. Steve and Mark are in the midst of a discussion about politics. After Mark has interrupted him for the second time, Steve says:

*"Mark, your constant interruption is very rude."* (evaluative)

*"Mark, do you realize that you have interrupted me before I had a chance to finish either of my last two statements?"* (descriptive)

2. A committee is charged with determining how to make enough money to pay for an addition to the meeting room. In the midst of discussion of various plans, Jeff and Mary get into an extended argument about how much money could be made by a bake sale. Susan,

---

[4]Jack R. Gibb, "Defensive Communication," *The Journal of Communication,* Vol. 11 (September 1961), pp. 141–148.

[5]Carl R. Rogers, *Client-centered Therapy* (Boston: Houghton Mifflin Company, 1951), p. 417.

Chapter Three:
Skills That
Establish a
Positive
Communication
Climate

43

sensing that the argument is causing many other members of the committee to lose interest, says:

*"Jeff and Mary—why don't you stop your stupid argument. You're boring everyone to death."* (evaluative)

*"Jeff and Mary—I feel very frustrated. While you two are discussing this one plan, others who are trying to get their ideas heard appear to be losing interest."* (descriptive)

Each of these two examples illustrates a different aspect of descriptiveness. The first is an example of description of behavior. **Description of behavior means accurately recounting specific observable actions of another without labeling the behavior as good or bad, right or wrong.** Steve's reply describes the behavior of Mark. Whereas telling Mark that his "constant interruption is very rude" is likely to create defensiveness, describing what Mark has done may help to build a positive climate. Mark will be less likely to believe that he is being attacked. The second example illustrates description of feelings of Susan ("I feel frustrated") as well as description of behavior ("others appear to be losing interest"). Because of the importance of description of feelings as a sender skill, we will discuss it in greater detail in Chapter 5.

The procedure for descriptiveness (describing behavior) is as follows:

1. *Get in touch with what you are seeing, hearing, or feeling.*

2. *Report only what you saw, heard, or felt.*

3. *Do not judge the merit of what you saw, heard, or felt.*

Now, expressing judgments may seem more fun; and, if your goal is to "get a person's goat," your expressed judgments may accomplish that goal. However, if you are interested in establishing a positive climate for good interpersonal communication, you will want to proceed descriptively. As a conversation develops, you may find an appropriate time to offer your opinion, but as opening statements for communication exchange, judgment and evaluation are more likely to create a negative climate rather than a positive one.

Descriptiveness is not an easy skill to learn or to use consistently. Do not be discouraged to find how often you slip into a judgmental pattern. However, we believe that, as you see yourself gaining skill in being descriptive, you will be rewarded by marked improvement in the communication climates in which you find yourself.

## Provisionalism

**Provisionalism is the skill of phrasing ideas tentatively rather than dogmatically.** There are few subjects on which any individual knows everything there is to know; likewise, there are few ideas that are so firmly accepted by everyone that some possibility for another way of looking at a subject can be ruled out. When you close and lock your mind about any subject, when you state something inflexibly as if all possible knowledge had been considered and as if you are so wise in your interpretation that no other view is possible, you are being dogmatic. On the other hand, if in your statements you recognize the possibility that more information may be forthcoming or an opposite view may be held, you are being provisional.

Dogmatic statements are likely to create a defensive rather than a positive climate. Dogmatic people are often viewed as "know-it-alls." Yet, even the most intelligent, the most thoughtful, the most knowledgeable persons sometimes say things that are only partly true or are even entirely mistaken. Provisional statements, on the other hand, help to create or to maintain the positive communication climate. How? By acknowledging that the other person has a viewpoint and letting it be heard even if it is not accepted.

Consider a situation in which two newly-weds are buying a television set. As they approach the subject of whether to pay cash or to finance it, the husband looks at the wife and says, "There's only one way to do it—and that's to pay cash." Or consider a situation where a man is trying to sew a button on his shirt. His mother watches him for a minute and then says, "Give me that—there's only one way to sew a button on so that it will stay." In each case the dogmatic statement is likely to cause a negative communication atmosphere. The wife may experience irritation, even anger, because her viewpoint has not even been asked for and the son may react with belligerent stubbornness because he believes his way is as good as any other.

How is provisionalism demonstrated in communication? One way is by recognizing that except for statements of fact, there are many possible opinions on any subject, and yours is not necessarily the same as one held by someone else. Be willing to state that your opinion is your view and not some universal absolute principle established at the beginning of time. Instead of saying "There's only one way to do it—and that's to pay cash," the husband might have said, "I was brought up to believe that paying cash will save me money." Notice that this statement allows for flexibility of action and/or belief. It does not close the door to discussion. Instead of saying, "There's only one right way to sew on a button," the mother could have said, "You probably have an idea of how to sew on that button, but I know a way I'd like to share with you that really helps a button to stay put."

Another way of showing provisionalism is by stating that something that seems to be true under these circumstances may not be entirely true or may not be true under all circumstances. Again, the husband could have said, "I've been brought up to believe that I can always save money by paying cash—I don't know whether that would be true in this set of circumstances." Likewise, the mother could have said, "I know there are several ways to sew on a button, but let me show you the way that has always worked for me in the past, although it may not work better on this particular garment."

Speaking provisionally may seem to you less dramatic than descriptiveness. Perhaps

**Chapter Three:**
**Skills That**
**Establish a**
**Positive**
**Communication**
**Climate**

**45**

it is. Just remember that a good communication climate is all too easy to destroy. Once the other person gets on edge or feels those nape hairs begin to rise, it might take a while to "clear the air." With just a little care in phrasing your statements, you can prevent a negative climate from developing and you can build or maintain a positive one.

The procedure for provisionalism? Keep it in mind:

1. *Consider what you are about to say.*

2. *Determine whether it contains a wording that shows an attitude of finality, positiveness, or allness of concept.*

3. *If it does, add a qualifying statement that recognizes (a) the statement is your opinion and (b) the statement may not necessarily be entirely true or true under this set of circumstances.*

## Equality

How do you feel when someone says something that you *perceive* as meaning that he or she knows more, is a better person, or in some way is speaking as a superior? Most people become very uncomfortable in reaction to such statements.

George Orwell needled the superiority attitude in *Animal Farm:* "All animals are equal, but some animals are more equal than others." The implication was that some animals were to be treated as superior, with special privileges. Some persons believe that their positions make them superior to those around them. The head of the department or the old-est member of the family may think that he or she is basically more intelligent, wiser, quicker, more mentally alert because of position—and this may be true. However, whatever the basis for the assumption of superiority, projecting it often results in a negative rather than a positive communication climate. This is particularly true when others involved are not at all convinced of that superiority.

A positive communication climate may well be achieved by projecting an attitude of equality rather than an attitude of superiority. **Equality means being on the same level, or seeing others as worthwhile as one's self.** It is usually manifested in the exclusion of any words or nonverbal signs that might indicate the opposite.

One way to alter statements that project delusions of personal superiority is to make statements issue-related. Instead of saying, "Listen, I know that LLG is the top stock to buy, I'm an expert in these kinds of things," try something like "LLG looks like a good stock to buy, it has paid solid dividends exceeding bank interest rates for the last eight years."

A second way is to be very conscious of sound of voice, facial expressions, dress, and manners. In words and actions, you need to show that you are a person—no better and no worse than others. By being willing to listen to others' ideas, by pitching in and working, by really hearing what is being said, and by respecting what others say, you show the attitude of equality.

In summary, the procedure for conveying an attitude of equality rather than an air of superiority is as follows:

1. *Consider what you are about to say.*

2. *Does it include any words or does it imply in any way that you as the sender of the message are in some way superior to the receiver of that message?*

3. *If so, recast the sentence so the content of the message remains but the intent is altered. Change sentences from, "Oh, that's what you are going to try—well, I tried it last year and found it's not a good idea" to "I hope it works for you—when I tried a similar procedure last year it gave me some problems."*

In these last few pages we have considered three specific skills that will work to build or maintain a positive communication climate. Now let us see whether you can demonstrate your understanding of them.

## Communication Session

*Reflection*

Think of the last time you had a discussion with another person. How did the interpersonal climate affect that discussion?

*Actualization*

Label the following statements as E (evaluative), D (dogmatic), or S (superior). In each case rephrase the statement so that it is descriptive, provisional, or equal. We have done the first one for you.

_D_ 1. "Maud—turn that off! No one can study with the radio on!"

"Maud—I'd suggest turning that radio off. Many people find they can study more efficiently if they eliminate potential distractions."

___2. "Did you ever hear of such a tacky idea as having a formal wedding and using paper plates?"

___3. "That advertising program will never sell."

___4. "Oh Jack—you're so funny wearing plaids with stripes. Well, I guess that's a man for you!"

___5. "Paul—you're acting like a baby. You've got to learn to use your head."

___6. A Walt Disney show? I don't want to see any kids' movie!"

___7. "You may think you know how to handle the situation; but you are just not mature enough. I know when something's right for you."

**Answers:** 1. D; 2. E; 3. E; 4. S; 5. E; 6. S; 7. S.

Chapter Three:
Skills That
Establish a
Positive
Communication
Climate

47

## Openness to Others—Self-disclosure

For years communication experts have attempted to determine the importance of openness in communication. Although there is considerable agreement that some openness leads to a positive communication climate, there is little evidence to document the degree of openness that is optimal for effective interaction. Although a lack of openness will not lead to a positive communication climate and may well result in a negative climate, too much openness may destroy the positive climate you have attempted to build or to maintain. Paul Cozby, in his review of self-disclosure literature, says that we should be very careful about any attitude that calls for people to lose their "freedom to have private thoughts because full disclosure is demanded by others . . ."[6]

We strongly disagree with those authors who demand total openness as a condition of good interpersonal communication. On the other hand, we recognize the importance of some degree of openness in order to maintain a positive communication climate. Our goal in the remainder of this chapter is to give you workable guidelines for your use of two very important communication skills, self-disclosure and receptiveness to feedback. First we will consider self-disclosure—later we will consider openness to feedback.

---

[6]Paul C. Cozby, "Self-Disclosure: A Literature Review," *Psychological Bulletin*, Vol. 79 (February 1973), p. 88.

### Sharing of Data

**Self-disclosure with another means sharing biographical data, personal ideas, and feelings that are unknown to the other person.** The first of these reveals facts about you as an individual. A statement such as "I was too small to make the team in high school" discloses biographical information; "I don't think the idea of rehabilitation of criminals is working" discloses a personal idea; "I get scared whenever I have to make a speech" discloses feelings. Through such self-disclosures others get to know you and understand you. Biographical disclosures are the easiest to make for they are, in a manner of speaking, a matter of public record. Disclosures of personal ideas and feelings are at the same time more threatening and more important. They are more threatening because they are not a matter of record—they are truly revealing of you as a person; they are more important because they represent the kinds of statements that enable someone to really know you.

The degree of self-disclosure you are willing to make is based in part upon trust. The more you trust a person, the more likely you are to reveal information about yourself that is personal. You may already have a pretty good operational definition of what it means to trust others. However, because the element of trust is so important to the development of the self-disclosure skill, we want to take some space to discuss it.

*Is self-disclosure safe?*

### Trust

Although we may know almost instinctively what it means to trust others, "trust" is a most difficult term to define. Giffin and Patton say that trust is "reliance upon communication behavior of another person while attempting to achieve a desired but uncertain objective in a risky situation."[7] If you rely on the communication behavior of another individual, the outcome of your interaction depends not only on your actions, but also on those of someone else. A willingness to rely on someone else is difficult because it entails risk. *Risk* is the possibility that you may lose

more than you gain in a given situation. So, it does not take much trust for someone to tell you that she had an appendectomy. If you tell someone else, she has lost little. If, however, someone tells you of her abortion, disclosing this shows a lot of trust, for if you reveal this to her employer or to her parents, it is likely to have serious consequences for her.

A person must have and must exhibit a certain amount of trust in others before he or she can be open with them. If you have more to lose than to gain, why should you trust anyone? Without some trust in your daily behavior, you would not be able to function. If you did not trust oncoming traffic to stay in its own lane, how could you ever take a car onto the street? If you did not trust the bank to credit your deposits and account for your money, how could you use a checking or savings account? And if you did not trust your friends, how could you talk out any of your problems, feelings, or decisions with others?

By trusting another person, you demonstrate the bond that exists between you and that person. In effect, you say to a trusted person, "I'm giving information that can hurt me, but in giving this information I am demonstrating my commitment to the value of our relationship."

Just as it is impractical to trust no one, it is folly to trust everyone. A person does not tell his or her deepest secrets to any enemy, to casual acquaintances, or even to some friends.

Nevertheless, some trust is crucial to deepening interpersonal relationships. Trust

---

[7]Kim Giffin and Bobby Patton, *Fundamentals of Interpersonal Communication* (New York: Harper & Row, 1971), p. 162.

Chapter Three:
Skills That
Establish a
Positive
Communication
Climate

**49**

should not be given blindly but should be given as a product of experience with others. If your experiences show that your trust was well placed, your trust in people continues and grows. If, for instance, Denny entrusts Carl with a package to be delivered, and Carl delivers it as promised, then Denny's trust in Carl is reinforced; if however, Carl fails to deliver that package as scheduled, then Denny may be less inclined to trust Carl in the future. Similarly, if Sheila tells Maureen a secret and Maureen guards it, Sheila's trust in Maureen is reinforced; if Maureen discloses it to others, Sheila may be less inclined to confide in Maureen in the future. Of course an individual's trustworthiness varies with the importance he or she places in the trust he or she has been given. Some people may be very trustworthy with secrets but not so trustworthy with material goods, whereas others may be trustworthy with material goods, but not with secrets. In your relationships, you expect trust to be reciprocal. The closer you come to another person, the more trust you place in that person, and the more you expect that person to place trust in you.

## Self-disclosure and Interpersonal Relationships

Now that we have considered the role of trust in the self-disclosure process, let us consider the ways in which self-disclosure is appropriate in interpersonal communication. To begin with, a degree of self-disclosure is necessary in the initiation and development of a relationship, since people feel closer to those they know the most about. How many times have you observed something like the following scene played out between two people who have met for the first time:

**Joan:** *Today is such a beautiful day—just right for tennis. You can play all day and still feel great.*

**Jill:** *Oh, you play tennis.*

**Joan:** *I sure do. I love it.*

**Jill:** *I play, too. How good are you?*

**Joan:** *Well, I've had a few lessons, and I think I do pretty well, but Chris Evert doesn't have to worry about me!''*

With this initiation of a conversation on tennis, Jill finds out whether Joan would be a good match and whether they might enjoy playing together. Now, whether they ever do play together may depend upon some other factors, but through the mutual self-disclosure Jill and Joan discover a common experience and a common enthusiasm. Through conversations such as these friendships are born. Had Jill replied "Well, I don't care for tennis, but I do like to hike on a day like this," the conversation would have taken a different turn, but still through the self-disclosure each would learn information about the other that would have suggested the possibility of some relationship.

Even in a relatively impersonal setting, self-disclosure can help people feel closer to others. For instance, you may feel closer to an instructor who becomes a "real person" to you. Through his or her lecture examples you get to know about the person's family, about his or her proficiency in cooking, about the way he or she sees the world, and about his or her interests, needs, and desires. The simple truth is that it is hard to like or even to warm up to anyone about whom you know nothing.

In ongoing relationships self-disclosure achieves a different purpose. It is through your communication and particularly your self-disclosure that *you teach others how to treat you*. The way you define yourself through your communication teaches others how they should act, react to, and communicate with you. For instance, if through your communication and your behavior it becomes apparent that you love to cook, then those around you will talk with you about cooking and seek to interact with you in subjects related to foods. If you hide your love of cooking, people will not know your feelings and may not talk with you about food, cooking, restaurants, or similar subjects. Have you ever heard something like this complaint: "I wonder why they don't ask me to go to that new French restaurant that just opened?" The person who makes such a statement may suspect that the lack of invitation indicates people dislike him, when actually it may be that they did not realize he was interested in fine foods.

The nature and degree of self-disclosure that you permit yourself is closely related to the level of the relationship you have with that other person. Relationships differ on a continuum from people we recognize but do not interact with at one end to people we are intimate with at the other end. The farther along the continuum, the greater the self-disclosure, but the fewer the people there are in that particular category. So, whereas there are any number of persons you may recognize but interact very little with, there are few with whom you are intimate and share some of your deepest secrets.

More important than the correlation between the amount of self-disclosure and the degree of intimacy is the stimulative effect of self-disclosure on the growth of a relationship. Growth is the increase of intensity of a relationship, based at least in part on the degree of self-disclosure. Thus, when you decide you really like what you know about another person and believe that the other person likes what he or she knows about you, you tend to *intensify* the degree of self-disclosure by revealing more intimate information about yourself. Now, here is where the nature of *risk* becomes very important. You may think: "If I reveal my fear of flying to Frank who goes in for hang-gliding as a hobby, Frank may not continue to like me." The dilemma is that if you do not reveal risky information, Frank will not understand and may misinterpret your behavior, and a relationship that might have grown to friendship or even intimacy if you had risked self-disclosure may never develop or may crumble. So often, the risk you think you are avoiding by not disclosing

Chapter Three:
Skills That
Establish a
Positive
Communication
Climate

51

becomes a two-edged sword. You may be cut by self-disclosure, but you also may be cut by the lack of it.

Whether or not you choose to disclose, *you must be prepared to accept the consequences of your communication behavior.* If you are not willing to face the risk of rejection, you should not disclose. However, if you are not going to disclose anything about yourself, others probably will not reciprocate. If disclosure does not take place, relationships cannot grow. If Charles finds himself missing the close relationships with girls he admires, his failure to develop such relationships could be a consequence of choosing not to disclose information about himself. So, at least in part, Charles must bear the responsibility for lack of close relationships.

### Guidelines for Self-disclosure

If you are not used to disclosing information about yourself, doing it is not easy. The advice to "go and self-disclose—but not too much," is not very meaningful. Let us consider some useful guidelines in determining appropriate self-disclosure. As you read these guidelines, keep in mind that the goal of self-disclosure is "to be perceived by the other as the one I know myself to be."[8]

---

[8]Sidney M. Jourard, *Healthy Personality* (New York: Macmillan Publishing Company, 1974), p. 181.

1. *Self-disclosure should come when you believe the disclosure represents an acceptable risk.* There is always some risk involved in disclosing. But if you trust another person, you will perceive the disclosure as "safe." Incidentally, this guideline explains why some people engage in self-disclosure to bartenders or people they meet in travel. The disclosures they make are perceived as *safe* (representing reasonable risk) because the person either does not know them or is in no position to use the information against them. It seems to us very sad that some people do not trust their husbands, wives, or other members of the family enough to make these disclosures.

2. *Self-disclosure should move gradually to deeper levels.* Since receiving self-disclosure can be as threatening as giving it, most people become very uncomfortable when the level of disclosure exceeds their expectations. As a relationship develops, the depth of disclosure increases as well.

3. *Intimate or personal self-disclosure is most appropriate in an ongoing relationship.* Disclosures about deep feelings, fears, loves, and so forth are most appropriate in an established relationship. When someone discloses deep secrets to an acquaintance, he is engaging in potentially threatening behavior. If disclosure is made before a bond of trust is established, the person making the disclosure may be risking a great deal. Moreover, some people are embarrassed by and sometimes hostile toward others who try to saddle them with

personal information in an effort to imply a relationship where none exists.

4. *Intimate self-disclosure should continue only if it is reciprocated.* When a person discloses, he or she expects disclosure in return. When it is apparent that self-disclosure will not be returned, you should limit the amount of disclosure you make.

5. *Consider the reaction of the other person before you disclose.* Some persons are not capable of handling disclosures that alter the nature of their perception of a friend. If Joe has a friend who is strongly opposed to premarital affairs, it may not be in the best interest of Joe's relationship with this friend to reveal that he is having such an affair.

## Communication Session

*Reflection*

**Think of one secret that you hold about yourself. How many people know it? How do you decide whom to tell? What have been some of the consequences (good and bad) that have resulted from sharing that secret?**

*Actualization*

**Working alone, label each of the statements below L (low risk), meaning you believe it is appropriate to disclose this information to almost any person; M (moderate risk), meaning you believe it is appropriate to disclose this information to persons you know pretty well and have already established a friendship relationship with; H (high risk), meaning you would disclose such information only to the few friends you had great trust in or to the person or persons you regarded as your most intimate friends; or X, meaning you would disclose it to no one.**

____ 1. **Your hobbies, how you like best to spend your spare time.**

____ 2. **Your preferences and dislikes in music.**

____ 3. **Your educational background and your feelings about it.**

____ 4. **Your personal views on politics, the presidency, and foreign and domestic policy.**

____ 5. **Your personal religious views and the nature of your religious participation.**

____ 6. **Habits and reactions of yours that bother you at the moment.**

____ 7. **Characteristics of yours that give you cause for pride and satisfaction.**

____ 8. **The unhappiest moments in your life in detail.**

Chapter Three:
Skills That
Establish a
Positive
Communication
Climate

53

____ 9. The occasions in your life when you were happiest—in detail.

____10. The actions you have most regretted taking in your life and why.

____11. The main unfulfilled wishes and dreams in your life.

____12. Your guiltiest secrets.

____13. Your views on the way a husband and wife should live their marriage.

____14. What to do, if anything, to stay fit.

____15. The aspects of your body you are most pleased with.

____16. The features of your appearance you are most displeased with and wish to change.

____17. The person in your life whom you most resent and the reasons why.

____18. Your favorite forms of erotic play and sexual lovemaking.

____19. The people with whom you have been sexually intimate, and the circumstances of your relationship with each.

*Discussion (optional)*
Working in groups of five to seven, discuss your labeling of the statements. You are not required to make any of the disclosures, only to discuss circumstances, if any, under which you are likely to make them. The purpose of discussion is to see whether any consensus can be gained on the labeling.

## Openness to Feedback

Another factor contributing to effectiveness as a communicator is receptivity to feedback from others. Feedback is the verbal and non-verbal response to you and your communication. You tell a joke and someone laughs—that's feedback; you ask various friends what they think of your new hair style, and they say they like it—that's feedback; you lean close to that someone you care for and he or she pulls away from you—that's feedback. Feedback is sometimes open and obvious, such as a statement by Jan that she likes your taste in clothes or a groan from Tom when you tell a story; at other times feedback is very subtle as in a pulling back, a slight frown, or a slight shift in position. It is through feedback, especially the type of feedback we refer to as "constructive criticism," that we learn who and what we are.

Our degree of sensitivity and openness to constructive criticism feedback to a large extent determines our effectiveness in our relationships with others. Let us take a very obvious example: If after a lunch at an Italian restaurant that features garlic bread with their pasta you find your friends shying away from close contact with you, you may become aware that your garlic breath is offending them. You then can decide what you want to do about the situation. If you are insensitive at that particular time, you may not catch the cues that are being sent—or if you are generally not open to feedback, not willing to acknowledge the cues, you will not profit from the feedback.

Now, feedback of itself does not require alteration of behavior, but sensitivity and openness to feedback make possible a conscious, rational choice about whether or not one will respond to that feedback.

Why are people so inclined to be closed to feedback? For a very simple reason—any implied criticism can be threatening. Since few people like to be criticized, the first tendency for most is to become defensive. For instance, when a friend shies from your garlic breath, you may see that as a putdown of you as a person, and it may make you angry. Everyone has a vested interest in himself. If a person is reasonably normal in behavior (and most people are), he or she thinks pretty highly of himself or herself and is protective of that self. Still everyone can be a better person and a more effective communicator. Many of the cues that come your way give insights into minor weaknesses that can be corrected and strengths that can be maintained.

In Chapter 4 we will consider the skills required to *give* useful feedback. For now, let us look at ways you can demonstrate your receptivity to feedback. **By receptivity, we mean creating a climate in which others feel comfortable in giving you feedback.** How can you create such a climate? Although you will probably get feedback even when you don't ask for it, when you want feedback you can so indicate through several verbal and nonverbal cues:

1. *Ask for feedback only when you are sincerely interested in an honest response.* For instance, if

*If you do not want feedback, do not ask for it.*

you ask a friend "How do you like this coat?" but you really only want the friend to agree with *your* appraisal, you are not being honest. Once others realize that your request for feedback is not really honest, that all you really want to hear is a compliment, valuable feedback will not be forthcoming.

2. *Try to avoid contradiction between your verbal and your nonverbal cues.* For instance, if you say, "How do you like my paper?" but your voice tone indicates that you do not really want to know, the other person may be reluctant to be honest with you.

3. *Give positive "strokes" to those who take your requests for feedback as honest requests.* For instance, if you ask a friend how he or she likes your spaghetti and get the response: "The pasta seemed a little overcooked," and you get annoyed and say, "Well, if you can do any better you can fix dinner next time," your friend will learn not to give you feedback even

Chapter Three:
Skills That
Establish a
Positive
Communication
Climate

55

when you ask for it. If you do not want feed-back, do not ask for it.

4. *Outline the kind of feedback you are seeking.* Instead of asking very general questions about ideas, feelings, or behavior, phrase your questions specifically. Instead of saying, "Marge, is there anything you don't like about me?" (which the other person is likely to consider a "loaded" question), you might say, "Marge, when I'm being critical do I get a cutting or hostile tone to my voice?" Now Marge can speak to the specific behavior in question.

5. *Think of feedback as being in your best interest.* No one likes to be criticized, but it is often through valid criticism that we learn to grow. When you get negative feedback (even when you expected positive), you should not look upon it as destructive to you personally but as a statement that reveals something about yourself that you did not know. Whether you will *do* anything about the feedback is up to you—but you cannot make such a decision about altering negative behavior if you do not know the negative behavior exists.

6. *Check out what you have heard.* Don't jump to conclusions about the meaning of feedback. When a person says something about your be-havior, make sure you understand exactly what is meant. Consider the following con-versation:

**Jack:** *Marge, when I'm being critical do I have a cutting tone to my voice?*

**Marge:** *I don't know—it may be a little sharp.*

**Jack:** *Do you mean that when I criticize a person he is bothered by the sound of my voice?*

**Marge:** *I can see where they would be. You do get a funny sound to your voice.*

The answer to the second question gives fur-ther clarification to Marge's perception.

## Communication Session

*Reflection*

1. Are people inclined to give you feedback? Under what circumstances?

2. What are some of your personal ways of encouraging or turning off feedback? Are they effective?

*Actualization*

1. Write down one to three specific attitudes or behaviors of yours that you would like feedback on. For instance:

Does the way I dress make me look younger than I am?

Do you think I talk too much at meetings?

Did my analysis of Paul's plan help the discussion?

Do I do anything to give the impression of being superior to my friends and acquaintances?

2. Ask a close friend for feedback on one or more of the attitudes or behaviors you have listed. Note how you react to this feedback.

*Discussion*

1. In your discussion group, consider how each of you identify another person's openness to feedback. What do they say and/or do?

2. How do each of you know when someone does not want feedback? What verbal or nonverbal cues do they emit?

## Payoffs

After studying this chapter, you should now be able to

1. Define empathy—both in terms of recognition and response.

2. Assess your own levels of empathy and sensitivity.

3. Define descriptiveness.

4. Incorporate descriptiveness into your communication behavior.

5. Define provisionalism.

6. Incorporate provisionalism into your communication behavior.

7. Define equality.

8. Incorporate equality into your communication behavior.

9. Define self-disclosure.

10. Explain the relationship between self-disclosure and trust.

11. Recognize self-disclosure statements.

12. Discuss the importance of self-disclosure in developing and maintaining relationships.

13. Discuss the consequences of self-disclosure.

14. State guidelines for determining appropriateness of certain self-disclosures.

Chapter Three:
Skills That
Establish a
Positive
Communication
Climate

57

15. Make appropriate self-disclosure statements.

16. Discuss the importance of receptivity to feedback.

17. Explain methods of demonstrating openness to feedback.

18. Ask for feedback from others.

## Suggested Readings

**Jack R. Gibb.** "Defensive Communication." *Journal of Communication,* Vol. II (September 1961). This landmark article provides an excellent analysis of communication climates.

**Sidney M. Jourard.** *The Transparent Self,* rev. ed. New York: D. Van Nostrand Reinhold Company, 1971. Jourard's book is basic reading in the field of self-disclosure.

**W. Barnett Pearce** and **Stewart M. Sharp.** "Self-disclosing Communication." *Journal of Communication,* Vol. 23 (December 1973), pp. 409–425. Not only does this article provide an excellent overview of the subject, but also it contains a good review of the research.

**Chapter Four:**
**Receiving Skills**

Some people perceive the receiver as having a passive role in the communication process. We have heard statements like "Roland's no lecturer—he can't make me understand" or "Martha's just so vague—I can't understand her." Behind such statements is the implication that the success or failure of communication is due primarily if not solely to the sender of the message. Although the sender must certainly shoulder his part of the burden of successful communication, the receiver has definite responsibilities.

Many receiving skills are a type of *feedback*. Feedback is the verbal or nonverbal response to what a person is, to what a person has said, or to what a person has done. You laugh at a joke; you pull back from someone who has bad breath; you say that you like your roommate's drawing; you cry during the climax of a five-handkerchief movie. Every one of these instances represents response.

One type of feedback is *automatic response.* If your instructor were to tell you that you were the best student he had had in all of his years of teaching, you might blush or smile. These would be automatic instantaneous nonverbal responses. Your blurting out "Wow!" "Thanks!" or "You're kidding!" would be a virtually automatic verbal response. Verbal responses are more likely to be subject to some control. By the time we are adults, we have had years of practice in censoring verbal responses. Still, our emotions sometimes get the best of us, and we blurt out what we are thinking regardless of what it might be.

A second type of feedback might be labeled *task-maintenance response.* Such responses hold a dual purpose. The task function of this type of feedback is to respond to the content of the original message. Content is the denotative substance of a message. At any given time you may hear or not hear, understand or not understand, agree or disagree with any message. You can also seek more details, you can object to what is being said, or you can ignore the message entirely. These

*The receiver has responsibilities.*

types of responses are directed at the content of the message. The maintenance function of task-maintenance response serves to confirm or to destroy the sender's perception of his self-worth. Statements that show you empathize with the person, that show concern for his or her feelings, or that somehow focus on the relationship between the communicators rather than on the substance of the message are maintenance-type responses.

A third type of feedback, the kind that provides the source with new information about himself, is *feedback on personal style.* This is directed not necessarily only at what the person has said but also at what he may have done or what you perceive him to be.

In this chapter we will first focus on the skill of listening, the skill that provides us with data to which we can respond. We will then consider five important task-maintenance skills: paraphrasing, supporting, questioning, interpreting, and evaluating. Finally, we will consider in some detail the personal-style feedback skill.

At this point you may be wondering why we discuss receiving skills before sending skills. We are doing so mostly because receiving skills are somewhat easier to put into practice; and because, instead of calling for you to frame new ideas, you need only react to those that have already been presented. Now let us consider each of these skills individually.

## Listening

Listening provides us with data to which we can respond. Through the sense of sight we grasp the meaning of visual nonverbal cues that illustrate, clarify, and occasionally countermand the apparent meaning of verbal messages. The principal instrument for recording verbal messages, however, is the ear.

You may already be aware that in your daily communication you spend more time listening than you do in speaking, reading, or writing. A recently completed study of college student communication habits shows that college students spend 22 percent of their time speaking, 20 percent reading, 8 percent writing, and 50 percent of their time listening.[1] Yet of these four skills, people tend to be most complacent about their listening. Studies indicate that although most people have the physical capabilities of recording audio impulses, many are not really good listeners. Receiving audio stimuli is hearing; **listening means making sense out of what we hear.** Research studies have shown that most of us listen with only 25 to 50 percent efficiency.[2]

In our analysis of listening, let us first consider those listening factors that are a function of your heredity and environment.

### Hearing Acuity

Some people have real hearing problems. Estimates are that as many as 10 percent of any adult audience have some hearing difficulty. If you know you have a hearing problem, you may now wear a hearing aid or you may have learned to adapt to the problem, but if you are not aware of the problem, poor hearing alone may limit your listening effectiveness.

If you suspect that you may have a hearing problem, your school probably has facilities for testing your hearing acuity. The test is painless and is usually provided at minimal if any cost to the student.

### Vocabulary

Listening and vocabulary are definitely related. If you know the meaning of all the

---

[1]Rudolph Verderber and Ann Elder, "An Analysis of Student Communication Habits," unpublished study, University of Cincinnati, 1976.

[2]Ralph G. Nichols and Leonard A. Stevens, *Are You Listening?* (New York: McGraw-Hill Book Company, 1957), pp. 5–6.

words you receive, you are likely to better understand what is being said and have better retention. However, if you do not know the meaning of some words used by the sender, you will not understand them, and your listening may well be affected. Many "poor students" have average or better intelligence, but are handicapped by a poor vocabulary. If you have a below-average vocabulary, you must work that much harder to develop listening skills. Or work to improve your vocabulary.

When Sally uses a word that Paul does not understand, he may sit in silent ignorance rather than taking a step toward improving his vocabulary by asking Sally to define the mysterious word. Is Paul's behavior like yours? Perhaps you fear appearing foolish for not understanding the word in the first place. Isn't it even more foolish to respond to something you don't understand? The tendency to respond as if we really understand is illustrated by results of a telephone survey conducted to ascertain whether people were continuing efforts to save energy. Most respondents answered "yes" to questions about turning out unneeded lights, keeping thermostats at 68 degrees, and driving at 55 miles per hour; however, a surprising number also said "yes" to a question about installing a "thermidor" on the family car. Think how foolish these people would feel if they found out they had confirmed that their engines were now equipped with seafood casseroles! You may feel foolish to ask; you are likely to behave more foolishly if you do not ask.

## An Ear for Language

If your family is articulate and given to verbalizing, there is a good chance that you have a natural "ear for language," that you have a grasp of good thought structure, and that you have had much experience with various kinds and levels of listening. If you have not developed an ear for language at home, then your ear may not be tuned to the difficult kinds of listening that you may encounter at school.

You may have some listening problems, but you can improve your listening ability. The following suggestions can be put into practice if you are willing to concentrate and practice.

1. *Get ready to listen.* Listening efficiency increases when the listener follows the apparently elementary practice of really being ready to listen. "Getting ready" involves both mental and physical attitudes. Mentally you need to stop thinking about any of the thousands of miscellaneous thoughts that constantly pass through your mind; all your attention should be directed to the sender and to what is being said. In effect, the sender is in competition with all these miscellaneous thoughts and feelings. Some of them may be more pleasant to tune into. Anticipation of an exciting evening; thoughts about a game, a test, or what's for dinner; and recreating in your memory scenes from a memorable movie or television show may offer more attractive pleasures than

listening to factual data, yet attention paid to such competing thoughts and feelings is one of the leading causes of poor listening.

Physically, you need to adopt a posture that is most conducive to good listening. Since physical alertness encourages mental alertness, you may find that how you stand or how you sit affects how messages are received. You may also find it helpful to look the speaker in the eye as he or she talks with you. A visual bond between sender and receiver helps form a mental bond.

2. *Make the shift from speaker to listener a complete one.* In a classroom setting in which you are planning to be a listener, it is relatively easy to get ready to listen. In conversation, however, you switch roles from speaker to listener and back to speaker again quite frequently. If as listener, you spend your time preparing your next contribution (that is, thinking about how to say something clever or trying to recall some fact you can use to make your point), your listening efficiency will take a nose dive. We have all experienced situations in which two persons talked right past each other under the guise of "holding a conversation." In comedy routines such situations are often hilarious. In real life, the results of such "communication" are often pathetic—each of two participants broadcasting with no one receiving! The next time you are conversing, check yourself—are you "preparing speeches" instead of listening? Perhaps putting the sender's ideas in your own

words will help you stay tuned in. Although making the shift from speaker to listener may be most difficult to put into practice consistently, it is especially important.

3. *Listen actively.* Because you think faster than most people talk, you can utilize your thinking capacities to make you a better listener. As noted in points 1 and 2, if you let

*Listen actively.*

your mind wander or if you prepare replies while you are supposed to be listening, your efficiency will go down. On the other hand, if you use your time to raise questions about the nature of the material, if you try to couple what the speaker is saying with your own experience, and if you mentally repeat key ideas or associate key points with related ideas, you may be able to raise your listening efficiency. Too often people think of the listening experience as a passive activity in which what they remember is largely a matter of chance. In reality, good listening is hard work that requires concentration and a willingness to mull over what is said.

4. *Withhold evaluation.* By this we mean that you need to control your emotional responses to a speaker's content. Are there any words or ideas that are red flags for you, words whose mere utterance causes you to lose any desire to listen to the speaker? Do you react to such terms as "chauvinist," "Libber," "gay"; "Democrat," "Republican," "Communist"; "Catholic," "Jew," "atheist," "Jesus freak"; "black," "white," "Chicano"? Would any of these words turn you off? Often, poor listeners (and occasionally even good listeners) are given an emotional jolt by a speaker invading an area of personal sensitivity. At this point all you can do is to be wary. When the speaker trips the switch to your emotional reaction—let a warning light go on before you go off. Instead of tuning out or getting ready to fight, work that much harder at being objective. Can you do it? If so, you will improve your listening.

In the above list, we have been concerned primarily with what you can do to improve your listening skills related to comprehension and retention of information. Now let us put your listening skills to the test.

## Communication Session

*Reflection*

**Under what circumstances do you really listen? Can you differentiate when you are really listening from when you are not?**

*Actualization*

**Ask someone to read the following information to you once, at a normal rate of speech. Then give yourself the test that follows. Although the temptation is great to read this item to yourself— try not to—you will miss both the fun and the value of the exercise if you do.**

**Today is your first day on an office job. A fellow worker gives you the following information:** Since you are new to the job, I'd like to fill you in on a few details. The boss probably told you that typing and distribution of mail were your most important duties. Well, they may be, but let me tell you, answering the phone is going to take most of your time. Now about the typing. Goodwin will give the most, but much of what he gives you may have nothing to do with the department—I'd be careful about spending all my time doing his private work. Mason doesn't give much, but you'd better get it right—she's really a stickler. I've always asked to have tests at least two days in advance. Paulson is always dropping stuff on the desk at the last minute.

The mail situation really sounds tricky, but you'll get used to it. Mail comes twice a day—at 10 A.M. and at 2 P.M. You've got to take the mail that's been left on the desk to Charles Hall for pickup. If you really have some rush stuff take it right to the campus post office in Harper Hall. It's a little longer walk, but for really rush stuff, it's better. When you pick up at McDaniel Hall, sort it. You'll have to make sure that only mail for the people up here gets delivered here. If there is any that doesn't belong here, bundle it back up and mark it for return to the campus post office.

Now, about your breaks. You get 10 minutes in the morning, 40 minutes at noon, and 15 minutes in the afternoon. If you're smart, you'll leave before the 10:30 classes let out. That's usually a pretty crush time. Three of the teachers are supposed to have office hours then and if they don't keep them, the students will be on your back. If you take your lunch at 11:45 you'll be back before the main crew goes.

Oh, one more thing. You are supposed to call Jeno at 8:15 every morning to wake him. If you forget, he gets very testy. Well, good luck.

**Answer True or False**

1.___ **Mail that does not belong in this office should be taken to Harper Hall.**

2.___ **Mail comes twice a day.**

3.___ **You should be back from lunch by 12:30.**

4.___ **Paulson is good about dropping work off early.**

5.___ **Mason gives the most work.**

6.___ **Goodwin gives work that has little to do with the department.**

7.___ **Your main jobs according to the boss are typing and answering the telephone.**

8.___ **Mail should be taken to McDaniel Hall.**

9.___ **The post office is in Harper Hall.**

10.___ **You get a 15-minute morning break.**

11.___ **Call Jeno every morning at 8:45.**

12.___ **You don't have to type tests.**

**Answers:** 1. F; 2. T; 3. T; 4. F; 5. F; 6. T; 7. F; 8. F; 9. T; 10. F; 11. F; 12. F.

## Paraphrasing

**Simply defined, paraphrasing is a restatement of the content or of the intent of the sender's message showing what the receiver understood from that message.** Before we get into the specifics of the paraphrasing skill, we had better discuss the difference between *content* and *intent*. Content is the substance of the message the source sends; intent is how the source feels about the content. Let us consider an example to illustrate the difference. Dora says, "My zipper is broken." The content is the fact that the device used for keeping material together, the zipper, has ceased to function properly—it is broken. The intent of the message is the feeling Dora conveys through making the statement. If tonight Dora is going to an important dance with her favorite boy friend—and if she bought this dress to impress him—Dora is likely to be upset by the break and how she makes the statement will convey that feeling. If the garment is old or inexpensive and easily replaced with another similar garment Dora has access to, she may not be particularly upset; in fact, she may even look at the incident as a comical happening. In any event, how she states the fact of the broken zipper will convey a somewhat different feeling from the statement that showed she was upset. A good paraphrase will show the receiver's understanding of the content of the message or of the intent of the message or perhaps both.

Now let us get back to the wording of good paraphrases. Some people mistakenly interpret paraphrasing as mere repetition:

**Fred:** *The big game's tomorrow.*

**George:** *The game's tomorrow, huh.*

Repetition shows that George received the words intact. It does not show that George really got the message. In order to paraphrase a message effectively you as a receiver should

1. *Actively listen to the message.*

2. *Decode the message.*

3. *Reencode the message into your own symbols.*

4. *Try making your statement either more general or more specific than the original message.*

Let's try again:

**Fred:** *The big game's tomorrow.*

**George:** *Yeah, Superbowl Sunday.*

**Fred:** *Naw, I mean the university Ping-Pong championship.*

Note how George took Fred's "big game," a general statement, and reencoded it into what he considered to be the specific "big game," the Super Bowl. This allows Fred to correct George's misperception of his original message.

Are message confusions very common? Of course they are. Think of the number of "communication breakdowns" you may have had just the past few days that were caused by misunderstanding of apparent meaning. You have to go to the bookstore so you ask a friend, "Can I get you anything?" "Hey,

yeah," he replies, "get me some paper for my notebook." So you do. When you return with the paper, he cringes. "Something wrong?" you ask. "You got me this great big pack of narrow-lined three-ring paper—I use wide-lined two-ring!" This simple mistake could easily have been avoided had you originally paraphrased: "I take it you want regular three-ring paper with the narrow lines."

Paraphrasing can make you a better listener, not only by helping you sharpen understanding of message content, but also by helping you sharpen understanding of message intent:

**Fred:** *The big game's tomorrow.*

**George:** *I bet you're looking forward to that.*

**Fred:** *Yeah, the first time I've ever made the finals.*

When you are seeking to understand or clarify the intent of a message, your paraphrase should reflect what you consider to be the motivation behind the original statement. In our example, George perceives that the reason Fred wants to talk about the big game is that he is happily anticipating it. Thus George's paraphrase allows him to check out the accuracy of that perception.

Let us examine a few more examples to aid you in understanding various applications of this skill.

**Instructor:** *I just don't care for the start of a new term.*

**You:** *(How would you paraphrase this statement?)*

On the surface this appears to be a straightforward expression of attitude. However, as with most statements, there is more to what the instructor is saying than these few words can really communicate: (1) He just might not like teaching very well, or (2) he might not like meeting new students, or (3) he might not like the chore of keeping new records. So, to really get an understanding of what he meant, you will need to paraphrase. You might have decided to try the following:

**You:** *Because you're uncomfortable with all the new faces.*

**Instructor:** *No, I enjoy meeting new students. I hate making out new class lists—all the paperwork.*

Occasionally it will take more than one paraphrase to pin down the message. Consider the following:

**Gayle:** *Wow, that guy is weird.*

**Pat:** *You mean he hassles you.*

**Gayle:** *No, he just says the strangest things.*

**Pat:** *And what he says bothers you in some way.*

**Gayle:** *Well, yeah. I really kind of like him but I just never know what he's going to say next, and I just feel uncomfortable.*

You may be thinking that if a person said what he really meant in the first place you would not have to paraphrase. You might be right; however, because language is such an imperfect means for communicating ideas and feelings, people are seldom able to phrase what they mean in such a way that another person can always comprehend it.

## Communication Session

*Reflection*
Think of the last time you had a "misunderstanding." Would paraphrasing have helped avoid that misunderstanding?

*Actualization*
1. Try paraphrasing the following statements. To get you started, we have done the first one for you.

Art: **It's Sally's birthday, and I've planned a really big evening.**

You: **(content) I get the feeling you're going somewhere special.**

You: **(intent) You seem really excited about it.**

Angie: **Professor Jones is a real bore.**

You: **(content)**

You: **(intent)**

Guy: **I don't watch much TV.**

You: **(content)**

You: **(intent)**

Sarah: **Mom and I aren't getting along.**

You: **(content)**

You: **(intent)**

Aileen: **Tomorrow's going to be a bad day.**

You: **(content)**

You: **(intent)**

2. Work in groups of three. A and B will hold a conversation on a topic such as "Why I'm majoring in _____," or "The advantages or disadvantages of living in dorms," or "Dealing with drug abuse on campus." C will observe the conversation. For this exercise, neither speaker is allowed to state his ideas until he paraphrases what the other person has just said to the other person's satisfaction. At the end of three to four minutes, the observer (C) discusses the paraphrasing of the two participants. Then, for 3 to 4 minutes B and C converse and A observes; for the final 3 to 4 minutes, C and A converse and B observes.

*Discussion*
After the exercise is completed, the participants discuss how they felt about paraphrasing and how the paraphrasing affected the conversations.

## Types of Responses

We respond to others in a variety of ways. Answering questions, changing the subject, showing understanding, giving opinions are just a few. As we are trying to show, the kind of response made often affects the climate of the particular interpersonal relationship. Especially when one of the communicators is very emotional about what he or she is saying, you cannot really afford the luxury of purposely creating disharmony. Within your response choices you have a wide range of potential for heightening the bond of communication or severing that fragile bond between others and you.

In order to be a good receiver, you must first listen to the message intently, then by use of the paraphrase you should make sure you have decoded properly. Only then are you really ready to respond further. Now we will consider four common classes of responses. After examining them, you should be able to identify the type of response you give and be able to determine how effective it is likely to be in getting information and in cementing the bonds of your interpersonal relationships. We want to focus our examples on responses to emotion-laden sender messages since careless response to these can cause the greatest interpersonal friction.

### Supporting Statements

**When you say something that soothes, reduces tension, or pacifies, you are being supportive of what a person has said or done.** Supportive statements are intended to help the sender feel better about himself and/or what he has said or done. Being supportive does not mean lying to a person or telling him only what he wants to hear. It does mean honest, sincere efforts to point out the good in the person, his thoughts, or his actions. Making supportive statements calls for you to (1) actively listen to the message and (2) reply in a way that supplies a reinforcement of sender value—a reinforcement that is directly related to the issue that causes the sender concern. Consider the following two examples:

*Alice does not get the job after what she thought was a good interview. While talking to Hank she says, "I know I should have gotten that job, now I don't know what to do." Hank looks at her and says, "Don't give up. You'll get a job if you keep thinking positively."*

*Shirley hangs up the telephone with tears in her eyes. "That was Norm—he called to break our date, but he wouldn't even tell me what was wrong!" Barbara replies, "I can see why you'd feel upset—I'd be hurt too if a person gave me no reason for breaking a date."*

In both of these examples, the receivers replied with supportive statements aimed at helping the person to accept the disappointment, sadness, or anger that was felt. Each response was an attempt to create a climate that would allow the original sender to accept her feelings. In circumstances such as these, there is nothing that can change reality. Alice did *not* get the job and Norm *did* break the date at the last minute. Even if Alice does need to sharpen her interviewee skills and even if Shirley needs to have better control of her emotions, now is the time for consideration of their feelings as described or as expressed. Under such times of negative emotions, most of us need from others a bit of soothing, something to help us cope better with our problems.

In summary, the procedure for making supportive statements is quite simple:

1. *Listen closely to what the person is saying.*

2. *Try to empathize with the person's feelings.*

3. *Phrase a reply that <u>confirms</u> the person's right to those feelings. Later in the conversation you may be able to say something that will help the person overcome the particular problem involved.*

### Questioning

Sometimes before a person can properly respond to what another has said or has done, he or she needs to have more information about the situation. **Questioning is a common method of getting that additional information.** In addition to getting information, careful questioning may serve to help a shy person "open up." Of course, questioning is a valuable response skill only when it is well done.

Questioning is a particularly appropriate response when what is said is sketchy (when necessary data are omitted), when the use of a term is uncertain, or when a receiver has no idea of the sender's feelings about what he or

she is saying. Let us briefly exemplify each of the three kinds of common questions.

1. Questions that encourage the person to give more details:

> **Ann:** *There I was in the middle of dressing when Tom came to the door.*
>
> **Nell:** *What happened next?*
>
> **Fred:** *They turned down my proposal again.*
>
> **Sam:** *Did they give you any reasons for their actions?*

2. Questions that seek to clarify the meaning or the use of a particular word:

> **Martha:** *I don't mind Paul being late, but recently he's been late so frequently!*
>
> **Adelle:** *How frequently do you mean?*
>
> **Phil:** *Norm has just been acting obnoxious lately.*
>
> **Bob:** *What has he been doing that's obnoxious?*

3. Questions that encourage the sender to share how he or she is feeling:

> **Cal:** *What a day —to top it off Marge broke our date.*
>
> **Pete:** *Did that really make you feel bad?*
>
> **Norm:** *Billy didn't win, but he did come in second.*
>
> **Kay:** *Were you disappointed that he didn't win?*

For questioning to succeed as an appropriate response, it must be perceived as an honest effort to discover information that will aid the questioner in helping with the particular problem. If the person perceives the questions as actual or veiled attacks, the questioning will be construed in a negative way. For instance, if in reply to Fred's statement, "They turned down my proposal again," Sam had pointedly replied, "Well, did you really explain it the way you should have?" Fred might very well perceive the statement as attack on Fred's ability to state his proposal in the best light. Rather than helping the situation, this might well have a very negative effect.

Let us look at guidelines for asking helpful questions:

1. *What is the motivation for your question? If the answer is that you need information to be helpful in reply, then continue. If you have some other reason, maybe a paraphrase or some other response is more appropriate. If you are just curious (nosy?) perhaps you need to curb your urge to question.*

2. *What is it you need to know? Is it more details? how a word is used or defined? how the person feels?*

3. *Phrase the question in a way that achieves the goal without creating defensiveness in the sender.*

4. *Respond with a tone of voice that is sincere—not a tone that could be interpreted as sarcastic, cutting, superior, dogmatic, or evaluative.*

Questioning might be a necessary response, but the information sought should be relevant to the prevailing issue and it should come out of a spirit of inquiry and support and not from a real or an apparent need to make the person look bad.

## Interpreting

In many circumstances an appropriate response is interpreting. **Interpreting is an attempt to point out an alternative or hidden meaning to an event.** Like questioning, interpreting can be perceived positively or negatively by the sender depending upon the nature of the interpretation.

**Polly:** *I just don't understand Bill—I say we've got to start saving money and he just puts me off.*

**Angie:** *Perhaps he feels bad about not saving money and feels that you are putting him down.*

**George:** *I take her to dinner, a great show, and when I get to her door she gives me a quick little kiss and says "Thanks a lot" and rushes in the house!*

**Martin:** *I wonder whether she might not be afraid that if she says any more you'll get the wrong idea about what kind of a girl she is?*

Both Angie and Martin are trying to interpret the situations in a way that will allow Polly and George to see possible meanings for the actions. Oftentimes we are quick to judge the meaning of a situation. An interpretation helps us to see other possibilities. The interpretations are not necessarily right, but they do provide alternative explanations.

Similar to questioning, a good interpretative response is formed in language that is supportive of the sender. We are often confused or perplexed by someone else's words or actions. Regardless of the strength of our self-concept we may be inclined to view the words or actions negatively. The interpretation gives us choices, stimulates thinking, and helps the sender to reason out what has taken place.

When you have a need to interpret, you should examine your motive for the interpretation. In the first place, you are not a mind reader—you cannot know for sure why something was done or said. Your goal should be to help the sender make some sense out of the action—to be a help, not a hindrance to the thinking process. Interpretation works best as a response when it comes with words that are perceived as supportive. In summary then, a procedure for interpreting could be stated as follows:

1. *Consider your motivation for the interpretation. As with questions, when you desire to interpret, you should assure yourself that your goal is to help the situation.*

2. *Phrase an alternative to the sender's interpretation—one that is intended to help the sender see that other interpretations are available.*

### Evaluating

**An evaluative response places a value judgment on what has been said or done.** It indicates relative goodness, righteousness, or appropriateness. Although the noted psychologist Carl Rogers believes that an evaluative response is bad whether it is favorable or unfavorable,[3] we believe evaluation can be constructive.

Negative evaluative statements are most detrimental to an interpersonal situation, because they are likely to cause defensiveness. Let us look at two typical negative evaluative responses:

**Garth:** *We can get the money if we could get every one of our supporters to give just two dollars.*

**Mel:** *That's a stupid idea.*

**Barbara:** *My car just has not been sounding right lately.*

**Jackie:** *You probably haven't been using the right kind of gas.*

The statements "That's a stupid idea" and "You probably haven't been using the right kind of gas" are likely to be perceived as attacks on person. For most of us, verbal attacks (or what we perceive as attacks) arouse anger and we are ready to fight back.

Sometimes constructive criticism really is called for. People who want to improve their golf game may hire a pro whose job it is to give constructive criticism; in this class you probably expect your instructor to "evaluate" your use of the various skills. Two elements of these situations allow for constructive criticism or evaluation. (1) The context is such that

---

[3]Carl R. Rogers, *Client-centered Therapy* (Boston: Houghton Mifflin Company, 1951), p. 417.

one person is expecting evaluative feedback from another. Both of the settings described are learning situations in which a learner has an expectation of evaluation. (2) In each situation one person is (directly or indirectly) asking for evaluation. Even so, the way the evaluation is given has much to do with how well it is received. Procedures for offering constructive evaluation are as follows:

1. *Make sure the context calls for or allows evaluation to be given.*

2. *Precede a negative statement with a related positive statement.*

3. *Focus on only one behavior at a time.*

4. *Include what the criticized can do to improve.*

The final section of this chapter considers feedback skills in much greater detail. For now, take the following as a good rule-of-thumb: *Avoid evaluation unless solicited —when evaluation is solicited or when the context calls for it, proceed with caution.* In most emotional circumstances a person is not looking for judgment—he or she is looking for help, support, or understanding. When evaluation is called for—and the use should be seldom—it should be used with great care.

## Communication Session

*Actualization*

1. **Let us summarize this section by examining a situation. Your goal is to identify the type of response.**

**Situation: Joyce is leaving a class in which she has just received her test score and grade. Although she knew she hadn't received an A, Joyce is very disappointed with the D grade that appears on her paper: she feels she should have had at least a C if not the B she was expecting. Jerry, her boy friend, is waiting for her as she comes from class. Upon seeing him, a look of anger comes into her eye and in a trembling voice she says, "He gave me a D—that stinkin' Morten gave me D!"**

Jerry might make any of several responses. Five possible statements are given in the list. Label each response as A, paraphrase; B, supportive; C, questioning; D, evaluating; and E, interpreting.

___1. **Come on, Joyce, you knew you hadn't studied enough when you went in to take the test.**

___2. **I know you feel bad, Joyce, but it's not the end of the world—you may be able to raise the grade by the end of the course.**

___3. **You're really disappointed with the D grade on this test, aren't you?**

___4. **Did he give you the reasons why he gave the D? Did he write any comments?**

___5. **A D is a low grade, but he may well have given it to you to motivate you to do better next time.**

2. **Supply an S (supportive), a Q (questioning), an I (interpreting), and an E (evaluative) response to**

each of the following statements. We have completed the first one for you.

George: (In a dejected voice) I didn't get the scholarship.

S: George—I'm sorry to hear that—anything I can do to make you feel better?

Q: Is that an official statement?

I: Maybe it was given solely on need.

E: You would had if you would have deserved it.

May: Mother says I am not to see Herman anymore!

S:

Q:

I:

E:

Jerry: They just fired my favorite teacher.

S:

Q:

I:

E:

Greg: I lost my car keys!

S:

Q:

I:

E:

Angel: The police just arrested my brother.

S:

Q:

I:

E:

3. Working in groups of six, have a dyadic role-playing conversation beginning with one of the statements above as a catalyst. The other group members should tally the number of paraphrases and S,Q,I,E responses made by each role player. After five minutes, another dyad should role-play another set. After all group members have participated, each member should receive the tally of how he did.

*Discussion*
**Discuss how the number of responses per category influenced the outcome of the role-playing.**

**Answers: 1. D; 2. B; 3. A; 4. C; 5. E.**

## Response to Personal Style

As we mentioned earlier, another kind of feedback—response to personal style—**provides the source with new information about himself.** This is directed not necessarily only at what the person has said, but at what he may have done or at what you perceive him to be. If Carl says, "Bill, you really smile a lot" or "Ann, were you aware that you didn't let him finish his point?" Carl is feeding back information that the source may not have. On this level, the riskiest yet potentially most profitable kind of feedback occurs—feedback directed toward giving new information to another about his or her behavior. "Jed, are you aware that when you criticize someone your voice gets a very cutting tone?" and "Jack, are you aware that whenever Alice comes into the room you get a very strained look on your face?" are statements of feedback about behavior.

Whether or not your feedback will have positive or negative effect may depend on your usage of the feedback skill that is often referred to as "constructive criticism." Anyone who is interested in improving interpersonal communication should be open to personal-style feedback; however, the way it is given may affect willingness to remain open to this feedback. Carelessly worded personal-style feedback may cause a person who is leery of openness to return to a closed position to avoid possible hurt. As a potential sender of personal-style feedback, you should become sensitive to right ways and wrong ways

as well as right times and wrong times for giving this type of feedback.

To some persons, the idea that criticism is important to personal growth implies that they have the license to become "supercritic"; you know the kind—the person who says: "Don't get angry, I'm only telling you this for your own good" or "I know it's a small point (and I know that I have already told you 756 things that are wrong with you), but while I'm at it, let me tell you one more thing that's wrong." These may sound like exaggerations—but such expressions are used in interpersonal communication far more than they should be.

Personal-style feedback is an important skill but very difficult to perfect, because the effect feedback will have is often determined by one's sensitivity to the situation and to the other person. Too often, persons who are insensitive or just careless give feedback that is inappropriate.

The following eight guidelines, based in part upon National Training Laboratory material,[4] may help you determine when and how to give feedback.

1. *Personal-style feedback is most valuable when the original sender indicates a readiness for feedback.* Too often, people are told something "for their own good" when they are not interested in hearing about it. Even an open person

---

[4]Several of these suggestions were first articulated in the *1968 Summer Reading Book* of the National Training Laboratories Institute for Applied Behavioral Sciences.

is not always receptive to whatever you might want to say. If a person tends to be particularly sensitive, you must be very careful about the timing of your approach. Look for signs of receptiveness; there may be indications that some response would be welcomed. Even when you feel fairly certain that the time is right, proceed with caution.

2. *If you want personal-style feedback, ask for it.* Just as you may not be sure whether the other person is ready for feedback, so that other person may not be sure whether you are ready. Be specific in your requests, such as "Do I frown when I speak?" or "Did I make myself clear on that point?" or "Does that idea sound any good at all?" Since most of us do try to protect the feelings of others, your friends may not respond to you (especially in a negative way) unless you ask them to do so.

3. *If you would like to give personal-style feedback but are not sure whether a person wishes to hear it, ask him.* You might say, for example: "I've got some comments for you on the way you handled the meeting—would you like to hear them?" *Caution:* Even if the person says "yes," be careful how you proceed. He may have said "yes" because he was curious or because he could not hurt your feelings by saying "no." Begin sensitively. If you are going to be negative, do not give him the whole of it, all at once. Probably one or two points are all that need to be mentioned, and they should be stated delicately (see point 8 below).

4. *Personal-style feedback can be and often should be positive.* For some reason, when most of us

think about feedback, we are inclined to think negatively—as if the only things that should be of concern are things that are wrong. In fact, it is not a bad idea, even when you are planning to give negative feedback, to start with something positive. But use a little common sense. We do not mean "Say, Jack, that's a nice shirt you have on—now, about that crummy meeting you just ran . . ." The positive statement should be important and should be related to a substantive point. If you cannot make a positive substantive point, then don't fool around with some worthless opening comment just to "be nice."

5. *Personal-style feedback should be specific and not general.* It is not very helpful to hear such comments as "your description of the place just didn't sound right." If the description lacked vividness, say so; if it was unclear, say so; if it was not complete enough to create a picture, say so. The more specific the feedback, the more directly the source of the message will be able to deal with the problem.

6. *Feedback should be given at the earliest possible time.* It just does not help a person very much to hear about something that he did last week or last month. The time to deal with a problem is when it is fresh. If you have to spend all of your time recreating the situation, you are not going to have the best climate for dealing with the feedback.

7. *Direct feedback toward behavior the receiver can do something about.* It is frustrating to be reminded of some shortcoming over which we have no control. Telling a person he would be

a better basketball player if he were taller may be true, but it will not help him improve his skill. Telling him he needs to hold his arms in a different position when he shoots a basket is something he can work on.

8. *Feedback should be given in a way that is descriptive and not evaluative or judgmental.* For instance, saying "That's a stupid idea, Joe" would not be effective for a lot of reasons, not the least of which is that calling Joe stupid will make him angry. Your goal is not to anger the person, but to help him. Saying, "Joe, when you get into a debate you speak so quickly that I have a hard time understanding you" is better than saying, "Joe, you talk too fast."

## Communication Session

*Reflection*

**Think of the most recent times you have given someone feedback:**

**1. What mistakes, if any, did you make in giving the feedback?**

**2. If you were to do it again, how would you proceed differently?**

*Actualization*

**Consider the following two situations. Work out an appropriate phrasing of feedback for each:**

**1. You have been driving to school with a fellow student whose name you got from the Transportation Office at school. You have known him for only three weeks. Everything about the situation is great except that he drives too fast for you.**

**2. A good friend says "you know" more than once every sentence. You like her very much, but you see that others are beginning to avoid her. She is a very sensitive girl who does not usually take criticism well.**

*Discussion*

**In groups of three to six, share your ideas on how you would phrase the feedback. Be especially sensitive to methods that seem particularly good.**

## Payoffs

As a result of working with these skills, you should now be able to

1. Differentiate between hearing and listening.

2. Apply the four-step process for improving listening efficiency.

3. Describe the three types of feedback responses.

4. Paraphrase both the content and the intent of a message.

5. Identify and present appropriate supportive, questioning, interpretive, and evaluative responses.

6. Understand the rules for giving personal-style feedback.

7. Give personal-style feedback in a supportive manner.

## Suggested Readings

**Larry L. Barker.** *Listening Behavior.* Englewood Cliffs, New Jersey: Prentice-Hall, 1971. You should find several chapters of this book particularly helpful to you.

**Ralph G. Nichols.** "Do We Know How to Listen? Practical Helps in a Modern Age." *Speech Teacher,* Vol. 10 (1961), pp. 118–124. This article contains several helpful hints for good listening.

**Carl R. Rogers.** *Client-centered Therapy.* Boston: Houghton Mifflin Company, 1951. This book is especially good for its detailed analysis of evaluative responses. Rogers is a pioneer in the field of the study of empathic communication.

**Chapter Five:
Sending Skills**

Your communication will be significantly improved if you learn to send your thoughts and feelings more accurately. Since most interaction is spontaneous, learning to sharpen sending skills will require careful thought and practice. Although a few people achieve the goal of instant intelligibility, most of us need all the help we can get.

In this chapter we will consider basic sender skills. The first, separating fact from inference, is a perceptual skill that actually precedes the encoding process; the next five, dating, indexing, accuracy in symbol selection, use of specific and concrete symbols, and fluency, are cognitive skills that will help you sharpen sending of your ideas. The final two, crediting and describing feelings, are affective skills that will help you to better communicate your feelings.[1]

## Separating Fact from Inference

In Chapter 2, we considered how the perception process affects communication. An essential skill for practical application of the perceptual process is the separation of fact from inference. Consider the following three statements: "Take your umbrella, Jack. It's raining like crazy out there." "Let's cross to the other side of the street—there's someone standing in that doorway!" "Moving this sofa should be a snap for us; it's light as a feather." All three of these statements have at least one thing in common: they ask for a course of action based upon what appear to be facts. Yet a sender's communication can be totally distorted and the action called for can be totally inappropriate if, instead of *facts*, his communication is based upon inferences.

A fact is a verifiable statement—usually

something that is directly observed; an inference is a conclusion drawn from or about the phenomenon being observed. **Separating fact from inference means being able to differentiate between a verifiable statement and a conclusion drawn from or about the phenomenon observed.** Ellen's reporting that she saw Hector run from his house, start his car quickly, and without pausing race his car down the street would be relating facts; if, in addition, she chuckled and said, "Ol' Hector's late again," this last statement would be an inference because Ellen is concluding Hector is "late again." Maybe he is not late at all! Suppose, for example, that he was just notified of a sudden illness in his family and was rushing to the hospital. Not only would Ellen's inference be wrong, but also it could result in further inappropriate action.

Transmitting effective messages depends not only on how accurately you perceive your world, but also in whether you can separate the facts from the inferences in your perceptions. If you have difficulty distinguishing facts from inference, you will have difficulty in thinking logically, shaping messages, and ultimately in communicating. Thus, the starting point in accurate message sending is recognizing whether you are communicating on the basis of facts or inferences. Studies show that many people are unable to make this differentiation in their communication.[2]

---

[1]Many of the skills in this chapter were developed by the general semanticists. For a more in-depth study of this theory, we recommend several books listed at the end of this chapter.

[2]For a discussion of a recent study, see "How Hints Are Transformed into Facts," *Psychology Today*, Vol. 9 (April 1976), p. 114.

There is nothing inherently wrong with drawing inferences—people must make them in order to make sense out of the world. However, (1) you should know when you are inferring and when you are reporting observation; (2) you should recognize that although your inferences may be true, they need not be, and so they should not be stated as if they are; and (3) you should not act as though your inferences are facts.

Failure to separate fact from inference can cause embarrassment, discomfort, and occasionally disaster. If Jane and Marsha cross the street to avoid the forbidding-looking man standing in the doorway they may be embarrassed to find that the menacing "man" is only a shadow. The embarrassment is small price to pay for caution. On the other hand, if Rex talks Bill into helping him move the sofa downstairs because "it's light as a feather," the sofa could be badly damaged or both fellows could be injured if the sofa turned out to be so heavy that they lost control of it going downstairs.

Confusing inference with fact can be disastrous. Consider this situation: Tom and Larry are driving north in a hurry because Tom is late for an appointment. Larry, the driver, stops at the stop sign at the intersection of Main and Corry. Cars coming east-west on Corry have no stop sign at the intersection. As Larry pulls to a stop, a car appears from Larry's left traveling west to east—the car's right turn signal is blinking. Tom nudges Larry and says, "Go on, Larry, he's turning here." The result of Tom's con-

fusion of inference and fact could be hundreds of dollars in repair bills and possible disaster. The blinking turn signal does not guarantee that the car will indeed turn right onto Main. The signal could have been turned on by accident; it could have been turned on because the car was going to turn into a driveway just beyond the intersection; or the signal could have been turned on early to designate a turn at the next intersection.

So, what communication effect does the skill of separating fact from inference have? (1) It helps you eliminate embarrassment; (2) it helps you keep from creating the impression that what you are saying is fact; and (3) it helps you avoid making statements that may be costly for both you and others.

Of course, before you can verbally separate fact from inference you must be sure you understand the difference. Our exercises focus on differentiating between the two.

## Communication Session

*Reflection*

Do you seem prone to fact-inference confusion? If so, design an action plan to help you overcome this problem.

*Discussion*

In groups of four to six, share past experiences where fact-inference confusion caused problems.

*Actualization*

Read the following statements. Assume that all information presented in them is definitely accurate and true. Then follow the instructions given below no. 1.

1. The only vehicle parked in front of 725 Main Street is a red truck. The words "Bob Jones TV Repair" are spelled in large white letters across the side panels of the truck.

Read the following statements made in reference to the data above. Indicate each statement as F—Fact or I—Inference.

___1. "Tom, there's a red truck parked in front of 725 Main."

___2. "Yeah, I see it. It belongs to Bob Jones the TV repair man."

___3. "Looks like the people living at 725 need their TV fixed."

___4. "Well if it can be fixed, Bob Jones will fix it."

2. Two people came hurrying out of a bank with several large bundles, hopped into a long black car, and sped away. Seconds later, a man rushed out of the bank waving his arms and looking quite upset.

___1. "The bank's been robbed!"

___2. "Yes indeed—we saw the robbers hurry out of the bank, hop into a car, and speed away."

___3. "It was a long black car."

___4. "The men were carrying several large bundles."

___5. "Seconds after they left a man came out of the bank after them—but he was too late, they'd already escaped."

3. Tom and Susan walked side by side across campus. A man with long hair came running down the walk panting, bumped into both Tom and Susan as he squeezed between them, stumbled slightly, and then disappeared into the crowd.

___1. "That man sure seems in a hurry."

___2. "Well, he's lost whoever was chasing him."

___3. "He sure was panting."

___4. "He'd been running for a long time."

___5. "He stumbled as he squeezed between them."

___6. "That's when he hurt his leg."

___7. "He really gave them a good shove as he went between them."

---

**Answers to 3:** 1. I; 2. I; 3. F; 4. I; 5. F; 6. I; 7. I.

**Answers to 2:** 1. I; 2. I; 3. F; 4. I (men?); 5. I.
Jones.).

**Answers to 1:** 1. Fact. 2. Inference (Beware of inferences in fact clothing! Just because it says "I see it," don't be fooled. Bob Jones may have just sold this truck and the new owner may not have had time to change the lettering.); 3. Inference (Someone may need his TV repaired, but from the statements we don't know that as a fact.); 4. Inference (If there is something wrong with the repairman may fix it—the repairman may or may not be Bob

## Dating

One basic fact of the reality of our life is that all things are subject to change. Notice your textbook, for instance. For as long as you own it, the words will remain the same—but the book will change. The more you work with it the more "used" it becomes: the cover will develop cracks, pages will show thumb prints and coffee stains, corners will be bent or torn. Like your book, some things in your environment will show only superficial changes; but others will change markedly even within short periods of time: The New York Yankees of the 1970s are not the Yankees of the 1950s; that 1967 Buick in the used-car lot is not the same car that it was in 1967; your father is not the same as he was twenty years ago (and neither are you); and your baby brother is different from what he was last week.

All this seems obvious, doesn't it? Nevertheless, in dealing with and communicating about people, ideas, and objects, there seems to be some satisfaction in seeing them as constants and our language seems to facilitate talking about the elements of our world as statics. This tendency can be seen especially well in evaluative statements:

**Carol:** *I don't like mushrooms.*

**Candy:** *When's the last time you tasted them?*

**Carol:** *Oh, about five years ago.*

**Ray:** *Your interest in the Chi Chi's amazes me—they're just a bunch of jocks.*

*Dating is a helpful skill.*

**Hal:** *I didn't know that.*

**Ray:** *Sure—when I was in college some twenty years ago most of the varsity athletes were members of Chi Chi.*

Are these uncommon examples? We don't think so. Your senses record certain data and you draw conclusions. Having once drawn the conclusion, you often no longer think about it. By saying "I don't like mushrooms," Carol makes a "forever" statement about tastes when in reality everyone's tastes change over a period of time. Ray's statement about Chi Chi's was true once but whether it was ever true again is not accounted for in the statement. Yet, in both cases, Carol and Ray are freed of the responsibility of reevaluation. Such mind sets are comfortable for people, but highly damaging to communication.

If your communication is based upon outdated facts, then your communication will be faulty. As a concerned communicator, what skill can you utilize to sharpen the accuracy of your communication? We find the skill of *dating* helpful. **By "dating" we mean including when the data were true.** For instance, "I didn't like mushrooms the last time I tasted them—and that's been about five years ago." "When I was in college some twenty years ago, the Chi Chi's were a bunch of jocks" (or, better yet, "had a high percentage of athletes").

You have no power to keep things from changing. In order to be accurate in your communication, best you accept the inevitability

of change. So, recognize the potential for change by dating statements you make.

## Indexing

A skill akin to yet somewhat different from dating is *indexing*. One of the great powers of the human intellect is the power to generalize. Generalization allows us to take what we have learned in or about one situation and apply it to similar situations. This is one of the abilities that distinguish man from lower animals. When George reports that he caught five beautiful bass along the shore where a fallen tree provided a certain environment that seems attractive to bass, Charlie is likely to seek out a similar setting for his fishing. When Arlene notices that her boy friend really seems entranced by the fragrance of the new perfume she is wearing, she is likely to wear it again when they are together. When the defense notices that the offense has run several plays to the left side of the line, they are likely to take measures to shore up that side of the line. All these are examples of the values of generalization.

As important as generalization is to our functioning in society, at least two common communication problems relate directly to our misuse of this power. One problem is the tendency to characterize all members of a particular classification exactly the same. This particular problem is called "allness." For instance, if your experience with one Chevette proved that it was economical and easily maintained, you may have a tendency to grant those characteristics to *all* Chevettes; if you have known an older house that was in need of repair, dingy, and "old fashioned," you may have a tendency to assign those characteristics to *all* old houses. A second and related problem is the tendency to assign a characteristic of one person to another person just because both are within the same classification. For instance, if Pat is a lazy teenager, your boss may think that Phil, another teenager, is also lazy; if Barbara, a sorority girl, is a poor student, your instructor may think that Imogene, another sorority girl, is a poor student.

Generalizations do not take into account individual differences. Now, through technology it is possible to produce items that are *virtually* identical. However, even small objects that have no moving parts have certain individual differences even if they are microscopic in nature. When we move to larger complex objects with many moving parts, the likelihood of identity is even less. We know enough about assembly-line production to realize that in assembly human error alone is enough to create tremendous differences in the finished products. No one is exactly like any other person who has ever lived; we know that even identical twins have many individual differences.

An easy way of taking individual differences into account when you are shaping messages is to use an indexing system. **By "indexing" we mean verbally accounting for those individual differences.** If you are going to talk about actors you must recognize in your thinking that each actor is an individual with individual differences: Jerry (an actor) is not the same as Don (actor$_2$) who in turn is not the same as Jack (actor$_3$). Notice, not being the same is shown by the indexing: actor$_1$, actor$_2$, and actor$_3$. Then when you talk about the classification of actors and individuals within that classification, instead of saying "All actors are a little weird, so you can imagine what Jerry is like," you might revise your statement to "Although I believe most actors are weird (general statement), Jerry may not be (indexing statement)."

Consider the methods of indexing used in the following statements:

*"Chevettes are supposed to be economical and very easily maintained—this particular one may or may not be."*

*"Barb is an accounting major. Usually women accounting students are really intelligent and sharp. I hope Barb has those characteristics."*

*"I know Marge is a feminist, but that doesn't mean that she necessarily holds to all NOW beliefs."*

## Communication Session

*Reflection*
**Have you ever had communication difficulties because of lack of dating and indexing skills? What was the history of the incident?**

*Actualization*
**Working in groups of three to six, have two persons discuss topics like the ones below. The rest of the group should observe when dating and indexing are being used, how well they are being used, and when they should have been used. Each person in the group should have an opportunity to practice.**

| | |
|---|---|
| **Cars** | **Animals as pets** |
| **Food preferences** | **Truck drivers** |
| **Politicians** | **The generation gap** |
| **Job interviewers** | **Minority groups in college** |
| **Sororities and fraternities** | |

*Discussion*
**Are dating and indexing hard for you to do? Why?**

## Accuracy in Symbol Selection

Much communication difficulty is caused by the imprecision of language; we may compound this difficulty by selecting inaccurate symbols to represent our thoughts and feelings. **A goal of encoding is to select words to represent thoughts and feelings that are recognized by others in our culture as symbolizing those thoughts and feelings.**

Have you ever found yourself in the situation in which someone says something like "He's got such a rasping voice" and when you reply, "I don't think I caught the scratchy quality," the person says, "I didn't really mean rasping, I meant more like nasal." Our problem of word selection is made even more difficult by the shades of meaning that so many words can represent. Take the simple verb "said." Notice the changes in meaning you can get by using each of the following words to complete the sentence, "No," Mark—"growled," "pleaded," "whispered," "shouted," "blurted," "answered," or "asked."

Perhaps you have a semantic bias and take the position that words don't mean—people mean. That is, you take the position that words do not have an inherent immutable meaning that everyone recognizes, agrees to, and honors specifically. Well, we take a similar view. Meaning depends a great deal upon the entire context in which a word is used. Still, our language developed as a result of people agreeing to use certain words to represent certain ideas and feelings. You call a four-legged object with a flat surface upon which people sit a "chair" rather than a "plick," a "glumph," or a "sarfrace" because at some time in the past most people who spoke English started to use "chair," rather than some other word, as a word meaning something people sit on. Likewise, you know that "growling" an answer and "purring" an answer mean two different things. The more sensitive you are in selecting words that precisely represent common shared meaning, the more likely that you will be understood as you wish to be. For instance, consider the following passage:

*Gail says: "Mary's an all right student. Certainly better than a lot of others. And she's into what she's doing enough so that the stuff she comes up with does the job."*

Notice how much sharper her meaning would be if she said:

*"Mary's a good student. Her 2.9 average is well above the university median. And she concentrates enough on her major courses to make a good impression on the speech faculty."*

When the elder William Pitt, regarded by some as one of England's greatest speakers, was a teenager, he gained an understanding and appreciation of language by reading a famous dictionary of the day through in its entirety *twice*. Even today, dictionary reading is not a bad way to sharpen your understanding of words. An interesting method of practice is to play "synonyms." Think of a word, then list as many words as you can that mean about the same thing. When you have completed your list, refer to a book of synonyms, like *Roget's Thesaurus,* to see which words you have omitted; then try to determine the shades of difference among the words. Refer to a dictionary for help—it is useful to look up words even when you are sure you know their meanings. You may be surprised to find how many times a subtle meaning of a familiar word escapes you. Now, the goal of this exercise is not to get you to select the rarest word to project an idea—the goal is to encourage you to select the word that *best* represents the idea you wish to communicate.

## Using Specific and Concrete Symbols

Specificity and concreteness go hand in hand in sharpening meaning by reducing choice on the part of the listener. When you are not careful, you may tend to use general and abstract words, words that allow the receiver the choice of many possible images rather than a single intended image. The more the receiver is called upon to provide his own image, the more likelihood the meaning he or she sees will be different from the meaning you intended.

"General" means an entire category; "specific" means one item within the category. When someone says "car" to you, what do you see? It may be any of a number of four-wheeled vehicles used primarily to transport people. In your mind you may see a large car or a small one, a sedan or a coupe, a Buick or a Datsun. If someone says "new Aspen," the number of choices you can picture are reduced. If the person says "new blue Aspen station wagon," the likelihood that you and the sender will picture the same image is considerably better.

Whereas *"general* versus *specific"* deals with object language, *"abstract* versus *concrete"* deals with ideas or values. Concrete language turns an abstract idea or value into clearly pictured behavior. When people say they are "loyal," for instance, you may think of the dictionary definition of faithful to idea, person, company, and so on. However, what "loyal" means in a particular situation is hard to say. What is an act of loyalty to Jim may not be an act of loyalty to you. Thus, to avoid ambiguity and confusion, a person might say, "They always buy the products made by their employer." Now the receiver would have a concrete picture of loyal behavior of a group of employees.

Semanticists speak of levels of abstraction. In some instances you can take an idea from a general abstract level and move it to a specific concrete level through a series of stages. Earlier we talked about cars. We could set forth a continuum, going from the very abstract generalization of vehicles, to motor vehicles, to passenger cars, to station wagons, to Aspen wagons, to the very concrete specific of my blue Aspen station wagon. Or, follow another progression: She likes to have fun; she's a sports enthusiast; she enjoys ball games; she likes to participate in ball games; she plays paddleball every lunch period.

Now, when you select a general or abstract word to encode your message you are inviting confusion. The receiver may have to go through numerous paraphrases to help sharpen the meaning of the message you were trying to send. On the other hand, if you select specific or concrete words to encode your messages, there is a much greater likelihood that the receiver will share your meaning with little additional effort. In summary, then, **speaking in specific and concrete symbols means using words that indicate a single item within a category or a single representation of an abstract value.**

## Fluency

Language, as imperfect as it is in representing accurately our thoughts and feelings, is still remarkably capable of approximating sender meaning. It is the users of language who are primarily responsible for language working less efficiently than it could or should. Few Americans can send as much as one minute of message without cluttering their sentences with some of the most popular nonfluencies. *Nonfluencies* are vocalized sounds that occur in a message but add no substantive content to the message. To be instantly intelligible—and that is the goal of a sender—his language needs to be fluent. He needs to **speak in smooth, uncluttered sentences, avoiding**

**such common nonfluencies as vocal segregates, "you know," and empty expletives.**

Vocal segregates are the "uh's," the "er's," the "well's," and the "OK's" that are so hard to eliminate from our speech. They are often caused by a fear of momentary silence. In some instances, this fear of silence is real. Americans have been taught that it is impolite to interrupt another person until the flow of sound stops. A problem occurs for the speaker when he pauses for the right word or idea. The split second it takes for him to come up with the word may be perceived by others as "dead air time." For fear that another person may perceive the pause as a full stop, the sender often fills that dead air time with sound. More often than not, the sound has no meaning. For some, the customary filler sounds are "uh" or "er"; for others, they may be "well uh" or "um." Although the fear of being interrupted may be real (some people will seek to interrupt at any pause), the intrusion of fillers is a terrible price to pay for occasional interruption.

Equally prevalent, and perhaps even more irritating than the vocal segregates, is the incessant use of "you know." The "you know" habit may begin with a teenager seeking to find out whether what he is sending is already known by a receiver. For some, "you know" may be a source of identification; the sender seeks to show that sender and receiver have common knowledge as a binding element. We believe that for most people, however, the adulteration of sentences with "you know" is just a bad habit, especially when "you know" becomes a filler of time and serves absolutely no communication purpose.

For the most part, excessive use of "you know" is an irritant that may force receivers to be poor listeners in self-defense. It has been our experience that no matter how irritating the use of "you know" may be, the receiver is unlikely to acknowledge his irritation. Seldom if ever does anyone say openly to another person anything like "Your use of 'you know' at every break in thought really causes me great difficulty in listening to you and concentrating on your ideas." Yet passages like the following are quite common:

*You know, the way things are going now, you know, I doubt that, uh, I doubt that we're ever going to get things, you know, straightened out.*

In addition to one "uh" and one repetition, that sentence contains three "you knows." We wish such uses were exaggerations. Unfortunately, they are not. Perhaps you should start pointing out this irritant in others' speech; most important, you should monitor your own speech for such use and do what you can to eliminate it. How should you proceed? We will offer a workable plan after we have considered the third common nonfluency.

To some, especially in informal and relatively intimate situations, a third nonfluency becomes nearly as prevalent as the first two discussed; this nonfluency is the empty expletive. Students of language are aware that language usage has become increasingly more permissive during the last ten years. Whereas at one time certain four-letter words were seen only on walls or spoken only by "coarse," "vulgar," or "crude" persons, now even highly educated individuals hold some special affection for one or more of these all-too-common words. It is not, however, use of four-letter words that mars communication, it is the use of the expletive as a nonfluency— the use of the expletive indiscriminately with no apparent meaning.

Perhaps you have a friend or acquaintance for whom some pet expletive has lost all meaning other than to fill space between words or take the place of other more precise words. When the expletive is used, not to convey thought, but to fill space, it becomes a nonfluency.

For purposes of illustration, let's invent a new expletive—one that can stand for any that you enjoy or resent. This new word is "trid." Now, if on some dim morning you are jolted from sleep by the alarm, fumble out of bed, and in a rush to the john stub your toe on the dresser, shouting "Oh, trid!" may have a therapeutic effect and certainly does express the pain and anguish you are experiencing. Perhaps even saying that the last test was a lot of "trid" is expressive. What we are talking about is the use of expletive as noun, verb, adjective, or adverb indiscriminately with no apparent meaning. For instance:

*Oh, trid. That was one tridden test. If I ever catch that tridder outside of the tridden class you can bet your tridden butt that I'll have something to say to that trid.*

Expletives may add a certain earthiness or even a certain sense of intimacy to a conversation—but at some point the usage reaches a point of diminishing returns—with most of us that point is exceeded far too often. When the expletive is used not to convey thought but to fill space it becomes a nonfluency.

Now, in any minute of conversational sending, most of us may well use one or more nonfluencies; few of us can completely avoid their use. However, with some practice, you can limit their occurrence in your speech and thus become much more fluent. Remember, although they may not be willing to tell you about it, most people are distracted or irritated by nonfluencies. If you are not being listened to the way you think you should be, it could be that people are tuning you out because listening to you carefully is actually painful! So, what do you do? We offer the following three-step method.

1. *Become aware of usage.* In self-defense, perhaps, your ear seldom hears your own nonfluencies. You may believe that you never use them, when in fact they may be a major part of your sending style. There are two ways of learning to be aware. One way is to tape-record yourself talking for several minutes

and then listen to the recording. Turn the recorder on and talk about the game you saw yesterday or the test you took or any of the kinds of things you are likely to talk about with a close friend. When you play it back, your ear will begin to pick up your uses. A second way is a little more traumatic, but we believe brings about quicker benefits. Have a close friend listen to you and raise his hand or drop a penny in a tin can every time you say "uh" or "you know" or use an empty expletive. You may find the experience traumatic or nerve-racking, but soon your ear will start to pick them up as fast as the listener.

2. *In practice sessions see how long you can go without using a nonfluency.* Start out by trying to talk for fifteen seconds. Continue to increase the time until you can get to two minutes. In these practices, meaning may suffer. You may spend a disproportionate amount of time avoiding nonfluencies. Still, it is good practice.

3. *In regular conversation mentally note your usages.* You will be making real headway when in the heat of conversation you can *recognize* your own nonfluencies. When you reach this stage, you will find yourself beginning to avoid their use.

It is hard work—but it is worth it. Conversation would be a lot more pleasant if everyone would work to reduce nonfluencies by just 50 percent.

## Communication Session

*Reflection*
**Which of the language skills mentioned so far (accuracy in symbol selection, use of specific and concrete symbols, or fluency) causes you the greatest difficulty? Why?**

*Actualization*
1. **Working in groups of three, have two members of the group discuss some topic of common interest. The third person should stop either person if he or she should use a general or an abstract word in any statement. When stopped, the person should substitute a specific or concrete statement for the general or abstract. The observer will have to be on his or her toes—we are so used to general-abstract language that sometimes we do not even notice it.**

2. **Working with groups of four to six persons, each person should try to talk continuously for two minutes. When it is your turn, you can select your own topic—talk about such matters as a movie you saw recently, the success of your school team, difficulties you are having with a particular course, and so forth. Whenever you use a nonfluency, one of the members of the group will drop a penny in a tin can. At the end of your two minutes, the pennies will be counted. Give everyone in the group two chances. See who can contribute the fewest pennies. The "penny in the tin can" device can also be used in the specific-concrete actualization above.**

3. **Design a plan for improving your use of the language skill that is most difficult for you. Make a commitment to yourself to work on it.**

*Discussion*

**In groups of four to six persons, discuss the following:**

*1.* **Why is it easier to be general and abstract rather than specific and concrete?**

*2.* **Why are people unlikely to express their displeasure at others' nonfluencies?**

*3.* **What do you consider to be the most irritating nonfluencies? Why do they bother you?**

## Crediting

**Crediting means identifying the source of a particular statement or feeling.** In a term paper, you give credit to those from whom you have taken words verbatim or paraphrased, thus giving credit to the original source and avoiding plagiarism. In interpersonal communication, you credit for two similar reasons: you credit the person whose ideas you are using to confirm the positive nature of the individual; and you credit your own feelings to differentiate them from the feelings of others. There are two skills that help us reach these two goals; let us examine each of these two skills separately.

### Crediting Others

As we have mentioned many times before, one of the goals of interpersonal communication is to build and maintain relationships. People get along better with others when they believe that they are recognized as individual persons—when others recognize their personal worth. Yet we as senders of information often act (usually inadvertently) to chip away at the very relationships we are trying to build or to maintain. **Crediting others means verbally identifying the person whose ideas you are using.** Consider the following illustration. Bart and Mike are discussing ways of making money—Mike suggests buying a valuable item (a television set, a canoe, whatever) at discount and then selling raffle tickets. Bart expresses his interest in the idea. The next day at a meeting of the entire fund-raising committee of seven members, Bart says "What about buying a television at discount and selling raffle tickets? We could probably make a couple of hundred dollars!" The group responds immediately with such comments as "Great idea!" and "Let's do it!" At this point, what is Mike, the originator of the idea, likely to be feeling? If he says, "That was my idea," the group may think less of him for quibbling over whose idea it was. If he says nothing, he is likely to feel resentful toward Bart. In this instance, it was Bart's *responsibility* to give credit to Mike for originating the idea.

Is this important? Of course it is. Think of the times you were hurt because an idea of yours was not credited. Giving credit to others is an essential skill of interpersonal communication. Had Bart just said, "Mike had a great idea—what about buying a television at discount and selling raffle tickets?" the group's reactions would probably have been the same, but Mike would feel much better because his idea would have been properly credited.

### Crediting Self—Making "I" Statements

When you talk, others assume your statements represent your ideas or feelings. Although people are willing to divulge most of their thoughts, they are not so willing to divulge or at least not take credit for their personal feelings. Instead of crediting self, they wrap their feelings in impersonal or generalized language or attribute them to unknown or universal sources. **Making "I" statements means identifying yourself as the source of a particular idea or feeling.** Consider the following paired statements:

*"Everybody knows the Reds have the best team."*

*"I think the Reds have the best team."*

*"The Omega Omega's are a great sorority."*

*"It is my belief the Omega Omega's are a great sorority."*

*"Nobody's going to take the word of a kid against an adult."*

*"I'm not going to take the word of a kid against an adult."*

Each of these examples contrasts a generalized or impersonal account with an "I" statement. Note, as in the second example above, **an "I" statement can be any statement that has a first person pronoun such as "I," "my," "me," or "mine."** For purposes of accuracy of information and for purposes of helping the receiver to understand fully the nature of the message, it is essential to credit self by making "I" statements. Why are people so reluctant to do so? Saying "Everybody knows the Reds have the best team" means that if the receiver doubts the statement he is bucking the collective evaluation of millions of Americans. Of course, everybody *does not* know the Reds are best; in this instance, the statement really means that one person holds the belief. Yet, because a person feels that his or her feelings or beliefs will not carry much power, he or she may feel the need to use unknown or universal sources for those ideas or beliefs. Similarly, people use collective statements such as "everybody agrees" and "anyone with any sense" in order to escape responsibility for their own feelings and thoughts. It seems far more difficult for a person to say, "I don't like Herb" than it is to say, "No one likes Herb."

To avoid misunderstandings and false generalizations, you need to develop the skill of making "I" statements. Everyone has a right to an opinion. If what you are saying is truly your opinion, then let others know and be adult enough to take responsibility for what you believe or feel.

## Describing Feelings

Each of us has had years of practice at stating our ideas. A more difficult skill that is essential to good communication, but is less likely to be a part of your communication repertoire, is describing feelings. If others are to interact with you, they must be as aware of what you are feeling as of what you are thinking. **The skill of describing feelings involves making statements that put your emotional state into words.** Yet too often you withhold your feelings, thus confusing those with whom you want to communicate. Consider the following situations:

*Mary is looking at dresses. She selects one that is obviously higher priced than Ted can afford. A feeling of panic builds in Ted as he realizes Mary may really want that dress. "How do you like it?" she asks. Ted replies, "It's OK, but I'm not sure about the color."*

*During an exciting part of the movie, Kathy, caught up in the action, begins to crunch the ice of the soft drink she is sipping. Randy is getting more and more irritated as Kathy crunches. After about three minutes, he looks at her and says: "Kathy, cut it out!"*

*Steve calls Bill into the office to tell him that he will be in charge of this year's United Appeal drive for the company. As Bill listens to Steve outline his duties, Bill thinks of all the work he already has to do. The more he thinks of it, the more frightened he becomes that this new responsibility will be just too much for him. He begins to perspire and his whole body begins to tremble. Steve says, "Bill, are you all right? You look a little shaky." Bill replies: "I guess maybe I have a cold coming on—go ahead."*

*Candy is helping Ken with a calculus problem. Candy is very enthusiastic in her explanation of the way the problem works. Ken is becoming very frustrated because he is just not getting it, even with Candy's explanation. Candy says: "See, that's not so hard after all, is it?" Ken replies: "Thanks, Candy—I appreciate your help."*

In each of these four examples, communication was blocked by the failure of at least one of the persons involved to describe feelings. The strong silent type, the model of manliness, may be effective for poker, but it is a bad model for communication. Most of us just are not very good mind readers—and when we try to be, we often get in trouble.

The key to good communication is sending messages that really describe your state of mind at the moment. Despite the merit of this statement, describing accurately how you are feeling at the moment is difficult. Moreover, the more personal and the stronger your feelings are, the less likely you are to describe them. For example, even when you are asked directly, "How do you feel about this?" you are probably inclined to respond, "OK," regardless of your actual feelings. Yet revealing how you feel is often essential to effective communication.

Failure or refusal to reveal feelings is often a result of one of the following assumptions: (1) You believe that if you really tell your feelings you will reveal too much about yourself and thus be vulnerable; (2) you believe that your feelings will in some way hurt the other person; and (3) you feel guilty about the feelings you have. Let's examine the fallacies behind each of these assumptions:

1. *The belief that if you really tell your feelings they will reveal too much about you and you will be vulnerable:* True, revealing feelings does involve a certain amount of risk, but more often than not the positive outcomes of taking the risk far outweigh the fears of disclosure. For instance, Joe really likes Doris. He would like to get to know her a lot better—he would like to ask her to go for a drink after class. But Joe

fears rejection. What if he asked Doris and she laughed at him or said, "Get lost"? Rejection hurts. But what if Doris would really like Joe to ask her for a date? His fear of taking risk may prevent establishment of a lasting friendship.

2. *The belief that your feelings will in some way hurt the other person:* The fact is that the other person may be hurt far more by your failure to reveal your feelings. Isn't Kathy better off hearing that Randy is irritated by her crunching than she is to be told without warning: "Kathy, cut it out"?

3. *The belief that you have feelings you should not be having:* The fact is that you have these feelings whether you think you should or not. Maybe Ted should not panic about the price of a dress, but he does feel panic; and unless the feeling comes out in a descriptive statement, it will come out some other time in some other way.

People are often caught up in a communication dilemma, which can be stated as follows: A person is not inclined to let another into his or her real world of feeling unless the other is a close personal friend; yet, close personal friendships are not likely to develop unless people are able to let others into their world of feeling. At first this looks like an impossible dilemma to deal with, but, if you examine it carefully, you will see that your perception problem comes with what is often meant by "real world of feeling." Most people think of a total either-or situation. Either you hold everything in or you let everything out. It is true that you would be downright foolish to be completely open and honest with everyone you happen to meet. Few people wish to hear the innermost feelings of someone they have just met. As a result, most people go to the other extreme—revealing nothing of themselves even to those with whom they want to be closest. Improved interpersonal relations then come with improved interpersonal communication, and you begin by describing feelings.

Why is describing feelings so important? Because it is an aspect of self-disclosure that is fundamental to interpersonal communication and interpersonal growth. If you will recall our discussion of self-disclosure, we said: *You teach people how to treat you.* How many times have you experienced discomfort,

anxiety, or mental anguish caused by people who borrow possessions from you because you "don't mind," by people who tease you a lot because you "take it so well," by people who are always relying on you to get things done because you do them so well "without putting up a fuss," or other similar behaviors.

Are these people really bent on causing you pain? Or is it because *you have taught people how to behave toward you* either by reinforcing their behavior with positive action or by not doing or saying anything that tells them to behave otherwise. How often have you heard someone comment on such behaviors as teasing by saying "Oh, don't worry about it—she really enjoys it"? Some persons are not very sensitive to their fellowman; they do not catch the nonverbal behaviors that give clues to the true feelings of others. However,

*Describing feelings must begin somewhere!*

all the blame cannot be placed on lack of sensitivity of others—when behavior is reinforced by positive *action,* perhaps other people believe they are behaving the way the person *wants* them to.

Failure to describe prevents correction of faulty perceptions. For example, let us say that a friend of yours begins, affectionately, calling you "Slim" as a nickname, but you, understandably, do not care for it. Soon, whenever your friend says, "So tell me, Slim, where should we go for lunch?" or "Hey, Slim, what are you up to tonight?" you find yourself getting uptight. If you keep your anger to yourself (whether because you do not want to hurt your friend's feelings or because you just tend to keep things inside of you or for some other reason) your friend may not realize that he or she is making you angry. Your failure to disclose your feeling of dislike for the nickname will reinforce your friend's behavior—since you say nothing, you may give the impression that you like it. Soon, others may start calling you "Slim." So in many similar instances, describing feelings may become almost a necessity for self-defense—for, as we said, you teach others how to treat you.

Describing feelings is a start in opening your real self to others. You can make such statements as "Cliff, when you borrow my stuff without asking, it makes me very angry"; or "Rick, I know you think I don't mind it when you tease me about how I talk, but really it makes me feel very uncomfortable and embarrassed about what I say"; or "Maria, I get

the feeling that you think it's a compliment to my ability to get things done when you leave me with the final details, but I really resent being left with those jobs."

What steps should you take in order to assure an accurate description of your feeling? First, you must realize what you truly *are* feeling. This sounds easier than it sometimes is. Often when someone does something that hurts another, instead of describing a hurt the injured person reacts with anger. Why? Because if you show hurt you are vulnerable, whereas by being angry you can protect yourself and make the other suffer. While this may protect you from further hurt, it also creates a communication breakdown. After you have diagnosed your feeling, you then should encode it. Be careful to (1) make sure it is an "I" statement and (2) make sure it contains a feeling.

We need to describe feelings in order both to send messages more accurately and to begin to open ourselves up to reach our fullest communication potential. How can we start in a way that will not be too risky for us but will tell others that we want to share a part of ourselves?

A good starting point is with positive feelings. You may not find it difficult to say, "The sun's out today—I feel great." By beginning with a conscious effort to state your positive feelings, you will soon discover that such statements are accepted by others and make you feel better and help other people learn how to treat you. Success with positive statements will make it easier for you to try to describe your negative feelings. Try to get in the habit of including how you feel with each statement you make. You will discover that a statement such as "The sun isn't out today— I'm feeling a little depressed" is not that hard to make. Practice by communicating positive and less threatening negative feelings. As you see how your communication improves, you will be encouraged about describing your feelings more accurately on all levels.

## Communication Session

*Reflection*
**Do you describe feelings or do you express them? When? Under what circumstances?**

*Actualization*
*1.* **For each of the examples on page 94, change the final sentence into a well-phrased description of feelings.**

*2.* **Work in groups of four to six. Each person role-plays a situation (for example, your roommate borrowed your car without asking permission; he comes in the room later and, giving you the keys, says, "Thanks for the car") and then tells how he feels about it. Other members of the group paraphrase what he has said until feelings have been described fully. Exercise continues until each member of the group has had practice with describing feelings.**

*Discussion*
**After completing the actualization, the group should discuss how they feel about describing feelings. Is it difficult or easy? Why? How do circumstances affect your attitude toward describing your feelings?**

## Payoffs

Now that you have studied this chapter you should be able to

1. Discuss the consequences of fact-inference confusion.

2. Separate facts from inferences in communication.

3. Discuss the consequences of not dating statements.

4. Explain the importance of indexing statements.

5. Date and index statements as necessary.

6. Discuss the accuracy of the statement "words don't mean, people mean."

7. Use specific and concrete language in place of general and abstract language.

8. Discuss the abuse of vocal segregates, "you know," and empty expletives.

9. Devise a plan to rid yourself of your non-fluencies.

10. Define crediting and discuss its goals.

11. Credit statements of self and others.

12. Explain the importance of description of feeling statements.

13. Describe your feelings to others.

## Suggested Readings

**John C. Condon, Jr.** *Semantics and Communication,* 2nd ed. New York: Macmillan Publishing Co., 1975. This short paperback provides an excellent explanation of semantics.

**William V. Haney.** *Communication and Organizational Behavior: Text and Cases,* 3rd ed. Homewood, Illinois: Richard D. Irwin, 1973. This is an updated version of a classic work in the field of semantic application. Haney supplements and illustrates his points with easy-to-read case studies. Well worth a careful reading.

**David W. Johnson.** *Reaching Out: Interpersonal Effectiveness and Self Actualization.* Englewood Cliffs, New Jersey: Prentice-Hall, 1972. See especially pages 90–98 for a discussion of describing feelings.

**Chapter Six:**
**Nonverbal Communication Skills**

*Helen moves forward smoothly on the tennis court to take the high easy bounce and put the ball away. Instead of the super shot she anticipates, she hits the ball into the net. She groans and throws her racket onto the ground in disgust.*

*As he picks up his fifth card in the hand of draw poker, George breaks into a wide smile—quickly he looks around the table to see whether anyone caught the smile, and he resumes his "poker" face.*

*"No doubt about it, Maggie, you were terrific,"* Suzi says with a sarcastic sneer in her voice.

*Allison rushes through her bath, hurries her make-up job, dresses frantically, and finishes at the stroke of eight. "Made it!" she says to herself as she moves down the stairs and into the livingroom to await Jeff. As 8:30 comes and goes, Allison is doing a slow burn as she paces the floor in front of the door.*

In each of the preceding examples, the main character uses nonverbal channels as the primary means of communication. Discussing nonverbal communication separately from verbal communication may seem somewhat artificial since in the real world both occur simultaneously. Nevertheless, in order to stress the importance of all the dimensions of nonverbal communication, we will separate them for purposes of analysis in this chapter.

We have heard it said that actions speak louder than words. Actions are so important to our communication that researchers have estimated that in face-to-face communication as much as 90 percent of the social meaning may be carried in the nonverbal message.[1] Because people are so much less aware of the nonverbal structure as compared with the verbal, we will begin with a basic analysis of the differences between verbal and nonverbal messages. We will then look at the various

---

[1] Albert Mehrabian, *Silent Messages* (Belmont, California: Wadsworth Publishing Company, 1971), p. 44.

elements that make up nonverbal communication, and finally we will discuss the skill of perception checking, which is a means of improving nonverbal "listening."

## Verbal versus Nonverbal Communication

There are four primary differences between verbal and nonverbal communication.

1. *Verbal communication is symbolic; nonverbal communication is not symbolic.* By "symbolic," we mean that people agree to a common meaning for a given set of letters or vocal sounds. Nonverbal communication, on the other hand, is not symbolic. For example, tilting your head to one side does not have a generally accepted meaning.

2. *Verbal communication is discrete; nonverbal communication is continuous.* When a person talks, communication begins when sound starts to emanate from his mouth and ends when vocalization stops. A person's nonverbal messages, however, continue for as long as a person is in your presence.

3. *Verbal communication is a single-channeled phenomenon; nonverbal communication is multichanneled.* Have you ever tried to listen to two or three conversations at once? How much do you miss as you try to tune in on other conversations around you? Most of us have trouble listening to more than one conversation. Why? Because one conversation is all your brain can process from that channel

(hearing) at one time. Nonverbal messages come to you by means of a variety of channels, so you are able to consume and digest much more information about your environment at the same time.

4. *Verbal communication is controlled; nonverbal communication is spontaneous.* The process of encoding allows you to think about and to plan what you say—usually you control what you choose to send verbally. Your nonverbal communications are usually spontaneous; you may control what your hand or eyes or head is doing, but usually you are not aware of the nonverbal signals you are sending.

These contrasts are not meant to give the impression that you have two communication systems, verbal and nonverbal, operating totally apart from each other. The fact is that verbal and nonverbal communication form a total unit. Before moving into an explanation of the specific elements of nonverbal communication, let's look at how verbal and nonverbal communication interrelate.

1. *Nonverbal communication supplements verbal communication.* This supplement may be repetition. Gesturing to show the height of a person or gesturing to point out a direction may well essentially repeat the verbal statements. Sometimes the supplement is complementary to the verbal. The dejected look accompanying the statement of failure or the smile accompanying a statement of success are complementary. The supplement may be for

emphasis. When your coach grips your arm tightly as he says, "I want you to try harder," the grip emphasizes the meaning explicit in the words.

2. *Nonverbal communication takes the place of verbal communication.* When the team comes into the dressing room after a game, the looks, posture, tones of voice tell the story of the game—no one needs to ask who won. When nonverbal messages are substituting for verbal, verbal communication is sometimes needed as a correcting device. When you come slouching home and someone says, "Did you have a great day?" you may (or may not) feel inclined to correct the impression through verbal communication.

3. *Nonverbal communication contradicts verbal communication.* When you yell at people but tell them you love them; when you perspire profusely but claim you are not nervous; when you shout and say you are not angry, your verbal and nonverbal messages are contradictory. So, which is to be believed? According to most communication scholars, nonverbal communication defines the communication in most social settings. This means that observers are more inclined to believe what is expressed nonverbally, because it is less subject to conscious control. When you say, "See how happy I am" and force a smile, you fool no one. On the other hand, when you say you love a person even when you are shouting, the verbal message may be true. Nonverbal clues are accepted as defining meaning especially when the non-

verbal message is represented by a sarcastic tone of voice. Such statements as "That was a great movie!" said in a sarcastic tone are always perceived as negative, regardless of the positive nature of the words themselves.

In this next section we will examine several elements of nonverbal behavior. Although Larry Barker and Nancy Collins[2] have identified some eighteen categories, we will limit our discussion to four: the environment, personal style, body motions, and paralanguage.

## Communication Session

*Reflection*

1. **Consider your communication with your two <u>best</u> friends. To which are you likely to be more sensitive, their verbal or their nonverbal communication? Why?**

2. **Consider the times that other persons did not believe what you were telling them. Were their actions based upon what you said or how you said it?**

*Discussion*

**In your discussion groups, consider when you are most likely to pay attention to a person's verbal communication? to his nonverbal communication?**

[2]Larry L. Barker and Nancy B. Collins, "Nonverbal and Kinesic Research," *in* Philip Emmert and William D. Brooks (Eds.), *Methods of Research in Communication* (Boston: Houghlin Mifflin Company, 1970), pp. 343–372.

## The Environment

When we speak of the environment as an aspect of nonverbal communication you may be rather surprised. Does the size of the classroom or the arrangement of the chairs or the distance you stand from another person really have any effect on the kinds and amounts of communication you have with others? Researchers tell us that they do and we think some of their findings will be of use to you as you go about the day-to-day problems of trying to cope in an environment that may not be conducive to good communication. We can divide the environment into three kinds of space: fixed-featured space, semi-fixed-featured space, and informal space. In addition, we can note how color, temperature, and lighting affect the environment.

### Fixed-featured Space

The types of buildings that you live and work in are fixed-featured space. Anything in your home that cannot be moved is considered part of this space. If, for instance, you live in a dormitory room in which the desk, bed, chest of drawers, and closet are all attached to walls, the only objects in your environment that are not fixed-featured space may be you, your desk chair, and your personal belongings. These aspects of your environment affect your interpersonal communication. The amount of time neighbors spend talking with one another differs between people whose homes are less than 20

feet apart and those whose homes are farther apart. Moreover, people who live in apartment buildings tend to become acquainted with neighbors who live across the hall and next door but are less likely to know those who live on different floors. Also, your chances of knowing more people who live in your building are greatly enhanced if you live near an access point like an elevator, a staircase, or a door.

Not only does fixed-featured space often determine with whom you will communicate, it also can help or inhibit the kind of communication that will occur. Have you ever tried to throw a party for twelve persons in a room big enough to accommodate 200? What happens? In this situation, the space is too large for the individuals to develop the intimate atmosphere that such a party needs. Conversely, have you ever tried to carry on a conversation on a crowded elevator? It is difficult because the space is too small for all the people who are squeezed into it.

### Semi-fixed-featured Space

Semi-fixed-featured space is characterized by objects that tend to remain in a fixed position unless they are moved. Your desk, your chairs, your table are objects in your room that are positioned to create an environment. How you arrange these objects reveals a great deal about your interpersonal relationships. The atmosphere of a classroom with several rows of chairs all facing the lec-

*Space utilization reveals a great deal
about relationships.*

tern differs from that of a room in which chairs are grouped into one large circle or four or five small circles. In the first environment, most students anticipate a lecture format. In the second, they might expect a give-and-take discussion, with the instructor and members of the class participating. In the third setting, they might expect the class to be working on group projects.

The arrangement of furniture in your livingroom at home creates an effect. The presence of a television set in that room often determines that all chairs and sofas are faced toward the set, with none turned toward other seats. This room arrangement invites television viewing, but discourages human interaction.

Consider a situation that may be familiar to you—a conference with your instructor

during his or her office hours. You can tell a lot about your instructor and about the kind of climate he or she is trying to establish just by the arrangement of the office and where you are asked to sit. If the visitor's chair is across the desk, the instructor may be implying, "Let's talk business—I'm the learned expert and you're just a student." If you would like to be more informal, the barrier of space (and the desk) could hinder communication. If the visitor's chair is at the side of the desk, the instructor may be indicating, "Don't be nervous—let's just chat." Of course, you must be somewhat tentative about the conclusions you draw; the instructor may have so little assigned office space that he or she has no option about arrangement! Still, the use of space is a pretty good index of how a person will treat you and how he or she expects to be treated. People expect space utilization to conform with their perception of the nature of the setting. When a person utilizes space in ways that appear to violate norms or are different from expectation, the result may inhibit communication. The next time you enter a room, be aware of the semi-fixed-featured space and how it affects you.

### Informal Space

Where do you sit in any particular class? Where do you sit at the family dinner table? Is it always in the same seat or the same area? Does your father have a livingroom chair that is his? How do you feel when someone plops his or her books on your desk? What is your behavior when you are in a crowded elevator? These questions all have one thing in common—they are concerned with how we use and feel about informal space. Studies about proxemics, the way people communicate with informal space, have shown that you need to be aware of how others regard space and how you can use knowledge of space to improve your communication.

One way of regarding informal space is as territory. Although you may not consider the territory one controls as the principal means of determining personal value (at times in the past—and still to some degree in the present—the amount of land owned determined status), you may still subscribe to a territorial imperative in much of your daily routine. Whether you are functioning in an office, a classroom, a dorm room, or your home, you try to define a territory that is yours. How do you deal with your territory? Have you and your roommate divided your sleeping room in half? How about closet space? desk space? When you go into a new class, do you establish a territory that is yours? When you go to the library do you spread out your books and papers so the limits of your territory are defined? Have you ever used a "marker" (a notebook, an umbrella, your coat) to identify your space in a dining hall, a classroom, a movie? Have you ever asked someone to hold your seat or your place in line while you were gone? When you have occupied the same space over a long period, do you expect people to recognize it as yours?

For most people, the answer to *all* these questions is "yes."

You expect others to respect your territory and you are expected to respect the territory of others. When your territory is invaded, you might act defensively toward the invader. For instance, a person who sits too close to you in the dining hall or the person who places his books in your space at the library will rouse in you at least an urge to react with a cold stare or a harsh comment. Of course, persons who are not considered threatening do not provoke the same defensive reaction—still, even if the encroachment on your territory is made by a loved one, you might feel at least a little twinge of resentment.

So, your attitude about territory affects your behavior and your communication. For most people, the most important territory is the space around them. Edward T. Hall, a leading researcher in nonverbal communication, discusses a series of distances that are a key to four different communication situations.[3]

The four categories are *intimate space* (up to 18 inches), *personal space* (2 to 2½ feet—appropriate for casual conversation); *social space* (4 to 7 feet—for impersonal business like a job interview); and *public distance* (more than 12 feet). What about the space between 7 and 12 feet? That's flexible. These norms have been determined by observation of typical be-

---

[3]Edward T. Hall, *The Silent Language* (New York: Doubleday and Company, 1959), pp. 163–164.

havior. What do these distances mean to you?

By far the most important is the intimate distance, up to about 18 inches, which is regarded as appropriate for intimate conversation with close friends, parents, and younger children. What happens when you are forced into spatial relationships that violate this intimate distance? Consider once again your last ride in a crowded elevator as an example of just such a situation. Most people hold themselves rather stiffly, look at the floor or the indicator above the door, and pretend that they are not touching. Being forced into such an intimate-space situation is acceptable to most of us, provided all involved follow the "rules." When closeness is not required, having someone encroach upon your personal space causes a form of anxiety. For instance, in a movie theater that is not crowded, people tend to leave one or more empty seats between themselves and others. If you are sitting in a nearly empty movie theater and a stranger sits right next to you, you are likely to feel somewhat upset. If a person you do not know violates intimate distance in conversation, you may find yourself instinctively backing away.

## Color, Temperature, and Lighting

When it comes down to it, almost every facet of the environment has a communication potential. Three facets that people seem particularly sensitive to are color, temperature,

and lighting. Color is particularly important to how we behave. Studies have been designed to determine the relationship between color and mood. People are likely to react predictably to various colors: red—exciting, stimulating; blue—secure, comfortable, tender, soothing, calm, peaceful; yellow—cheerful, jovial; black—strong, masterful. Thus a designer who is trying to create an atmosphere that will promote peaceful serenity will decorate in blues rather than in reds and yellows. Likewise, a play area that is supposed to contribute to a stimulating environment will be done in reds and yellows rather than blues.

Of course a great deal of our reaction to color comes from expectation: mashed potatoes are supposed to be white; butter, yellow; and broccoli, green. At a dinner party recently, we served spinach noodles, which are green. Our guests sent some interesting nonverbal messages about that unorthodox noodle color.

The colors that you surround yourselves with do influence how you act and communicate in a particular setting. Each of us has certain color preferences—colors we like to wear or be surrounded by. If for some reason you are forced to live in an environment of color that you hate, you often will react with negative communication.

Temperature acts as a stimulant or deterrent to communication. The ideal temperature for communication is one that is perceived as neither too high nor too low. Most Americans are most comfortable when temperatures are between 70 and 75 degrees. If you doubt the importance of temperature, recall your grade school days when the June or September heat made listening to the teacher extremely difficult. Recently we attended a convention where some of the meeting rooms were unheated. The coldness of the rooms (about 60 degrees) made it almost impossible for people to relax and talk. Improper temperature seems to act like noise in the environment, making the sending and receiving of messages difficult.

*Soft, dim lighting is especially conducive to intimate conversation.*

Lighting has a similar effect. In lecture halls and reading rooms, you expect bright light—bright light is most conducive to good listening and comfortable reading. In a chic restaurant, a music listening room, or a television lounge you expect the lighting to be soft and rather dim. Soft, dim lighting is especially conducive to intimate conversation.

## Communication Session

*Reflection*

1. **Think of where you live (dorm, apartment, house). Which of your neighbors do you know best? Can you account for interactions with neighbors by the proximity of your fixed-featured space?**

2. **Define your territories. What do you do when those territories are invaded? What are your expectations about space when you are talking with an instructor? When you are talking with a good friend? When you are talking with a person for the first time?**

*Actualization*

1. **Work in pairs. Start on the opposite sides of the room (at least 20 feet apart). Begin to walk toward each other. (a) Stop at 12 feet apart and hold a conversation. (b) Stop at 7 feet apart and hold a conversation. (c) Stop at 1 or 2 feet apart and hold a conversation. (d) Continue until you feel too close. Step back until the distance seems comfortable. Notice how far apart you are.**

2. **Before your instructor arrives at class, change the semi-fixed-featured space in the classroom. For example, remove the lectern, change arrangement of the chairs, and the like. Note instructor's reactions to these changes.**

*Discussion*

1. **In groups of four, discuss what happened as people walked toward each other. What changes in behavior occurred as distances became smaller? Was there any difference in behavior of male to female? male to male? female to female?**

2. **Discuss how individuals in the group react to different colors and variations in heating and lighting. Under what conditions do you work best? rest best? listen best?**

## Personal Style

Your personal style is a presentation of yourself through such elements as the clothes you wear, the way you wear your hair, your body shape and how you react to it, and how you treat and react to others' treatments of time. Most people know by now that not all long hairs are anti-Establishment, that short skirts are not indicative of promiscuity, and size is not related to brutality—at least people say they know. Still, long hair, length of skirts, and size as well as numerous other physical qualities can and do communicate to your benefit and to your detriment. When a woman has her hair done, buys a new outfit to wear, and takes a maximum amount of time to make sure she looks just right, she is saying something about her attitude toward a job interview; likewise, the man who does not bother to shower and shave and puts on his rumpled sports coat over a dirty shirt is saying something about his attitude toward a job interview.

We sometimes laugh at Emily Post's and Amy Vanderbilt's statements on etiquette, but what they do is verbalize cultural norms. How a person acts in relationship to those norms does communicate.

### Clothing

You have the power to help yourself or hinder yourself by the way you dress for a particular occasion. Times change and values change, so what was proper dress ten years ago is not necessarily proper today. It is up to you to determine what is appropriate or expected; then you deviate from expectation at your own risk. The man who goes into an interview with a major oil company in a rumpled sweatshirt, levis, and tennis shoes had better have quite a lot going for him if he expects even to be heard, let alone to be hired.

People have the right to their individual differences, and we believe modern society is moving in the right direction in allowing a person to express himself or herself individually. Nevertheless, your clothes are still perceived by others as being clues to your attitudes and behaviors—clothes do communicate, however accurate or inaccurate you may believe that communication to be.

More basic than the clothes we wear is the body type the clothes adorn. Body types are considered in three classifications: endomorph, mesomorph, and ectomorph. The endomorph is soft, round, and fat; the mesomorph is muscular, hard, athletic and powerful; the ectomorph is thin, fragile, and brittle.

In a study done by Wells and Siegel,[4] 120 adult subjects were shown silhouette drawings of the three body types and asked to rate them on such paired adjectives as lazy—energetic; intelligent—unintelligent; dependent—self-reliant. The results showed that endomorphs are seen as older, lazier, weaker, but more warmhearted, good-natured, agreeable, and trusting; mesomorphs are seen as

---

[4]William D. Wells and Bertram Siegel, "Stereotyped Somatypes," *Psychological Reports*, Vol. 8 (1961), pp. 77–78.

stronger, more masculine, better looking, younger, taller, and more mature; ectomorphs are seen as younger, more ambitious, more suspicious, more tense and nervous, more stubborn, and quieter.

In addition to body type itself, height, skin color, and body hair also communicate. Americans seem to prefer tall men to short. Within races, skin tone from lighter to darker is also a variable. We are affected by amount of hair on face, arms, and body, as well as length of hair on the head.

Clothes, body type, hair, skin color, and height are all part of the personal style that you communicate to others. Whether your approach to these elements is conscious or unconscious, the interrelationship of these elements still affects your relations with people around you.

### Time

Interpersonal use of time also communicates. Modern American society is time-bound. Yet, many of us do not understand the communication effect of this phenomenon. Consider some of the peculiarities of our culture.

For each of us, there are durations of time that we regard as appropriate for certain events. For instance, Sunday sermons are 20 to 30 minutes long, classes take 50 minutes (Tuesday and Thursday classes of 75 minutes never seem right to many students), a movie runs roughly 2 hours. Television programs last 30 minutes and 60 minutes *unless* they are movies or sporting events. When the duration of an event does not meet expectations, that time itself becomes an obstacle to communication. You may get angry with the instructor who holds you beyond normal class time; likewise, you may become hostile if someone asks you to cut short your lunch hour or coffee break.

In addition to an appropriate length of time there is also an appropriate time of day for certain things to happen. People work during the day, sleep at night, eat at noon, have a cocktail at 5 P.M., and so on. You may make judgments about people who accept times for events that differ from yours. Joe is strange if he gets up at 4:30 A.M. The Martins eat dinner at 4:30 P.M.; the Smiths do not dine till 8 P.M.—you may consider both families peculiar. Adam works on his books from midnight till 4 A.M. and then sleeps till noon—you are aware that he is "different." So, *when* people do things communicates something to you.

Third, and perhaps most basic to your perception of people, is how they treat time designations. For instance, suppose you are throwing a party. When you invited people you told them to come at about 8 P.M. What do you think of Rob if (1) he arrives at 7:30? (2) if he arrives at 8 P.M. exactly? (3) if he arrives at 8:30? (4) if he arrives at 10 P.M.? Now, for sake of argument, let us change the setting. Suppose you have a test scheduled for tomorrow. After today's class, suppose that a group of five of you decide to study together. Since your place is as good as any, you say, "Stop by about 8 P.M." Now what do you think of Rob if he arrives at (1) 7:30? (2) 8 P.M. exactly? (3) 8:30? and (4) 10 P.M.? Depending upon how *you* see time, you will make a value judgment upon the basis of when he comes; moreover, you may view his arrival time differently depending upon the occasion.

Time does communicate. You must be sensitive to your own perceptions of time as well as those of others so that the variable of time facilitates or at least does not inhibit your communication. Let us see how you regard the variable of personal style.

## Communication Session

*Reflection*

1. Do you dress to achieve any special goal? If so, what? If not, does how you dress still affect your relations with others?

2. What is your body type? Do you believe the generalizations about body types on pages 110-111 accurately reflect your personality? If so, how? If not, why not?

*Actualization*

1. Next time you go to class, dress completely differently from your normal dress. Notice what effect, if any, this has on your communication with those around you.

2. Working in groups of four to six, have two people role-play various situations related to time and the rest of the group will share their reactions. Examples: A student is late for an appointment with a professor; your date is fifteen minutes late for your first date; your steady is fifteen minutes late for a date.

3. Each person in class should bring in a picture of a person taken from a magazine article or advertisement. Divide into groups of six. Each person in the group should write three to five adjectives about each of the pictures. Then the persons in the group should compare their assessments and discuss them on the basis of perception of clothes, body type, height, hair, and skin color.

*Discussion*

In your groups, consider how each person handles someone who violates his or her time boundaries.

## Body Motions

Of all nonverbal means you are probably most familiar with kinesics, the technical name for body motions, including facial expression, eye behavior, gestures, movements of the limbs and body, and posture. To the un-observant, all body motion may appear as random movement growing from peculiar-ities of culture, personality, or nationality (Italians talk with their hands; the British use few gestures). By careful study, however, you can begin to interpret with some accuracy the nonverbal clues. To analyze the various body motions, we will adopt the Ekman and Friesen categories of emblems, illustrators, affect dis-plays, regulators, and adaptors.[5]

### Emblems

These body motions or gestures take the place of a word or two or a phrase. Emblems are the exception to the rule of the nonsym-bolic nature of the nonverbal communica-tion. Their meanings are every bit as clearly defined and generally accepted as are verbal dictionary definitions. Thumbs up for "every-thing is Go"; extension of first and second finger in V shape for "peace"; the waved hand for "hi" or "how are you doing"; shaking the head for "no" and nodding for "yes"; shrug-ging the shoulders for "maybe" or "I don't

[5]Paul Ekman and W. V. Friesen, "The Repertoire of Non-verbal Behavior: Categories, Origins, Usage, and Cod-ing," *Semiotica*, Vol. 1 (1969), pp. 49–98.

care"; or rolling of the eyes for exasperation are but a few of the nonverbal emblems that people use consistently to replace speech.

Just as your verbal vocabulary consists of words that you know and use regularly in your daily speech, words that you can rec-ognize if others use them but that are not in your working vocabulary, and words that you have to look up, so your nonverbal vocabulary has these same three classifications. For in-stance, nearly everyone in our culture nods his head for "yes"; this is an example of a non-verbal emblem that each of us knows and uses regularly in daily communication. Exam-ples of emblems that you recognize but do not use are those that do not fit your personality, or do not have enough meaning for you. Many obscene emblems may be in your un-derstanding vocabulary even if you rarely or never use them. Likewise, there are many emblems that just are not familiar to you. New emblems come into vogue just as new words are constantly being coined (the gen-eration gap is reinforced by both verbal and nonverbal language usage). Moreover, some ethnic groups have sign languages whose meaning is known only to members of the group.

When do you rely on emblems to carry your messages? Emblems are probably used most when you are too far apart for speech to be heard and when there is so much noise present that you cannot hear, or when you just do not feel like verbalizing. Emblems also are used nearly exclusively when auditory receptors do not work properly (the deaf have developed an extremely elaborate sign language) or when people are trying to exclude someone who is not a member of the "in" group.

### Illustrators

These sets of nonverbal body movements or gestures are used to accent or emphasize what is being said verbally. Often when a person says, "He talks with his hands" or "He couldn't talk if we tied his hands," he or she means that the person's speech and body movements are totally complementary.

Researchers have classified illustrators as serving six different functions. Although the labels used to distinguish the classifications do not seem particularly important, since the differentiation of illustrators shows the complexity of our usage, let us name and illustrate each of these classifications.

*Batons* are movements that accent or emphasize a particular word. If you said, "I don't want to go to the movie," you might make a sharp downward gesture with one or both of your hands when you said "want." Nearly everyone has different gestures he uses as his batons. So, it is not the nature of the gesture that is important so much as where or how it is used. *Ideographs* sketch a path or direction of thought. If you said, "The progress of this class goes from good (and you pointed to an imaginary extreme) to poor (and you pointed in the opposite direction)" your pointing would be a form of ideograph. Again, the gesture itself is not so important as where

or how it is used. *Deictics* are movements that involve pointing to present objects. If when you said "Take this chair, for instance," you pointed to it by extending your forefinger, the act of pointing would be a deictic gesture. *Spatial movements* depict a spatial relationship. You might hold your hands about a foot apart when you said, "Why, it's only about this long" or you might hold your hand parallel to the ground as you said, "He already stands about this high." *Kinetographs* are movements that depict a body action. For instance, you might chuckle and say "Did you see the way he was nodding?" and while you were talking you would show the kind of nod you had been observing. The last classification is *pictographs,* which are actual drawings of their referents to illustrate such statements as "Here's the shape of the opening."

Like emblems, illustrators are used intentionally, and receivers process their use in determining meaning. Also, illustrators are socially learned and can be taught. Body action used in public speaking or lecturing is largely comprised of illustrators. In the old days, training of public speakers involved detailed study of illustrators. You have probably heard older people talk about "elocution," which was in part a study of how to gesture "properly." Today, when we teach public speaking, we talk of letting the body action follow naturally from the thought. We are not, therefore, advocating that you learn and put into practice a set of illustrators. Our goal is to raise your awareness of their use and if you use them inappropriately, or if your use calls attention to them rather than facilitating meaning, you should try to correct the use.

## Affect Displays

When you feel some strong emotion, you are likely to affect-display the nature of that feeling through a facial configuration or some concurrent body response. For instance, you get out of bed in the morning and as you walk sleepy-eyed to the bathroom you stub your toe. You are likely to show the pain with some verbal comment (do you have a pet word for these occasions?) and with an accompanying grimace. More often than not, these reactions—spur-of-the-moment emotional displays—are not intended as conscious communication. One of the apparent reasons for labeling the body motion a "display" is that your reaction takes place automatically whether you are alone or with others, and it will probably be quite noticeable.

Of all the body motions we have considered thus far, affect display is the kind by which you reveal most about yourself. Although the response you make is automatic, it is conditioned by a set of cultural, familial, and personal norms that alter the nature of the display. So if you are aware, you can learn a lot about a person by how he displays his emotions. The behavior you witness will probably be of four different kinds. Consider these carefully—they are very important to increasing your awareness of nonverbal communication.

1. *A person may deintensify the appearance of clues.* For instance when Jane is extremely afraid, happy, or hurt, she may feel she must attempt to look only slightly afraid, happy, or hurt. Perhaps Jim bangs his head very hard on the door frame getting in the car, but acts as if it only hurt a little.

2. *A person may overintensify or amplify.* When a person is only slightly afraid or happy, he or she may show extreme fear or happiness. A child (and sometimes an adult) who suffers a little pain may scream as though grievously injured.

3. *A person may take a neutral position.* If a person is happy, afraid, sad, or angry, he shows no difference. We call this the "poker face."

4. *A person may mask the clues.* This means that the person purposely looks different from what we would expect. If a person is happy, he may sneer or look angry. If he is angry, he may smile.

These display rules are usually learned—perhaps at home, perhaps in a social group, or perhaps in keeping with a self-image a person is trying to project. Especially in relation to family or social group, a person tries to conform to the established norms. For instance, if in your family it is considered bad form to show fear, then you learned from early childhood when you were afraid to deemphasize your display or to adopt a neutral posture or perhaps to mask the display. Of course, the stronger the stimulus, the harder it is to follow your personal rule. When you step sleepily out of bed and stub your toe, the display is likely to be directly proportional to the degree of pain. Ordinarily, however, your rules are your guide. Of course, you may portray yourself differently under different circumstances depending on how well you know the people present, what you think of them, and what you want them to think of you.

In this area of affect display, we as students of communication need to be very careful about the conclusions we draw. For if we do take the nonverbal behavior as the true meaning of the communication, we can be fooled. Later in this chapter we will discuss the principal means for clarifying perceptions of nonverbal behavior.

## Regulators

A less dramatic but equally important category of body motion comprises the *regulators*. These are nonverbal actions that regulate the flow of conversation by telling the speaker to continue, to repeat, to elaborate, to hurry up, and the like. Think for a minute. How do you know when someone has finished speaking? or when someone will continue speaking for a while longer? How do you know when you should talk more slowly? or faster? We pick up such communication clues from movements such as nodding of the head, shifting eye contact, slight head movements, shifts in posture, and raised eyebrows.

Regulating occurs on the periphery of our awareness. We usually do not know when we are doing these things, and we are not necessarily conscious of others' doing them. But, if we were restrained from doing them we would become quite frustrated—we expect and need these regulators.

Regulators penetrate awareness when their usage reaches a state that is described as rudeness. If while Maria is talking Carl gives signs of impatience, she may think, "How rude of him to do these things when I'm talking!" Or, if in the midst of what you think is a good conversation the other person gathers his things, puts his coat on, and starts to leave while you are in the middle of a statement, you probably would be upset. Yet, you do regulate communication on a subtler level constantly.

## Adaptors

In the fifth classification, which is the most difficult to define, are the *adaptors*. Researchers have called them adaptors because they are thought to be adaptive efforts to satisfy needs, perform actions, manage emotions, develop social contacts, or to perform many other functions. Of all the nonverbal movements we have discussed, these are the least capable of being coded—yet, in some ways they are the most fascinating. You may be familiar with one or more of the books that trade on the mystery of adaptors. A few years ago Fast's *Body Language*[6] had everyone who read it trying to "psyche out" the hidden messages that people were unaware of or were trying to repress. For a time, at least, such books heightened general awareness of the fact of adaptors and many readers pondered such problems as, for example, if Maggie crosses her knees, it may have something to do with her attitude toward the man she is with (or it may not) or the crossing of her arms may have something to do with her rejection of the other's ideas (or it may not). Usually, we just are not aware of adaptive behavior.

Yet, if people believe they sense something in your nonverbal behavior, their belief may greatly affect communication. When you talk with a person you may get an instinctive feeling of what he or she is like, what he or she is thinking, or feeling. For instance, supervisors who take off their coats, roll up their sleeves, and pitch in to help in an emergency tell something about themselves that is somewhat different from the messages sent by supervisors who dress rather formally, stand apart from workers, and shrink from getting their hands dirty. You doubtless have been attracted to persons who are vibrant with sex appeal or move with an easy grace or just seem relaxed and comfortable to be with. Sometimes you may have been repelled by persons who seem stern, strict, formal, and

uptight. Many of these impressions are responses to adaptive behaviors on the part of the persons in question.

In the following exercise, our goal is not to try to codify adaptors but to determine our own reactions to nonverbal behavior we perceive. Of course, in normal conversation we should check out the accuracy of our perceptions. As mentioned before, a means of checking our perceptions will be discussed later in this chapter.

---

[6]Julius Fast, *Body Language* (New York: M. Evans & Company, 1970).

## Communication Session

*Reflection*

Do you use many gestures when you speak? What emblems are most common to your usage? What kinds of illustrators do you use most frequently? What are your normal nonverbal means of displaying such emotions as anger, pain, surprise, boredom, and others? What do you do to show others that you have finished talking?

*Actualization*

1. Working alone, compile a dictionary of emblems. Classify them as (1) emblems used consistently and (2) emblems understood but seldom used.

2. Working in groups of three to six, share your lists. Is there any similarity? What are the bases of the differences? As a result of the comparison, develop a third classification: (3) emblems not known. Have you put any in this classification?

3. Working in groups of four to six, have each individual describe a game he or she has played, a place he or she has just been, where he or she had lunch, or the like. Give the person a maximum of two minutes to talk. Note the nature of the illustrators: Was body action used as a baton, ideograph, deictic, spatial movement, kinetograph, or pictograph? Was the usage above average, average, or below average? You will begin to establish a norm for average as others continue with the assignment. Compare the use of body movement as illustrators. Who uses more than others? Under what circumstances?

4. Working in groups of four to six, have each person role-play various emotional incidents— for instance, stubbing your toe, getting angry with a person for slighting you. In these role-playing situations, what displays are shown?

*Discussion*

Working in groups of four to six discuss the following:

1. What kinds of adaptive behavior seem to be conscious, or in the control of the person? What kinds seem unconscious?

2. What kinds of facial expression, posture, gesture, or movement are suggestive of being "sexy," "fun loving," "a bore," "pushy," and the like.

3. What seems to account for some people being more likely to use various kinds of body motions? Under what circumstances, if any, should people attempt to change the body motions they use?

## Paralanguage

Kinesic behavior relates to what you see; paralanguage relates to what you hear. In simple terms, *paralanguage* is the study of *how* something is said and not *what* is said. It is all of the vocalization that is *not* symbolic. We have all developed a sensitivity to certain vocal patterns. Let us consider some of the various elements of paralanguage that people become attuned to.

### Vocal Qualifiers

The voice is composed of pitch (highness or lowness of tone), volume (loudness), rate (speed), and quality (the sound of the voice). The first three of these are considered as *vocal qualifiers.* That is, we get from the voice levels meanings that supplement or occasionally contradict the words used. For instance, when people are angry they are likely to talk louder. Thus, when a person starts to talk loudly, he may be betraying a rising anger. Likewise, when people are trying to be particularly empathic, they may talk softer. Two people conversing very softly may—or may not—be very fond of each other.

The pitch and the rate tie in with volume to strengthen these beliefs. People often raise their pitch when they are anxious, nervous, or tense. This goes along with the increase in volume. Also, the low volume of intimacy will probably be accompanied by a low pitch as well. Along with raising their pitch and volume, people may also talk faster when they

are upset. Lower pitch and lower volume usually are accompanied by slower rate of speech. So, most often, the three work in concert to create the states you perceive as showing various emotions.

### Vocal Differentiators

These are special vocalizations. Such things as crying, laughing, belching, yawning, swallowing, and clearing the throat may have a definite meaning in and of themselves. Yawning may show boredom. Of course, some of these are related to phenomena that have nothing to do with communication; we also yawn when we need more fresh air in our lungs.

One set of vocal differentiators that we must become attuned to is the set we call the breakers. For instance, the nervous giggle, the quivering voice of emotion are both forms of breaking. Breaking refers to loss of control or insecurity. Thus when you perceive these becoming a part of a person's speech, you should realize he or she is coming under extreme stress for one reason or another.

### Vocal Segregates

Segregates are vocalized pauses (such as "uh-uh," "um," and "ah") that may have meaning, but may be nothing more than space fillers. By and large, they have a negative role in communication and should be avoided as much as possible. A person who uses vocalizations of this kind excessively becomes quite annoying. If you find yourself falling into habits of "uh," "ah," or "um" throughout your speaking, you should try to consciously hear them. When you can actually hear yourself using these, you can consciously prune them from your speech. Earlier we discussed vocal segregates as nonfluencies that inhibit the communication process.

## Vocal Quality

This is the area that seems most fruitful for study. The quality of a person's voice tells us a great deal about him. Some voices are whining; others are breathy; some are hard or strident; some are smooth and pleasant. Each of these represents the tone of voice a person uses naturally or the tone a person uses to communicate some special attitude. The key to communication understanding is awareness of changes in quality. Some people get very strident or harsh when they are angry; some people get very breathy when they are being intimate. To each of these different qualities, you may assign some kind of a value judgment about how the person is feeling or what he is thinking. Now let us examine your use and awareness of paralanguage.

## Communication Session

*Reflection*

1. **What happens to your voice in stress situations? When does your pitch go up? down? When do you talk loudly? softly? When are you likely to talk fast? slowly?**

2. **Are there any vocal segregates that you use frequently? Are you always aware of their use? Are you making some effort to reduce or eliminate their use?**

3. **What are the emotions you read in other voices? For instance, how do you know when a person is being sarcastic? angry? condescending? humble? happy? sad? spiteful? Are there consistencies? Can you be sure?**

*Actualization*

1. **Go around the room having each class member say the word "yes." Each member should have in mind a specific question he or she is answering "yes" to. After each person has said "yes" try to figure out what his or her reaction to the question was. Was he or she excited? tentative? angry? What other emotions?**

2. **Divide into groups of three to six. Have two persons role-play various situations: for instance, a student has received a low grade on his theme that he worked on for hours and he wishes to confront his instructor, a person who does not have much patience when talking with students. The rest of the group should listen for paralanguage.**

## Perception Checking

A perception check is to nonverbal communication as a paraphrase is to verbal communication. You have learned to use paraphrasing to clarify the meaning of verbal messages; the perception check is the skill used to clarify the meaning of nonverbal messages. **Basically, it is a verbal statement that tests your understanding of how another person feels.**

If all of us always said what we are thinking or feeling, perception checking would not be needed. Because some people do not verbalize what they are thinking or feeling and because what they do say sometimes seems at odds with other clues they are sending, you as a receiver must interpret the words and actions. There is no way of judging the accuracy of your perceptions without putting them to the test. Examine the following situations and the efforts at checking out perceptions:

*George, through various visual and auditory clues that connote displeasure (speaking in short, precise sentences with a sharp tone of voice, and the like), gives Bill his day's assignment. Bill says: "I get the impression that you're upset with me, George. Are you?"*

*Ted delivers a note to Mary from her friend Gary. As she reads the note, her eyes brighten and she breaks into a smile. Ted says: "You seem particularly pleased with Gary's note, Mary. Is that so?"*

*Al offers Suzy directions for revising the advertisement she has written for a new product—an advertisement that took her many hours to prepare.*

*As Al talks, Suzy's face reddens, her eyes seem to water, and she sets her lips. Al says: "Am I right that you're angry with the suggestions I'm making?"*

*Martin listens to what Greg says with virtually no expression other than a slight smile. As Greg speaks Martin occasionally nods and he looks Greg straight in the eye. Greg says: "I'm not sure whether your expression means that you're satisfied or unsatisfied with my proposal?"*

In each of the above examples, the final sentence is a perception check that is intended to test the receiver's perceptions of the nonverbal communication of the sender.

How do you phrase a perception check?

1. *Watch the behavior of another.*

2. *Decode the perception.*

3. *Ask yourself, "What does that behavior mean to me?"*

4. *Choose the appropriate symbols for encoding.*

5. *Check to make sure that the symbols are just descriptive—no evaluations should be made.*

After the perception check is made, the sender has a chance to speak to the accuracy of that perception.

When should you use perception checking? We recommend that you check your perceptions whenever someone's nonverbal cues suggest that he or she has experienced a mood change. The perception check will enable you to make sure you understand that mood change so that your response to it will be appropriate.

What happens when you respond without checking your perceptions? Let's examine a rather typical conversation based upon the situation described in the first example above.

If, in place of the descriptive perception check ("I get the impression that you're upset with me. Are you?"), Bill were to say: "Why are you so upset with me?" Bill would not be describing his perception—he would be making a judgmental statement related to that perception. Replying as if your perception is "obviously" accurate involves reliance on mind reading and few of us can read minds. When mind reading is substituted for perception checking, the result is all too often trouble. Perhaps you are thinking, "Well, I know when another person is upset with me." Perhaps you are correct in your certainty that you can properly identify such feelings accurately much of the time. If you do not respond at all, you are guessing that you know how the other person is feeling. If you choose the judgmental reply, any person so spoken to would be inclined to be rather defensive about his feelings that you appear to be challenging. In response he might say, "Who said I'm upset?" or more harshly, "What the hell are you talking about?" Such responses might soon lead to further emotional outbursts, and very little communication takes place when communicators lose their tempers.

Because a perception check is descriptive rather than judgmental, the original sender will be less likely to become defensive. The purpose of checking out any perception of behavior is to give a person the opportunity to deal with that perception—to verify it or to correct it. Let's carry through with George and Bill's conversation. When Bill says, "I get the impression that you're upset with me, George. Are you?" George may say either (1) "No, whatever gave you that impression?" in which instance Bill can further describe the clues that he received; or George may say (2) "Yes, I am," in which instance Bill can get George to specify what has been the cause of the upset. If George is not upset, then Bill can deal with what caused him to misinterpret George's feelings; if George is upset, then he is given the opportunity to explain why in more detail, and Bill has the opportunity of changing the behavior that caused George to be upset.

A perception check will not eliminate defensive behavior. There are times when the emotional stress is so great that calm, logical communication is nearly impossible. Through the use of perception checking, however, you can reduce the probability of defensiveness.

Of all the possible barriers to communication that we will discuss in Chapter 7, defensiveness is the easiest to elicit and perhaps one of the most difficult to deal with. We are all sensitive human beings; without giving it conscious thought, we become attached to our own ideas and feelings because they are ours. Then, when we believe that one of our ideas or one of our feelings is being questioned, challenged, or in some way attacked, our immediate reaction is to strike out at the attacker. If, however, we feel that a person is not attacking us, we may develop an empathic bond, and we are less likely to get defensive. Although we will have occasion to talk about defensiveness later, for now let us try checking perceptions in a way that is least likely to elicit a defensive reaction.

## Communication Session

*Actualization*

1. **Respond to the following situations with well-phrased perception checks:**

> Vera comes rushing into the room, throws her books on the floor, and sits at her desk with her head in her hands. You say:

> Bob comes out of the instructor's office with pale face and slumped shoulders. Glancing at you with a forlorn look, he shrugs his shoulders and says, "Everything's all right." You say:

> As you return Jim's tennis racket you borrowed, you smile and say, "Here's your racket." Jim stiffens, grabs the racket, and as he walks to put it away says, "Thanks a bunch." You say:

> In the past, your advisor has told you that almost any time would be all right for working out your next term's schedule. When you tell him Wednesday afternoon at 4 p.m., he pauses, frowns, sighs, and says "Uh, I guess that's OK." You say:

2. **Work in groups of three. A talks with B and C observes. A role-plays a situation, giving off various cues of feelings through words and actions. B uses perception checking to test perception of A's feelings. C discusses the conversation. The exercise continues until everyone in the group has a chance at being sender, receiver, and observer.**

*Discussion*
**After the exercise, each person discusses how it feels to check out perceptions. Did the perception checking help or hinder the communication? How?**

## Payoffs

If you understand the elements of nonverbal communication, you should now be able to

1. Discuss the differences between verbal and nonverbal communication.

2. Discuss how fixed-featured and semi-fixed-featured space affect communication.

3. Arrange semi-fixed-featured space that will invite good communication.

4. Explain how territoriality affects communication with others.

5. Explain your use of the four categories of personal space.

6. Discuss how color, temperature, and lighting may affect interpersonal communication.

7. Explain how you use time and how you react to others who use it differently.

8. Define kinesics.

9. Discuss the use of emblems, illustrators, affect displays, regulators, and adaptors in interpersonal communication.

10. Define paralanguage.

11. Discuss vocal qualifiers, vocal differentiators, and vocal segregates.

12. Explain the three most important functions of nonverbal communication.

13. Define a perception check and explain the steps involved in phrasing one.

14. Phrase perception checks that help facilitate the communication process.

## Suggested Readings

**Mark L. Knapp.** *Nonverbal Communication in Human Interaction*. New York: Holt, Rinehart and Winston, 1972. Of the three sources cited this one presents the best analysis of research studies.

**Albert Mehrabian.** *Silent Messages*. Belmont, California: Wadsworth Publishing Company, 1971. A short, highly readable book focusing on the role of nonverbal communication in social interaction.

**Lawrence B. Rosenfeld** and **Jean M. Civikly.** *With Words Unspoken*. New York: Holt, Rinehart and Winston, 1976. Heavy emphasis on the role of nonverbal communication in establishing and developing interpersonal relationships. Includes selections from popular fiction, songs, and magazines.

**Part C: Application of Skills to Problem** 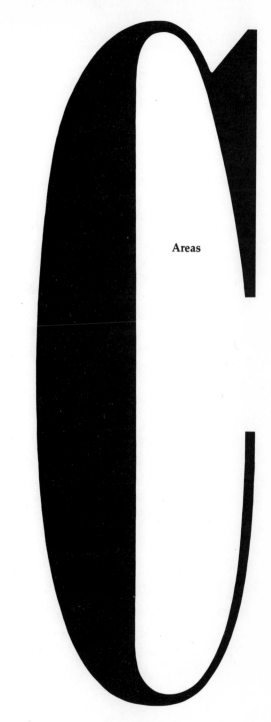Areas

**Chapter Seven:**
**Reducing Communication Barriers**

Despite your best efforts, communication will sometimes go awry. Perhaps the deck is stacked against you—perhaps the best-laid plans go astray. Whatever the reasons, barriers can and do occur. Our goal in this chapter is to consider several of the most common barriers in communication and give you some advice for reducing them. These barriers result from problems of information exchange, problems of distance between and among people, problems of attitude, and problems of

*By the time the message reaches*

strategies. We will start with the easiest to cope with, problems of information exchange, and work up to the most difficult, problems of strategies.

## Problems of Information Exchange

Any problem that gets in the way of one person's understanding of another is a barrier. Three relatively common barriers are transfer stations, information overload, and noise.

### Transfer Stations

A common barrier to information exchange is the dependence upon transfer stations. The imperfections of language as an instrument of communication are most evi-

dent in a situation in which communication occurs in chain-link fashion, as compared with one-to-one or one-to-many communication. Recall the game called Telephone (or Gossip) in which one person whispers a statement to another who in turn whispers what he thinks he heard to the next person and so on until it has gone through five or six transmissions. By the time it reaches the last person, the message may be so garbled that it is unintelligible.

In such a chain, each person acts as a transfer station. The original sender may have all the information he needs to communicate a relatively complex idea. When he encodes the message into language, he has already simplified, limited, and/or interpreted the original idea. The person who is the first transfer station for the message does not have benefit of

*the last person, it may be garbled.*

the entire background for the idea. He has only the words the first person used. He may not be able to remember all the words; he may not understand all the words; he may let semantic noise interfere with his understanding of the words. Nevertheless, he communicates what he now perceives as the message to the next person, who communicates what he perceives. As the message moves on down the line, each transfer station affords another opportunity for selection and interpretation. As we see from the game, if there are enough transfer stations (and it does not take many), the message can be distorted beyond recognition. Unscrupulous persons have used the technique to spread rumors for as long as people have used speech. Rumors are statements that are passed from person to person and usually embellished along the way, becoming

bigger, bolder, bloodier all the time. (It is interesting that messages with many facts are not only distorted in transmission but also shortened; messages that are storylike usually get embellished—certainly they are distorted, but instead of becoming shorter, they often become longer.)

The best way to avoid this barrier is to create a face-to-face communication setting with all those who must have the information. Even under the best of circumstances, pass-it-along, transfer-stations transmission distorts messages—the problem is how to minimize the distortion.

If you are caught in a chain-link communication put paraphrasing to work. Do not pass the message until you have taken the opportunity to get it right—both in content and intent.

## Information Overload

A second common barrier to information exchange results from information overload. Since you are a human being and not a high-speed computer, there is a limit to the amount of information you can process at any given time. You have probably had the experience of trying to get directions to a particular place in an unfamiliar area. When you think you are at least in the right area, you stop a pedestrian and ask, "How do you get to the stadium from here?" If he says, "Go three blocks north, turn to the right, and it's down a block or two on the left-hand side," you can probably process the information easily enough and will get to your destination with little difficulty. But have you ever had something like the following experience? The local character says to you, "Well, let's see, go three blocks north, turn right, go five blocks until you come to a Texaco station, turn left until you hit the third stop sign, turn left again, . . ." If you are like most people, you will probably go part of the way and then seek new directions. Regardless of how well you listen, you can be overloaded with details of information.

You can use selective perception, accepting only the input you want to perceive or are used to perceiving, to cope with the barrier created by overload. In practice, there should be a basis for the selection—perhaps a criterion that you can apply consciously to the volume of material. If you are the sender of information you can protect against information overload by limiting the details of the message, by grouping ideas, and by emphasizing the key points verbally or nonverbally. Of course, the more information you elect to send, the greater the likelihood for overload. If you are the receiver, you can use paraphrasing to check out your understanding. If you do not have the opportunity to paraphrase, you will have to rely on some selection process. Your mind will make a random selection anyway—if you are in control, you can determine which points will be retained. If you select consciously at least you will know why you attempted to retain the information you did.

## Noise

A final barrier we will consider in the group of problems of information exchange results from *noise*—both physical and semantic. As you will recall from our discussion of variables of communication in Chapter 1, physical noise consists of the external factors that clog the channels of communication, the sounds produced by things like jackhammers, lawn mowers, sirens, and "background" music. Sometimes even an almost imperceptible sound can be most distracting. Have you ever had the experience in a class where a fluorescent light overhead was buzzing? In the din of the chatter before class no one may really have noticed it, but when the class quiets down at the start of the lecture the buzzing seems to get louder and louder to the point where you can hear nothing else.

Some physical noise originates with the sender. For instance, if a person lisps or has some other speech impediment, you may find yourself listening to the lisp instead of to the ideas. Some people whistle as they speak, some scratch or play with their hair, some develop unusual facial expressions that appear incongruous.

Any noise that calls attention to itself may turn out to be a barrier. Why? Remember in our discussion of perception we talked about focus and the concepts of figure and ground? No one can focus on two competing stimuli at the same time. When one stimulus takes the position of focus, the other takes the position of ground.

As a receiver, there are only two things you can do. One is to eliminate the noise—turn off the buzzing light. The other is to turn up your power of concentration, issuing to yourself an order like "I will listen to the ideas—I recognize the distraction, impediment, or whatever, and I choose not to let it bother me." The former is, of course, more effective, but sometimes you are forced to do the latter. As a sender, you can talk louder, more enthusiastically, more vividly to try to compete successfully, or you can try to eliminate the distractions you are creating (if someone will tell you what you are doing).

At least you are conscious of physical noise. The second category—semantic noise—is more difficult to recognize and to deal with. You have semantic noise when a receiver gives to a word, phrase, or sentence different meaning than the sender intended. A citizen

*Semantic noise.*

attending a meeting of local taxpayers says, "We know where the problem is—it's downtown." The citizen may mean that City Hall, the seat of city government, is downtown, but if most of those listening regard downtown as the slum area inhabited by the city's poorer people, they may accept the statement as an attack on the residents and not on the administration. Semantic noise involves the use of words with multiple meanings or words that may evoke emotional reactions. Words such as "cops," ("fuzz"? "pigs"?), "Republicans" ("rightists"? "reactionaries"?), "Democrats" ("leftists"? "extremists"?) are typical examples of words that create semantic noise.

As a sender, your first job is to examine what you really mean to say and then encode it with care. Your second responsibility is to analyze the receivers of your communication to determine (as well as you can) whether they are likely to have the same meanings as you have for the language you have selected.

As a receiver, you may find paraphrasing an especially valuable corrective device. If you are not in a situation where you can use it, you must examine the entire context of the message to make sure that no noise is interfering with your ability to receive the message accurately. For instance, if you should hear an irate citizen saying that the source of the problem is "downtown," you should listen to how the speaker elaborates his points before you get set on the meaning.

## Communication Session

*Reflection*

1. **What is your reaction to information overload? Do you tune the person out? Do you become overly anxious?**

2. **How can you recognize yourself as the cause of information overload in others?**

3. **What words or idea groups cause semantic noise in you? Can you overcome this noise? How?**

*Actualization*

1. **Work in two groups of six—the rest of the class will be observers. Your instructor will give one person in each group a verbal message. The initiator will tell the message to one member of his or her group. In one group the message is to be passed chain-link method with no feedback from receivers. The message should eventually be told to all members, one at a time. In the other group, the receiver may paraphrase the message before attempting to pass it on to the next person. When the last person in each group has received the message, he or she writes the message on paper and gives it to the instructor. The instructor will read both messages to the entire group.**

*Discussion*

**What differences were present in the final messages? How can you account for relative accuracy or inaccuracy of the transmission?**

*Actualization*

2. **Work in pairs. One person gives a long series of directions. The sender should make the directions as complicated as possible. The receiver should paraphrase at will, stopping the sender and asking him to repeat when it seems appropriate. At the completion of the message, the receiver feeds back the directions as best he or she can.**

For a second round, the sender again gives a long series of directions, but this time the sender should do everything in his or her power to assist the receiver by emphasizing key ideas vocally, grouping details, repeating at key places, and so forth. This time the receiver may not interrupt either to paraphrase or to ask for repetition. At the end of the message, the receiver feeds back the directions as best he or she can.

*Discussion*
**Which method resulted in the greater accuracy? Why?**

*Actualization*
3. **While one person is talking, have another person hum in the background. Have the hummer increase the volume of the humming as the speaker proceeds.**

*Discussion*
**What was happening to each listener as the talk went on? What did each person do to maintain concentration?**

## Problems of Psychological Distance

The next class of barriers we will consider is a result of distance between and among people. This distance is not the linear distance of yards or meters, but psychological distance. Two such barriers are suspicion and gaps.

### Suspicion

Anything that keeps communicators apart can become a barrier. One attitude that results in the psychological separation of people is *suspicion,* a major barrier to communication. You doubtless know some persons who have such low credibility that you tend to be suspicious of any of their ideas, their motives, and/or their methods. Certainly some healthy caution is a good thing. If you were so naive that you trusted and believed everyone, some few would take advantage of you.

Still, there is a qualitative difference between withholding judgment of a person or his ideas and being so suspicious that you doubt everything regardless of how well it is supported. Suspicion, as we are using the word, is an unhealthy fear of the unknown, of the unusual, or of persons in authority. Suspicion is a barrier to effective communication, because it prevents us from gaining maximum value from what is being communicated. Instead of weighing and evaluating the content of a message, the suspicious person is bent on drawing conclusions that confirm his suspicion that he should be suspicious.

Avoiding suspicion is largely a matter of opening your mind to what is being said. This is not to be confused with accepting without questioning all that you hear. If you listen carefully, and completely, then you can make a decision on merits and not on how you feel about the person or the cause.

But by far the best way of coping with suspicion is by building a climate of trust.

In interpersonal relations, some degree of caution is probably healthy, but those relations and ultimately the communication rising out of them will be improved by the willingness to extend trust provisionally. For instance, Amber asks Vince to drop her paper off at class on a day she is sick. She extends a bit of trust. If Vince does what she asked, then Amber begins to see him as trustworthy and will be even more confident the next time she calls upon him for help. Since you do not have the time, energy, or power to do everything yourself, if in your relationships you expect the best to happen, you will usually not be disappointed. People need people. The development of trusting relationships can smooth the way for considerably more satisfying interpersonal relationships.

What if you are a person who feels that no one ever trusts you? Then perhaps you should look into your performance. If your roommate asked you to mail a letter and you said you would, but you did not, you should not be surprised if in the future your roommate does not trust you. Trust is a very fragile bond. The ordinarily suspicious person who has once extended trust and then gotten "burnt"

will revert to his suspicious nature. You build the bonds of trust by acting responsibly. Do what you say you will do; if you know you cannot perform, do not accept the task.

### Gaps

Perhaps the greatest psychological distance between persons or sets of people results from gaps. Communication means sharing meaning. When the frames of reference of two persons or two sets of people are based upon different experiences and are encoded by language that is not or cannot be accurately decoded, we have gaps. For instance, a person from New York asks for a soda (a word he uses for a carbonated soft drink) at a lunch counter in Nebraska and gets a glass filled with ice cream, carbonated water, and flavoring; or a person from the South asks for a poke (a word he uses for a bag or sack) in a northern grocery store and receives a shrug of the shoulders and "What do you want?"—or, from some literal-minded person, a jab in the ribs.

Our nation is a mixture of ethnic, social, religious, sex, age, nationality, geographic, and race groups. Although some think this blending ("the great melting pot") has helped to strengthen us as a nation, it also has resulted in significant barriers to communication between persons of different groups.

Theoretically, identical twins should have (and perhaps they do have) the greatest potential for mutually satisfying communication because their relationship is based on the greatest number of similarities. As individuals are separated from each other by time, space, race, religion, and so on, the potentials for communication gaps multiply. If the only difference between two persons is age, their communication problems should be fewer than if they are also separated by religion, sex, nationality, and social standing. Yet even a single gap, like age, seems unbridgeable for some persons.

Although gaps between people as individuals are difficult enough to deal with, they become even more difficult when the individuals are expected to function as representatives of a particular reference group bargaining with persons representing a different reference group. A student and a teacher may have some communication problems in classroom situations but not nearly so many as when the student as a representative of the student senate talks with the same teacher as a representative of the college administration. Likewise, Jack and Joe may often get along quite well and communicate admirably, yet when Jack becomes a spokesman for General Motors and Joe becomes a spokesman for a citizens' committee concerned about fuel conservation, the potential for communication gaps increases. Why? Because now they are responsible not only for their own individual differences, but also for the differences in standards of their groups. Communication is most effective when people function as individuals rather than as members of groups.

The problem of gaps increases tenfold

when we introduce the element of *stereotyping* into the communication process. When people look at others who have frames of reference different from themselves they feel a need to assign value judgments to those different frames of reference. You have heard such statements as "Youngsters are naturally hot-headed," "Women are more emotional then men," "Hard-hats are bigoted," "Blacks are shiftless," "Whites are racist," "The rich are insensitive," and so on. If the value judgments we harbor relative to such reference groups are negative, then the groups themselves represent to us inferior qualities and we tend to consider the individual members of those groups as inferior. Stereotyping is a method of classifying people without considering individual differences. Stereotyping is a barrier to effective communication because it reduces complex entities to a simple two-value system: Everything is either all good or all bad. "All youth are bad" does not allow for any gradations between "good" and "bad" and certainly does not allow for individual differences.

So, how do you deal with gaps and avoid stereotyping? First, you must recognize that communication does become more difficult as there are more differences between communicators. Good communication is seldom easy. When you are trying to bridge gaps (and you cannot bridge gaps without trying), you must realize that you will have to work at the communication. Second, determine to build your bridges of communication between individuals and not between groups. Instead of a battle between youth and old age, focus on a dialogue between, for example, Mark Jones, Jr., and Mark Jones, Sr. How can this be done? The key is the ability to look at the issue being discussed from the other person's perspective. Issue—marijuana. How does Mark Junior see "grass" (or whatever term he uses)? Why does he want it legalized? Then, how does Mark Senior see marijuana? Why does he oppose legalizing it? Why is he afraid of it, or is he? See the other as an individual. Viewing from the other person's perspective requires sensitivity. You must really listen as the other person speaks—paraphrase, put his ideas in your own words. Try to understand his ideas, point of view, beliefs, evidence. You may never be convinced about his position, but you should at least understand it, as best you can.

Prejudice is often nothing more than the refusal to look beyond a label. Try the indexing method we talked about earlier, for getting beyond the label. Remember, when talking about actors (Catholics, women, or any category) $actor_1$ ($Catholic_1$ or $woman_1$) is not $actor_2$ ($Catholic_2$ or $woman_2$), and so on. Bill may be black; Ted may be white. But Bill and Ted have individual characteristics that are more important than any preconceived group characteristic. When you see individual characteristics, you can examine, describe, and draw conclusions from the data about the individual.

## Communication Session

*Reflection*

Consider your communication in this class. Each person in class represents slightly different reference groups. Has group affiliation affected your communication with class members? Are you a man or a woman? Has this affected your communication? Are you a fraternity member, or a sorority member, an independent, or a commuter? Has this affected your communication? When you come to some "gap" that has affected your classroom communication, take time to think what you can do about it and how.

*Actualization*

1. At the first opportunity, ask someone you are ordinarily a little suspicious of to do something for you—mail a letter, buy you a pack of paper. After the experience, ask yourself whether your feeling about the person has changed.

2. Work in pairs. One member of the pair closes his eyes or blindfolds himself. The other person leads him on a five-minute walk. At the end of the five minutes, reverse the roles. After the exercise, discuss how you felt when you were leading—when you were being led. Did you become more confident as the walk proceeded? Why?

3. Do you stereotype? On the top of a piece of paper, write as column headings Republicans, Democrats, Jews, Catholics, Protestants, Whites, and Blacks. Under each heading jot down any adjectives that occur to you when you say that heading to yourself. Be honest—no one else need see your lists.

*Discussion*

In groups of four to six, discuss the kinds of gaps that affect your communication and how you can cope with those gaps.

## Problems of Attitude in the Interaction

A third class of barriers are those that result from attitudinal problems in the interaction—barriers that result from an attitude or barriers that create a negative attitude. In this section we will consider inappropriate responses, defensiveness, and emotional overreaction.

### Inappropriate Responses

A useful response is a verbal and/or non-verbal reaction that is a result of, relates to, or grows out of a sender's message. Many times, responses do not meet the expectation of the sender. We call such responses inappropriate, for rather than dealing directly with the communication, they significantly disrupt the flow of communication. They range from responses that totally ignore the person's statements to those whose sole purpose is to put down the sender for making such a statement. There are times, of course, when people intend to ignore or to put down, but often the behavior arises, not out of malice, but out of ignorance, insensitivity, or total absorption in self. The motive for using such responses goes beyond the scope of this text; yet we are interested in identifying inappropriate responses, showing why they are barriers, and offering suggestions for avoiding them. The following are some of the most common:

1. *Irrelevant response:* An irrelevant response is one that bears no relationship to what has been said—in effect it ignores the sender entirely.

**Bob:** *I'm really concerned with the way Paul is handling arrangements for the benefit.*

**Tom:** *Hey, the Russian gymnasts are coming to town—I've got to get tickets for that.*

When the sender is totally ignored it not only causes him to question whether he was heard, but it may well cause him to wonder about the worth of what he was thinking or saying—for anything important will not be ignored.

2. *Interrupting response:* When the receiver breaks in before the sender has finished, the response is interrupting.

**Bob:** *I'm really concerned with the way Paul . . .*

**Tom:** *I know—that Paul is something else, but I don't think there's any real problem.*

People are inclined to interrupt when they believe what they have to say is much superior to what the sender is saying, when they believe they know what the sender is going to say and they want the other person to know that they already know, or when they just are not paying careful attention. Any of these three common reasons connotes a lack of sensitivity or a dogmatic or superior attitude. As human beings we need to be able to verbalize our ideas and feelings regardless of whether they are already known or not. Constant interruptions are bound to either damage the sender's self-concept or make him or her hostile—and possibly both. Whatever you have to say is seldom so important that it requires you to interrupt the sender. When you do interrupt, you should realize that you are building a barrier. The more frequent the interruptions, the greater the barrier will become.

3. *Tangential responses:* Tangential responses are really irrelevant responses in tactful language. They are better in that at least the receiver acknowledges hearing the sender's statement. But the net result, changing the subject, is essentially the same:

**Bob:** *I'm really concerned with the way Paul is handling arrangements for the benefit.*

**Tom:** *Well, you know Paul—Hey, the Russian gymnasts are coming to town—I've got to get tickets for that.*

Even though Bob's statement has been acknowledged, Tom appears to be saying that the issue is not important enough to deal with. Again, such responses chip away at the sender's feelings of self-worth. Bob thought that he was raising an issue that was of great importance to everyone within the group. Either Tom has problems because he fails to see the gravity of the situation or Bob has problems with placing too much emphasis on Paul's methods. The real problem is that the conversation deals with neither of the possibilities. The issue is unresolved. The apparent withdrawal from discussing an issue is in itself a barrier.

4. *Incongruous response:* In the chapter on nonverbal communication we indicated that communication problems occur when nonverbal messages appear to conflict with the verbal messages. An incongruous response is a manifestation of this problem.

**Bob:** *Well, we really got some things done today.*

**Tom:** *Yeah, that was a great meeting* (stated in sarcastic tones).

On the surface Tom seems to be acknowledging and verifying Bob's statement, but his sarcastic tone causes Bob to wonder whether he is confirming Bob's ideas or whether he's making fun of them. Since nonverbal reactions are likely to override verbal meaning with most people, it is most likely that Bob will take Tom's words as sarcasm. If they are in fact sarcastic, a barrier begins to be built through Tom's insensitivity to Bob's honest statement of feelings. If Tom's words are sincere, a barrier begins to be built as a result of Bob's confusion about Tom's meaning.

5. *Evaluative response:* Although we have already discussed evaluation in some detail in Chapter 4, we list it here because it is often an inappropriate response that results in a barrier to communication. When something intervenes to stop the interaction on a content point, that something is a barrier—and few responses produce more barriers than evaluation:

**Bob:** *I'm really concerned with the way Paul is handling arrangements for the benefit.*

**Tom:** *Questioning Paul's methods is idiotic—he's done this kind of thing more than the rest of us put together.*

Tom's response is inappropriate because it changes the subject from whether or not Paul's handling of arrangements is appropriate to whether Bob makes idiotic statements or not. The barrier results initially because the statement has an air of irrelevancy to it, but, more important, it is an attack on Bob—an attack that probably will result in defensive behavior. We will consider defensiveness as a barrier in the next section in this chapter.

Although these are not the only five inappropriate responses they are the most common ones in building or strengthening communication barriers. How can inappropriate responses be avoided? First, you should really listen to the other person. If you spend your time thinking of what you have to say, your response is likely to be inappropriate— you are more likely to come up with an irrelevant or an interruptive response. If, on the other hand, you really listen to what is being said, you are more likely to acknowledge and to come to grips with the idea or feeling the sender is describing or expressing. Second, you should be sensitive to the needs of the other person. Start with the assumption that what a person says is important to that person —*even if it is not or does not seem to be important to you.* Then deal with the idea or feeling at face value. If what the person has said is not, in your opinion, very important (or worth talking about) then the honest impersonal response is one that verbalizes your ideas or describes your feelings.

**Bob:** *I'm really concerned with the way Paul is handling arrangements for the benefit.*

**Tom:** (Believing the point is not important) *I can see where you might be concerned, Bob, but I really don't see any major problem at this time.*

**Tom:** (Believing the point may be important to Bob but is not so important to Tom) *Bob, that may be a concern to you, but I'll tell you I'm so excited about the thought of the Russian gymnasts coming to town that I just can't get very concerned with Paul's methods.*

Notice that both of Tom's responses are honest. Bob should now understand why Tom is changing the subject or not taking Bob's ideas very seriously. Bob now has the option of letting the topic drop or trying to persuade Tom of its importance. At least, however, he has been acknowledged. If a barrier is going to be built it becomes Bob's responsibility as much as Tom's.

It is our belief that inappropriate response barriers are common because people just do not take the time to be sensitive to the needs of others. You need not compromise your ideas or feelings in any way. Just let the other person know why you are behaving as you are.

### Defensiveness

In several places in this textbook, we have considered the interpersonal skills that can be utilized to develop a positive communication climate. We stated that when such skills are not used or are misused the result may be a negative climate. Perhaps the major aspect of a negative climate is defensiveness. If you have understood all that we have discussed so far and if you have been able to put what you have learned into practice, you may well have been able to keep defensiveness from resulting. Still even with the best of intentions, defensiveness will occasionally develop in interpersonal encounters. In this section, we want to take a brief look at what creates defensiveness and stress again those skills that are most appropriate in alleviating or preventing it.

What is defensiveness? Defensiveness is a behavior that results when a person feels threatened. Although some people are constantly defensive, most often a defensive response is evoked by something that was said, was done, or happened. Each person is a fragile vulnerable human being; inside each of us there is a "sensing device" that when triggered shouts "Alert! Trouble ahead! Be wary!" A stranger walking toward Sara suddenly raises his arm. Sara is alert to danger and for a moment is seized by emotion. The stranger scratches his nose and returns his arm to "normal" walking position. Sara's mind analyzes the situation, discovers she is in no danger, and her nervous system returns to normal.

During the time Sara was reacting to her emotions, during her defensive period, she would have difficulty communicating in a normal manner. Remember that defensiveness is not caused only by apprehension about physical attacks—defensiveness, as we have already considered, is often provoked by verbal attacks or perceived verbal attacks as well. Jack Gibb found that defensive behavior is caused by interaction that is perceived by the individual as (1) evaluative, (2) control-oriented, (3) strategic, (4) neutral, (5) superior, and (6) dogmatic.[1]

How do you reduce defensiveness or prevent it from occurring? You should engage in communication behavior that lends itself to a positive climate. Gibb offers six behaviors that are directly the opposite of those cited above: (1) descriptive in language rather than evaluative, (2) oriented to problem solving rather than personal control, (3) spontaneous rather than patterned to strategy, (4) empathic rather than neutral, (5) implying equality rather than self-superiority, and (6) tentative rather than dogmatic. These and other alternative behaviors are discussed in Chapter 3.

### Overreaction

Everyone experiences emotional response. Emotional overreaction is a disproportionally emotional response to a stimulus. When you overreact, you temporarily lose control of your rational behavior. Any large doses of emotional response, particularly of negative emotion like anger, jealousy, and hostility that are injected into the communication process can short-circuit the process, creating nearly insurmountable barriers.

---

[1]Jack R. Gibb, "Defensive Communication," *Journal of Communication*, Vol. 11 (September 1961), pp. 141–148.

Basically, your life is determined by rational decision making. When an emotion becomes so strong that it short-circuits the thought process, it can and often does lead to inappropriate behavior. Pure emotion is powerful. You should be aware of that power.

Let us look at how emotional overreaction creates a communication barrier. Alfred and Sue offer different plans for raising money. The rational process calls for presentation and discussion of both plans so that they can be compared according to some standard of judgment and the best plan selected for implementation. However, if Alfred dislikes Sue, if he is hostile toward everything Sue stands for, he may be incapable of examining Sue's plan rationally—incapable of seeing any good arising from anything that Sue says or does. Moreover, his overriding hostility may well cause him to be excessive in his claims for the superiority of his plan—to the point where he might do anything to win. Alfred's extreme emotional reaction could prevent him from communicating with Sue—or with anyone else—about Sue's plan.

Now please do not misinterpret what we are saying. A world without emotional reaction would be a bleak and dull world indeed. But if you let your emotions run rampant, they will short-circuit the rational process, which in turn will block communication. When the lines of communication are blocked or broken, decision making is left to blind chance—and on issues that are vital to self, family, or nation, you need to give yourself better than a 50–50 chance.

So, what do you do about emotional overreaction? Obviously, the simple advice "Don't overreact" is not going to help. Our suggestions are three:

1. *If you feel yourself acting out of emotion, disengage.* If a decision is involved, let others make it—those who can examine it rationally.

2. *If the decision involves you, describe your feelings.* Maybe by airing your grievance with the person you can create a more rational climate. If you say, "When you talk I get very angry regardless of what you're saying," you are being honest, and honesty in communication is a good starting point for consideration of grievances.

3. *Force yourself to go through the steps of problem solving.* Define the problem, analyze the problem, list possible solutions, then select the best solution rather than letting the decision be made at a gut level. We will talk about this method in more detail in Chapter 10. You may not be able to do it very well, but it may give you just enough perspective to handle the situation adequately.

Of course the best solution is to deal with the emotion itself. What is it about Sue that Alfred hates? Is it the way she looks? The way she talks? The way she thinks? Is it Sue's reaction to Alfred? Perhaps if you can figure out the *what* and the *how* of your emotions before you are confronted with a potentially explosive situation, you can work out a means of dealing with them.

## Communication Session

*Reflection*

1. **Why do people use inappropriate responses?**

2. **Think of the last time you felt defensive. What caused your defensiveness? How might you have dealt with that defensiveness?**

3. **Identify a person to whom you seem to react with great hostility. What is it about the person that causes you to act the way you do? Be specific: Is it attitude? Describe the attitude. Is it dress? Describe the dress. Is it ideas? Describe the ideas. Is it a behavior? Describe the behavior.**

*Actualization*

1. **Working in groups of three, let two people start with a stimulus message like, "I'm really concerned about Pete's grades" and role-play a discussion on the topic. The observer should note any inappropriate responses and the results of them.**

2. **Work in pairs. One person should give a defensiveness-producing statement (for example, "You're wearing that ugly shirt or blouse again"). Then have the other partner try to change the statement into one less likely to arouse defensiveness (for example, "I don't think you look your best in that shirt or blouse"). After each corrective statement, both partners should discuss why the second statement was better or worse.**

*Discussion*

1. **How do you know that you are about to overreact? What clues do you give off to others?**

2. **Is it easy or difficult to avoid inappropriate responses? Discuss ways of making appropriate responses.**

3. **What causes people to respond inappropriately?**

## Problems of Strategies

The fourth classification of barriers, and in many ways the most difficult to cope with, includes those that result from use of strategies in communication. One of the most insidious of these strategies is the hidden agenda.

We assume that people are honest, open and aboveboard in their communication. Yet all too often the agenda for a communication event really is not what it may seem to be. What is an agenda? It is the subject matter to be discussed, the purpose for the communication. For instance, if the boss calls Sanders in to talk about his progress on the Morris account, the discussion of that account is the reason for the meeting—it is the agenda. For a family deciding whether to send the children to camp, making the decision is the agenda, the subject of the conversation. In normal conversation, the agenda is often made up as participants go along. It is usually flexible, and the conversation leads where it will. In more formal settings, an agenda arises from the situation at hand and people meet to accomplish what is on the agenda.

What then is a hidden agenda? A *hidden agenda* is a reason or motive for a communication event that is not disclosed to other participants. For instance, if the account executive called Sanders in to talk about the Morris account but really wanted to find out why Sanders had seemed so depressed lately, trying to discover the reason for the depression would be the executive's hidden agenda. In a meeting with many participants, each may have a hidden agenda that controls his behavior. For instance, if an office group meets to discuss a gift for their supervisor who is being transferred, Madge may not care about the gift—her agenda may be her willingness to go along with anything; Warren may have only thirty minutes on his parking meter so his agenda is to hurry the meeting along; Audrey may harbor a secret passion for the supervisor, so her hidden agenda may be to try to promote an exquisitely personal gift that will somehow show that she cares. A hidden agenda, then, is any strategy that is unknown to one or more of the parties in the conversation but that determines the nature or direction of the behavior of the individual.

Many people use the hidden agenda as a strategy to play psychological games with other people. A game is nothing more than one person's attempting to manipulate another person's behavior until the manipulator gets some payoff, usually a predictable behavior. Art knows that Madge gets angry when he turns off the television without asking her—so, he turns it off and acts very amazed when Madge loses her temper. Rachel knows that Steve is likely to become very uncomfortable with a discussion of his former girl friend, Doris. So in his presence, Rachel "innocently" asks, "Say, has anyone seen Doris lately?" In both cases, the person's hidden agenda was to create a painful experience. If the behavior gets the desired response, the person "wins." And it is this win-lose element that makes such statements games.

Are hidden agendas always barriers to communication? Usually, if not always. Although as a matter of tact or propriety you may sometimes stipulate one agenda when in reality you support another one, such deception all too often degenerates into manipulation. If Max is suspected of cheating on a test, the instructor may call him into the office ostensibly to talk about the subject for his next report but really with the intention of trying to get at the subject of cheating indirectly. In this instance, the hidden agenda may appear to be a proper procedure; but in terms of interpersonal relations, it includes elements of manipulation. Since the hidden agenda often is beneficial only to the person holding it, it can be detrimental to other persons involved or to the subject being discussed. The base for good interpersonal communication is a willingness of all parties to be open with each other. Disclosures of true feelings, attitudes, and beliefs are fundamental to good working relations among people. When hidden agendas are discovered, the fragile bond of trust can be frayed or perhaps even broken; and, once trust is gone, the chance for good interpersonal relations is gone. So although hidden agendas may appear expedient, we do better to avoid them as detrimental.

Then how do we bridge the gap created by a hidden agenda?

1. *Through direct confrontation:* "Bill, you called me in here to talk about the Morris account. Is that really what you had in mind?" Or, "Art, you know I get angry when you turn off the TV without asking—are you trying to

hurt me?" When the agenda is open, it can be handled. Often a direct confrontation will bring the subject into the open. Perhaps the subject is hard to talk about, delicate, risky— it does not matter. Get it out in the open.

2. *Through openness on the part of the initiator:* "Max, I called you in because I'm really concerned about your last test. My perception is that you cheated. Am I correct?" Openness leads to discussion of issues. Now instead of dealing in implication and innuendo, those involved know the issue and can talk about it.

## Communication Session

*Reflection*

Think of the last time you met with a group of people. Did you have a hidden agenda? How did it affect your communication?

*Actualization*

Give each of three or four people in a group a hidden agenda. Have the group then discuss a topic such as the nature of the gift for another group member's birthday. Note the way the hidden agendas are introduced. See whether the people involved can deal with them.

*Discussion*

In groups of four to six, discuss how you feel when you discover that you have been following someone's hidden agenda. How do you deal with those feelings?

## Payoffs

Now that you have finished this chapter on barriers, you should be able to

1. Describe the consequences of chain-link communication and know how to avoid them.

2. Explain the phenomenon of information overload and understand how to overcome it.

3. Explain how noise acts as a barrier to communication.

4. Overcome physical and semantic noise.

5. Explain how suspicion undermines the communication process.

6. Understand the reason for communication gaps.

7. Discuss how stereotyping acts as a barrier to effective communication.

8. Explain how gaps can be bridged.

9. Explain the types of inappropriate responses.

10. Define defensiveness and understand its principal causes.

11. Change defensiveness-provoking messages to supportive messages.

12. Describe how emotional overreaction creates barriers.

13. Cope with overreaction.

14. Define "hidden agenda" and explain the communication difficulties it creates.

## Suggested Readings

**Jack R. Gibb.** "Defensive Communication." *Journal of Communication,* Vol. 11 (September 1961). Gibb lists six attitudes that provoke defensiveness and contrasts them with six attitudes that will build a supportive climate.

**Irving J. Lee** and **Laura L. Lee.** *Handling Barriers in Communication.* New York: Harper & Row, 1956. This handbook that grew out of the Lees' work with organizational communication is sometimes difficult to come by, but well worth the effort to try to find it.

**Carl R. Rogers** and **F. J. Roethlisberger.** "Barriers and Gateways to Communication." *Harvard Business Review,* Vol. 30 (July–August 1952). Although the article is more than twenty-five years old, it still provides valuable insight into dealing with barriers.

**Chapter Eight:
Conflict**

Conflict—the clash of opposing attitudes, ideas, behaviors, goals, and needs. It is the rare person who can get through even one day without experiencing conflict. How do you react to conflict? Does it make you anxious? Do you try to avoid it at all costs? Do you thrive on it? Do you see it as a stimulating, necessary aspect of living? Conflicts will occur—make no mistake about it. How you deal with conflict determines the nature of your interpersonal relations and determines the degree of satisfaction you have with the outcome of the conflict.

We are not going to show you how to avoid conflict because conflict is not necessarily bad. Conflict occurs between people because each of us has different ideas, feelings, motives, and behavior. Conflicts are inevitable because of these uniquenesses. Thus, in order to teach you how to avoid conflict we would have to teach you how to avoid people! Moreover, conflict often can be constructive. Conflict forces choice, and in a good environment the process of choosing helps you to test relative merits of the attitudes, behavior, needs, and goals in conflict.

Since conflict inevitably will occur between friends as well as enemies and since most people cannot be or do not want to be hermits, you need to be aware of various methods of dealing with conflict. You will see that sometimes you can resolve conflict in a manner agreeable to all persons involved; sometimes you can cope with or manage conflict; and sometimes the best you can hope for is to keep the conflict from escalating to a type of interpersonal warfare. In this chapter we will consider methods for resolving or managing your conflicts.

## Kinds of Conflicts

You will be better able to cope with a conflict if you know whether it is pseudoconflict, content conflict, value conflict, or ego conflict.

### Pseudoconflict

Pseudoconflict is not really conflict but gives the appearance of conflict. It exists when a person believes that two goals cannot be simultaneously achieved when in fact they can be. If you are studying for tomorrow's exam in geology and a friend stops by to ask you to go out for a pizza with the gang, you may perceive these two actions as being in conflict. The tendency in a pseudoconflict situation is to put the choice between actions in an either-or framework, in this case *either* you study *or* you go out with the gang. This would be a real conflict if it is impossible to do both within the prescribed time period. More often than not, however, you are likely to set up a false dichotomy between choices when in fact it may very well be possible to accomplish both goals. Perhaps, in this example, you can find out where the gang is going and then say you will meet them in an hour or two; or you can go with the gang for a couple of hours and then come back and study. If either of these schedules for your evening is really possible, then you can dispel the pseudoconflict.

In addition to false either-or dichotomies, pseudoconflict can also result from misunderstanding. Suppose a husband and wife have agreed to clean up the apartment before going to play tennis. Yet before the job is finished, the husband puts on his shoes and starts for the door. When the wife, thinking he is breaking the agreement, asks "Where are you going?" the husband calls back to her as he reaches the door, "I'll be back in a minute, don't worry." If she is untrusting, his leaving without clearly stating the nature of his action may bring on a pseudoconflict. This pseudoconflict may be dispelled as soon as he returns, realizes her distress, and explains that he had no intention of running out before finishing the cleaning but just had to get a pack of cigarettes. If the explanation is accepted, the conflict disappears.

The plots of many simplistic situation television comedies are built on pseudoconflict played for all it is worth until at the end of the show a simple explanation eliminates the conflict. However, pseudoconflict becomes real conflict when the explanation (1) is not forthcoming or (2) is not satisfactory or (3) is not accepted. If the wife sees the husband's action as symptomatic of his "lack of concern for her feelings," a real conflict based upon the pseudoconflict may ensue. The conflict may then escalate into either a content conflict or an ego conflict.

Potential conflicts are often resolved by showing that no real conflict exists. Perhaps the very first thing to do when you perceive conflict is to determine whether that conflict is real.

### Content Conflict

A confrontation that is based on message accuracy is content conflict. It usually occurs in any of four sets of circumstances.

1. *The conflict may be over a fact.* Two or more persons may come into conflict over whether Johnny Bench drove in more than a hundred runs last year or whether Barbra Streisand won an Academy award for her performance in the movie *Funny Girl.* Conflicts over facts are easily resolved by looking up the facts. Still, those in conflict may continue to battle if no source is readily at hand. If you find yourself embroiled in a conflict over a fact try to avoid escalating the conflict. Try to disengage until a source for checking the fact can be found.

2. *The conflict may be over an interpretation of a fact or an inference drawn from a fact or series of facts.* Two or more persons may disagree over whether the rise in steel prices will trigger another round of inflation. The rise in steel prices is a fact; what will result from that rise is a matter of opinion based on interpretation of the fact or on inference drawn from the fact. Since there is no way of *proving* that a given interpretation or inference is correct the participants may determine which choice is more likely to occur.

3. *The conflict may be over a definition.* Two or more persons may come into conflict over whether the use of communication strategies to motivate people to buy a product is *unethical behavior* or *good salesmanship.* In this type of conflict, the antagonists agree on what is being done; the problem lies in how each person defines the behavior. Again, there is no way to prove the superiority of a given

definition. The conflict may be resolved by determining which definition can be best supported.

4. *The conflict may be over a choice among goals, actions, or means of arriving at goals.* Two or more persons may come into conflict over whether building a multilevel garage or utilizing available space more efficiently is the better solution to the campus parking problem. In this type of conflict, the opponents agree on the problem but disagree on the solution. Since you cannot prove that one proposed solution is better, the conflict will be resolved only when the parties involved agree that one solution can be better supported than the other.

Some authorities refer to content conflict as "simple" conflict. Because facts can be looked up, inferences can be tested, definitions can be verified, and competing goals can be weighed and evaluated, the conflict can be resolved rationally. Issues can be clearly stated and the potential for cooperative effort in resolving the conflict is present. The best procedure for coping with most content conflict is to follow the guidelines for conflict resolution that are stated in the last section of this chapter and are discussed in greater detail in Chapter 10.

Although content conflicts cannot always be resolved, they are still much easier to cope with than either value conflicts or ego conflicts. If you can keep personal emotions out of the conflict situation, you have the chance of amicable resolution.

## Value Conflict

Value conflicts arise when people differ in their views of life in general (or an aspect of life), and these differences are brought into focus on a particular issue. A person who believes that the government is responsible for each individual views life differently from a person who believes that each individual has the right and responsibility to take care of himself. On such issues as welfare, Medicare, and unemployment compensation these two persons would have value conflicts. Although people whose basic value systems differ can learn to get along on many levels, they will find it difficult if not impossible to resolve most conflicts resulting from their differences in values. For such people to get along they must seek areas for discussion where their values do not come into basic conflict, and about areas where the basic conflicts occur they are probably best counseled to agree to disagree on such issues.

Can value conflicts be resolved? Perhaps over a period of time. Our values change to some degree from one period of life to another—but these changes are not likely to occur very quickly. Is it bad for people with differences in values to debate those differences? No, provided each person recognizes that he is not likely to change the other person's values. Good friends can often argue over differences for the joy of good verbal combat. Persons who are anticipating a long-term intimate relationship by all means should discuss their value systems to determine whether basic differences in values will affect their ability to maintain a relationship.

### Ego Conflict

Ego conflicts are probably the most damaging to interpersonal relationships. Ego conflict exists when the persons in conflict view "winning" or "losing" the conflict as a measure of their expertise, personal worth, or image. Ego conflicts develop when in the dialogue over content elements one or both parties introduce personal or judgmental statements. In a discussion of whether Barbra Streisand did or did not win an Oscar for her performance in *Funny Girl,* the simple content conflict may be escalated to an ego conflict when one or both parties view the issue as stupidity versus supreme knowledge—that the eventual winner is the champion of supreme knowledge and the loser is relegated to the role of poor, stupid individual.

Who you are, what you are, what competence you have, over whom you should or do have power, and how much you know are likely to be a few of the factors involved in the make-up of your self-concept. When you view a conflict as somehow tied in with your personal worth, the conflict becomes an ego conflict. If you see yourself as a baseball expert, you may perceive conflict over a statement you made about baseball as an attack on your self-esteem; if you see your role as a protector of your brother, you may perceive conflict over whether your brother should be

allowed some special privilege as an attack on your ability to handle the responsibility. Once your ego becomes involved in the conflict, your ability to cope rationally is often lost. Before either party realizes it, emotions are involved, words are said that cannot be taken back, and the conflict gets blown all out of proportion.

Since conflict is hard enough to resolve without bringing in personalities and emotions, you must be careful to separate the content of a conflict from your potential ego involvement. This is, of course, easier said than done. In the next section, we will consider effects of cooperation and competition in conflict resolution—it is through the maintenance of cooperative attitudes that ego conflicts are avoided or resolved.

In this section we have tried to identify four common types of conflict. Before you move on to suggestions for resolving conflict complete the following exercises.

## Communication Session

*Reflection*
Identify the last three conflicts you had. Were they pseudoconflict? content conflict? ego conflict? or value conflict? What was the outcome of each?

*Actualization*
Decide whether the following are C (content conflict), P (pseudoconflict), V (value conflict), or E (ego conflict).

___1. Joe wants to live together while Mary wants the two of them to get married.

___2. Stan believes that since he is an insurance salesman Jerry should not dispute his position on annuities.

___3. George defends his failure to present an anniversary gift to Agnes by asserting that their anniversary is not today (May 8) but May 18.

___4. Martin calls to announce that he is bringing the boss home for dinner. His wife replies, "That will be impossible. The house is a mess and I need to go shopping."

___5. Jane says, "Harry, pick up your clothes—I'm not your maid!" Harry replies, "I thought we agreed that it's your job to take care of the house, I take care of the yard."

*Discussion*
Which of the above examples would be the most difficult to resolve? Why?

Answers: 1. V; 2. E; 3. C; 4. P; 5. C.

## Cooperation versus Competition

When a conflict arises, one of the first variables to affect the outcome of the conflict is whether the participants' attitudes are competitive or cooperative. If the attitudes of both individuals involved are competitive, then each is likely to be ego-involved. If Fred wants to live in an apartment off campus and his father wants him to live in the dorm, Fred and his father have a content conflict. If Fred and his father look at the conflict competitively, then for Fred getting an apartment represents winning and living in the dorm represents losing; from his father's viewpoint, if Fred lives in the dorm Dad wins and if Fred gets an apartment Dad loses.

The problems created by the win-lose dichotomy are multifold. First, one member of the conflict must lose. Losing is not pleasant and the reaction to losing, especially in a high-stake conflict, may be one in which the loser looks for a way to get revenge against the winner. Second, if the two people engage in several encounters and the same person always wins, the loser may become very dejected or hostile. If the loser becomes convinced that he or she will always lose, this may well cause a stumbling block to even the most intimate relationship. Third, and perhaps most important, winning or losing seems to become a measure of personal worth. Battle lines are drawn and neither party can "give in" without viewing it as a personal loss.

The alternative to the competitive attitude is the cooperative attitude. If the attitudes of those in conflict are cooperative, then each person looks for mutually beneficial ways of resolving the conflict. You may ask, "How can an outcome be mutually satisfying to Fred and to his father when Fred wants to live in an apartment and his father wants him to live in a dorm?" A mutually satisfying solution is one that meets the needs, wants, and desires of both persons. Why does Fred want an apartment? Why does his father want him to live in a dorm? Through cooperation, the reasons can be discovered. If Dad wants Fred to have good grades and stay out of trouble and if Fred wants to have privacy and a place of his own, then the two can see whether both sets of needs can be met. Assuming that no third choice exists that may be satisfying to both, through cooperative discussion they may achieve a compromise: If Fred lives in the dorm one term and keeps his grades up, he may move into an apartment the next term; or Fred may get an apartment now and, if he keeps his grades up and stays out of trouble, he can keep the apartment. A solution then can be mutually satisfying because it meets the needs behind the expressed preferences.

Cooperation means willingness to follow the steps of the problem-solving method: For now we will list these steps—(1) identify the problem, (2) analyze the nature of the problem, (3) suggest possible solutions, and (4) select the solution that best meets the needs determined in problem analysis—later we will show how they are put into practice. Does cooperation always result in conflict resolution? No, not always; but once the win-lose dichotomy is rejected, those in conflict

have the potential for working out their conflicts.

In some conflicts one person initially may look at the outcome competitively while the other has a cooperative outlook. In this situation, the nature of the conflict will depend upon whether the person looking at the conflict competitively draws the other person into the competition or whether the person looking at the outcome cooperatively influences the other person to cooperate.

A factor that influences whether a person will view a conflict cooperatively or competitively is the importance of outcome. Suppose Fred and Suzy are discussing plans for the evening. Fred suggests going to a movie. Suzy says she would just as soon stay home and watch television. Fred and Suzy have a content conflict over a choice of actions. If neither sees the decision as important, they are more likely to approach the conflict resolution cooperatively.

Suppose, however, that Fred and Suzy are discussing next summer's vacation plans. If Fred has been thinking for weeks about using the new fly rod he got for his birthday and he is excited about going off in the wild for a week of camping, boating, and fishing, where they go will be very important to him. If, on the other hand, Suzy has been thinking about going to a plush resort for a week of swimming and sunbathing and eating at exotic restaurants, the conflict that results may be fraught with potential hazards. Granted that neither will consider vacationing alone, on this issue, each has significant stake in the outcome. If they have time and money for only one week of vacation during the year, the chances that they will maintain a cooperative attitude are not very good. If competitive attitudes develop, then either Fred or Suzy will lose; and, on this issue, losing will hurt. On the other hand, even if both do their best to maintain a cooperative attitude, negotiating an amicable resolution to the conflict will not be easy.

For people who have been resolving conflicts between themselves for years, coming upon an issue that is not easily resolved can be a real shock. Oftentimes the degree of difficulty is primarily determined by the importance of outcome. So, the more important the outcome to you, the more careful you have to be to avoid becoming competitive.

If one person has a strong interest in the outcome and the other person does not, the conflict usually will be resolved in the direction of the stronger interest. The person with little vested interest is unlikely to offer much resistance to the other person even if a competitive attitude is present.

Let us now consider how you can proceed to keep competition from occurring or how you can deal with it in a way that results in a more cooperative and objective approach. Above all, you need to be aware of competitive statements. If you are on your toes, you can soon draw perceptive conclusions about another person's attitude toward a subject. When you ask whether the person is a Reds fan, and he or she replies, "Baseball is a ridiculous game befitting the intelligence of chil-

dren," you will have no problem drawing a conclusion about that person's attitude about baseball. Sometimes, however, we are wrong in our judgments. Since a wrong judgment might well initiate a conflict or heighten one that has begun, we should paraphrase the person's ideas or check out our perception of what the person is feeling. So, if in response to your comment about some candidate for public office, a person were to say, "Those Democrats are all alike," you might say, "Are you saying that you believe all Democrats are incompetent?" Such a paraphrase will not resolve a conflict, but it might clarify the situation if a conflict does exist and it might help to determine the exact attitude of the other person.

If a person approaches the potential conflict competitively, how do you go about bringing the person into a cooperative state so the conflict can be considered rationally? First, do not get into the elements of the issue at hand until you demonstrate to the other person that you wish to resolve the conflict in a mutually satisfactory way; and, second, avoid any statements that would escalate the potential conflict or result in defensive behavior.

Now, let us put these two suggestions into practice. In an apparent conflict over whether your roommate has the obligation to carry out the trash, you would not want to say, "Well, I'm approaching this problem in the spirit of inquiry, so why don't you get off that competitive kick you are on?" Such a statement will only result in the other saying, "What do you mean, 'competitive kick'?" and now you have a new conflict. Remember, your goal is to get the conflict on a cooperative level, without adding to any ego involvement and without compounding the issue. Some of the following wordings may be useful in demonstrating your resolve to be cooperative and in preventing the conflict from escalating:

*"I know you feel very strongly about what you want to do. Before we consider whether your plan is the answer, perhaps we could consider what we want to accomplish."*

*"I know I sometimes get a little hotheaded in conflict situations, and I'm going to try to look at this problem as objectively as I can, but I may need your help."*

*"You have good reasons for your belief, and I believe I have too. Perhaps if we share our reasons and then consider the consequences of each of our ideas, we can make a mutually satisfactory decision."*

These examples illustrate ways of putting the conflict in an objective cooperative context.

Remember, your language, both verbal and nonverbal, indicates your feelings not only about the issue, but also about the person with whom you are in conflict. If you approach a person with respect, openly, you should at least get a hearing, but if you demean a person's idea or the person himself by your words or actions, you are likely to create defensiveness, cause hard feelings, and perhaps destroy the entire relationship.

## Positive versus Negative Communication

Some communication modes are most associated with cooperative attitude, some with a competitive one; some modes are fundamental to good interpersonal communication and some are destructive. The positive modes are discussion and persuasion; the negative modes are withdrawal, surrender, and aggression or combat. Because the negative modes are likely when people react to conflict rather than analyzing it, we will consider the negative modes first.

### Withdrawal

A common negative mode of dealing with conflict is withdrawal, removing oneself physically or psychologically from the situation. Although withdrawal from engaging in inconsequential disputes and withdrawal from confrontations with individuals you communicate with infrequently may at times avoid unnecessary strife, withdrawal as one's primary mode of dealing with interpersonal conflict is harmful. Sometimes when a person senses conflict he will try physical withdrawal:

*Tom says to Doris, "Get your coat and let's get going—we'll be late for the movie." Doris replies, "Oh, I thought it might be nice to sit home, make popcorn, and watch a little TV." When Tom then says, "We already talked about going to the movie," Doris runs to the bedroom and slams the door. Doris offers an alternative to the movie. When Tom emphasizes the conflict, Doris withdraws physically.*

Withdrawal behavior does not alter the conflict—it is still there. Doris chooses not to deal with it by removing herself from the scene. If Tom follows Doris to the bedroom, the conflict will be resumed there; if not, the conflict will later resurface—probably in an intensified manner and very likely on the ego level.

Withdrawal need not be physical; it can also be psychological. Say, for example, that Marv begins to discuss with Otto a topic about

*Withdrawal is a common negative mode of dealing with conflict.*

which their values conflict. One way Otto might cope with this situation is to "not hear" what Marv is saying. Otto can think about the movie he saw last night or the date he is having this evening. He can do any sort of daydreaming. Thus, by not hearing Marv, Otto can escape the conflict, and when Marv finishes his statements, Otto might change the subject to something less threatening.

Psychological withdrawal may be less painful than coming to grips with the issue being considered, but it is no answer to conflict.

## Surrender

Another negative mode of communication is surrender. When the surrenderer senses conflict, he or she might choose to give in immediately to avoid the conflict. The prevailing attitude of the surrenderer is that actions, goals, and choices are never worth arguing about. This avoidance or occasionally "martyr" reaction can be seen in the following example:

*When Jeff says, "I think we ought to take the money and put it in savings bonds," Marion replies, "I was really hoping we could get the colored TV we've been talking about." Then when Jeff says, "OK, we'll talk about it—we have mentioned a TV, but with the economy the way . . ." Marion, seeing that conflict is developing, then says, "Oh, no need to discuss it—go ahead and put the money into bonds."*

Banking the money may not be meeting Marion's needs, but rather than express those needs or even consider the comparative advantages of the proposed courses of action, Marion immediately gives in. Sometimes people who feel persecuted play the reaction into a martyr role with statements that seem to say "Do it your way—it's just not worth arguing about. I can bear the suffering." Even though the other person gets his way, surrender can be infuriating. It can often result in making the first person angry because the other person will not disclose what he or she is really thinking.

## Aggression

The most common escalating reaction to conflict is to become aggressive. Through aggression a person attempts to force another to accept his ideas. When conflict or the suggestion of conflict is perceived, one person strikes out at the other. Aggression is sometimes physical:

*Bart says to his son, "It's time for you to go to bed, David." When David replies, "I don't want to go to bed now," Bart says, "Get to bed before I beat the living daylights out of you." At the hint of conflict with his six-year-old, Bart loses his patience and threatens to strike out aggressively at him.*

Aggression need not be physical. It can also be verbal. Consider the following exchange:

*Quinn says, "The game is going to start soon, let's get dressed." Dolly replies, "I don't know if I feel up to going to a game today." Quinn then says, "Right. Any time we talk about going to a game, you're not up to it. Well, maybe I can find someone who is."*

A verbal aggression is every bit as threatening as physical aggression.

Aggression is characterized by threat of or actual punishment should the aggressor not win the conflict.

*Thought is short-circuited, and the person lashes out.*

Aggression is an emotional reaction to the conflict. Thought is short-circuited, and the person lashes out physically or verbally.

With each of the above reactions either the conflict is escalated or it is obscured. In none is it resolved or discussed. With these negative reactions, simple conflict becomes ego conflict and may grow into a power struggle. The greater the degree of escalation or withdrawal, the more complicated the conflict and the more difficult resolution of that conflict becomes. Now let us examine the two most positive communication modes of dealing with conflict.

### Discussion

**Discussion is verbal weighing and considering of the pros and cons of the issues in conflict.** It depends upon mutual desire of the participants to talk through the various aspects of the conflict. It is a product of cooperative rather than a competitive attitude toward the conflict. It requires an objectivity in the presentation of the issues, an openness in stating feelings and beliefs, and an openness to acceptance of the solution that proves to be most logical and in the best interests of the needs of both parties. Discussion works best in a climate of mutual respect where neither party is so ego-involved that objectivity is impossible.

The form of conflict discussion is **an orga-nized procedure for solving problems** that includes: defining the problem, analyzing the problem, suggesting possible solutions, selecting the solution that best fits the analysis, and working to implement that decision. In everyday give-and-take practice of the discussion method, all five steps are not always considered completely nor are they necessarily considered in the exact order. Its use requires that when two people perceive a conflict emerging they step back from that conflict and proceed systematically in its resolution. Sound ideal? or impracticable? Well, it is difficult. But when two people have agreed to commit themselves to *trying,* beneficial results can be achieved.

Consider the discussion and its analysis, shown on pages 162-163. Although this is not a real example, it illustrates the discussion method. Both persons have set aside personal needs. Each considers the other's opinion. They weigh and consider together. Is the conflict over? Perhaps not; they have not bought the car yet, but they seem to be on the right track of making a cooperative decision. Ego involvement seems to have given way to cooperative analysis. In Chapter 10 we will make a more detailed analysis of the problem-solving method.

What happens if both parties try, but still discussion breaks down? When two people cannot arrive at the same decision through objective weighing and analyzing, then one person may seek to influence the other through persuasion.

## Persuasion

As a means of learning to cope with conflict, you will want to learn to use the various means of persuasion. Although we will make a more detailed analysis of persuasion in the next chapter, we want at least to familiarize you with those means now.

Persuasion is the attempt to change either the attitude or the behavior of another person. Suppose that at the point of their discussion where Doris says, "Don't we need room?" Jack would reply, "Enough to get us into the car together, but I don't see why we need more than that." If he made such a statement, they would be approaching a new conflict position. Doris might then have said, "Jack, remember the other day when you were cussing out our present car because it doesn't have much back-seat room? We carry a lot of stuff. I do food shopping, you're always carrying equipment for the men at the lodge, and there are a lot of times we invite another couple to go somewhere with us." With statements like these she would be making persuasive attempts to influence Jack.

Persuasion takes a variety of forms and relies primarily on reasoning, development of an emotional climate (motivation), and credibility of the persuader. *Reasoning* involves the presentation of logical arguments in support of the point of view. In our example, Doris offered reasons why Jack would profit from a roomier car. If you voted for Jones because he has the best qualifications and a good public office record, your action is a result of reasoning. *Development of an emotional climate* involves the presentation of the information in language that excites or stimulates the emotions of the listener. When, in our example, Doris spoke of "carrying equipment for the men in the lodge," the language had an emotional thrust—it played upon Jack's needs as a responsible member of his group. If you voted for Jones because his position on crime in the streets meshed with your anxieties about personal safety, you were persuaded to vote as you did by motivational factors that played upon your emotions. *Credibility* is a personal means of persuasion that grows from your belief that the sender of the message is knowledgeable on that subject, likable, and trustworthy. If you voted for Jones because your best friend urged you to do so, you have been persuaded by your personal belief in your friend—by your friend's credibility.

When two people in conflict take adversary positions—that is, each attempts to prove his point to the other—debate occurs. Debate is a type of dual persuasion in which competition is more common than cooperation. Many so-called discussions that people have are really informal debates, wherein neither party accepts the merits of the other's position, but instead attempts to demonstrate the strength of his or her own position. As a result, debates rarely do much to solve the conflict between participants. Still, people sometimes find it useful to debate anyway—

## Discussion and Analysis

**Doris:** *From what you say, we really need to get a new car.*

**Jack:** *Yeah, the time has come.*

**Doris:** *Well, we've talked about getting a station wagon—let's go ahead and do it.*

**Jack:** *What do you mean a station wagon—you know I've been looking forward to a sports car.*

**Doris:** *Oh-oh—I can see we're looking at this differently. Before one of us goes off the deep end, let's see if we can't talk this out. We agree we're ready to get a new car, right?*

**Jack:** *Yes.*

**Doris:** *OK—If there's a hassle it's over what kind. Look, let's both of us say what we think we need in this new car.*

**Jack:** *All right—we need a car that gets good gas mileage.*

**Doris:** *I'll buy that, but maybe we'd better be more specific. What is good gas mileage?*

**Jack:** *At least 30 miles per gallon.*

**Doris:** *I think we need good gas mileage, but that's really limiting choices, isn't it? How about at least 20 in the city?*

**Jack:** *OK. And it's got to look nice—be a little jazzy.*

**Doris:** *That's good, and it has to be roomy enough so that we can get in luggage on trips and have room for Judy.*

**Jack:** *I don't know—*

**Doris:** *Don't we need room?*

The family car has gone haywire. Both Doris and Jack are in agreement on that, but we can see that making the decision is going to result in conflict. At this particular point either we'll see some negative mode (withdrawal, surrender, aggression) in action, or we'll see something said to put the conflict in a problem-solving climate.

Doris takes the first step to try to put the conflict in a problem-solving framework.

Jack gives verbal agreement. Let's see if he is really cooperative, or whether he is saying he is cooperating as a strategy.

Jack and Doris seem to be cooperating.

Here they are stating criteria that are important in making a rational choice.

**Jack:**   *I guess so —I'd like to think we didn't, but I get your point. I'd like air conditioning.*

**Doris:**   *Definitely —and a nice exterior.*

**Jack:**   *That's what I meant when I said 'look nice.' How high can we go?*

**Doris:**   *You're better with figures than I am —what do you think?*

Notice how Doris seeks help from Jack in determining various limits.

**Jack:**   *Let's say we get around $1,500 in trade. I think that's possible. Maybe $3,000 more?*

**Doris:**   *So about $4,500 top?*

**Jack:**   *Give or take a bit.*

**Doris:**   *OK, let's consider some of the kinds of cars. Can we get a sports car with room?*

Now they begin testing specific types of cars against the criteria they have agreed upon.

**Jack:**   *Not a real sports car —but we can get a sporty car. Can we get a station wagon that gets 20 miles per gallon in the city?*

**Doris:**   *A compact would, wouldn't it?*

**Jack:**   *Maybe, but would it really have the kind of room you're talking about in the back seat?*

**Doris:**   *Maybe we need a medium sized car that looks kind of sporty.*

Both seem to agree that their original choices will not fill the bill. Compromise seems likely.

**Jack:**   *So we can discount a station wagon?*

**Doris:**   *And a sports car?*

**Jack:**   *OK.*

it gives each person a chance to be heard even if there is not much impact on the other.

Debate is an important communication form, but it does not work too well in interpersonal communication. Debate belongs in the legislative assembly and the law court where as a result of the debate other legislators, a judge, or a jury will make decisions on particular issues.

## Communication Session

*Reflection*
1. **Indicate which of the above means, if any, is typical of your communication in a conflict setting.**

2. **Analyze a conflict that you were involved in recently.**

   a. **What was the attitude of the participants: cooperative or competitive?**

   b. **How important was the outcome to each participant?**

   c. **How complicated was the conflict?**

   d. **What communication modes were used in dealing with the conflict?**

*Actualization*
Break into groups of six. One person in each group should be named as an observer. Your instructor will give each of the five participants an envelope. In this envelope are pieces of a puzzle. The task of the group is for each person to construct a square. You may not be able to do this with the pieces in your envelope, so some sharing may have to take place. However, the following rules must be strictly obeyed:

1. **Absolutely no talking.**

2. **You may not take a puzzle piece from someone else.**

3. **You may not indicate in any way that you would like a puzzle piece that anyone else has.**

4. **You may give away puzzle pieces to anyone but you may not indicate where the piece might fit.**

5. **Your observer will enforce these rules. Observers will also get instructions from the instructor.**

*Discussion*
**What does this exercise demonstrate?**

_____

## Prearrangement of Procedures in a Conflict Situation

Much of the difficulty of conflict resolution in ongoing relationships arises because the parties do not have any procedure in mind. Just as people who have made plans for what they will do in case of a fire, a flood, or a tornado often weather the particular disaster in much better shape than those who have not, so parties to an ongoing relationship weather conflict better if they have a prearranged plan for conflict resolution.

At least one of the two parties will know when a conflict situation is about to occur. It is for him or her to remind the other of following the prearranged procedure. For instance, if two people have agreed to write out advantages and disadvantages of the conflicting actions or plans or ideas before the conflict heats up, then when a conflict does occur the prearranged procedure will take precedence over any actions. Sometimes the time involved in going through the prearranged steps is enough to get people past that explosive moment when each party is likely to say or do something he or she would like to take back later, but never can.

Many of the guidelines offered in this section can be put together into a package that will serve as a conflict resolution procedure. Following a plan encourages rational analysis to take precedence over emotional outburst or evaluative behavior. The plan you draw up might well contain provision for negotiation and if necessary, arbitration.

### Cooperation through Negotiation

Although we tend to see conflict in a win-lose context, sometimes we can find a way of resolving the conflict so that neither party wins all or loses all. This may be brought about by negotiation—by definition, **negotiation is the art of making trade-offs.**

Conflict often results when two actions are proposed and in fact only one can be accomplished. You cannot go to a movie and to a concert at the same time; you cannot eat at a Chinese and at an Italian restaurant at the same time; or, if you can only afford one house payment, you can't *buy* a house and *rent* a house at the same time. Even after you have considered every aspect of the conflict rationally, each person may still truly believe that his way is the best; then perhaps you should negotiate or "horse trade."

With some simple problems, negotiation is easily accomplished. For instance, "I'll tell you what, Joan, I'll go to the concert with you tonight if you'll go to the movie I've wanted to see with me this weekend" will probably achieve the desired results. Since in this case there need not be an either/or approach, both activities can be accomplished at different times.

For negotiation to work, the activities, goals, ideas, or whatever must be of fairly equal importance. For instance "Joe, if you'll let me make the decision on where to eat tonight, I'll go along with you on whatever movie you want to see" has a good chance of working. On the other hand, "Alice, if you

will let me decide on the kind of car to buy, I'll let you decide on where to eat" does not stand a chance. Obviously selecting a car is a far more important decision than picking a restaurant, a movie, or any other one-night activity. A person trying such a negotiation is not acting in good faith. Finding situations that are indeed parallel may be difficult, but when they can be found, they make an excellent base for negotiation.

If an issue truly is not negotiable, such as conflict about whether to rent a house or buy one, and you and the other person just cannot work out the decision cooperatively, you are not necessarily defeated.

### When Negotiation Fails, Seek Arbitration

**Arbitration involves the presence of an impartial person who, after hear both sides, will weigh and evaluate the alternatives and make a decision for you.** Labor unions and management sometimes go to arbitration. It may work for you.

For interpersonal conflicts, arbitration will work if you can agree on an arbitrator who in turn will agree to make the decision for you. It is important that the arbitrator be a person whose judgment you both trust. The arbitrator also should in some way be competent to make a decision on the issue. Your lawyer may act as arbitrator for you over whether to sue or not to sue about a car accident. Your financial counselor may arbitrate a conflict over whether to invest in a high-risk stock or a high-dividend stock.

Too often we seek to pull in a close friend or a relative to arbitrate. Not only does this person often not have the expertise needed for the particular issue, but more important, the friend or relative is not an independent, impartial agent. He or she may well be close to both parties, or may have a vested interest in the outcome. Calling on such a person puts him or her in a no-win situation (somebody may well be upset by his or her decision) or at best make the person feel very uncomfortable in the role.

If you do agree to arbitration, the verbal contract between you and the other person should include a clause saying that whatever decision is made, you will both willingly and happily comply. Remember you will have gone to a third person because the two of you were unable to come to a conclusion; if you are unwilling to abide by the decision, whichever way it goes, then you should not agree to arbitration in the first place.

In some circumstances the impartial third person will act as a facilitator rather than as an arbitrator. The difference is that instead of the person making the decision for you, the person will *help* the two of you (or you alone in the case of an intrapersonal decision) use the problem-solving method to make your own decision. Psychologists, psychiatrists, marriage counselors, and other clinicians are skilled in facilitating decision making. A good facilitator not only sees to it that you are following the steps of problem solving, but also helps you weigh and evaluate the variables. Even with a good plan there are at least three additional important considerations.

1. *Don't be intractable.* Interpersonal communication is not the place for "non-negotiable" demands. If you go into a situation with a defensive attitude or a "this is the way we're going to do it or else" posture, you are more than likely going to heighten the conflict. If, after calm appraisal, it appears that your way is not the best or at least not the only good way, you should try to avoid becoming so ego-involved that any modification of position would cause you to "lose face." Of course, willingness to back off from a position is easier said than done. However, by altering your stance on any issue, you pave the way for the other person to make some concessions then or later. If you are in a long-term relationship, it is better to think in terms of the betterment of the relationship than in the "winning" of a particular issue.

2. *"Win" and "lose" graciously.* This guideline is a logical follow-up to not being intractable. Regardless of any advice we can give, there will be times that you feel very strongly about your position, and having to abandon it or even to modify it will be a tremendous blow to you. Yet, the very worst thing you can do is to punish the other person for "making" you give in. For instance, if your attitude (if not your actual behavior) goes like this: "OK, Laura, I'll go to your ol' party, but, you'll see, I'll be just miserable the whole evening," you

are not going to have much fun—and neither will Laura. Moreover, Laura probably will resent your attitude. When a decision is made through objective discussion, both parties should feel an obligation to support the decision. Although our own defenses will not let us concede that the other person's plan is the better one for these circumstances, the continuation of the "war" during the implementation stages will only bring on new conflicts or heighten or regenerate older ones.

3. *Discuss conflict-resolution failures.* The ideal is to resolve every conflict as it comes up. ("Never let the sun go down on your anger.") However, there will be times when no matter how hard both persons try, they will not be able to resolve the conflict. If the person is a friend or a relative, and intimate—so that the relationship is especially important to you— after the heat of the conflict dies down, you should initiate steps to analyze the failure of the conflict resolution. You should consider such questions as "Where did things go wrong?" "Did one or more become competitive? or defensive?" "Did we fail to implement the problem-solving method adequately?" "Were the vested interests in the outcome too great?" By seeing why conflict resolution failed, you put yourself in a better position to cope more successfully with the next conflict.

Of course, conflicts will arise again and again. Yet, we should have no need to fear conflict. The presence of conflict as such does not mar any relationship; it is the way conflicts are dealt with that is the true measure of a relationship. Some careful analysis after a particular conflict may well save you additional strife in the future.

## Communication Session

*Reflection*

**What behaviors do you indulge in during conflict that make resolution difficult? What suggestions from this chapter will help you work on them?**

*Actualization*

**Working with a person with whom you have a close relationship, design a plan for dealing with conflict before it arises.**

## Payoffs

If you have fought your way through the content of this chapter, you should now be able to

1. Define conflict and understand the four most common types.

2. Discuss why ego conflict is so difficult to resolve.

3. Contrast a cooperative attitude with a competitive attitude.

4. Identify and understand the inappropriateness of withdrawal, surrender, and aggression.

5. Discuss the discussion method.

6. Apply the problem-solving method to a conflict situation.

7. Explain the role of persuasion in conflict resolution.

8. Explain how you might bring someone who views conflict competitively into a cooperative state.

9. Explain how negotiation can resolve conflict.

10. Discuss the role of arbitration in conflict resolution.

11. Devise a plan for dealing with conflicts in your relationship with a close friend.

## Selected Readings

**George R. Bach** and **Peter Wyden.** *The Intimate Enemy.* New York: Avon Books, 1970. A very readable and quite useful discussion of conflict in marriage.

**Fred E. Jandt.** *Conflict Resolution through Communication.* New York: Harper & Row, 1973. Of particular value are the two articles on conflict theory and the 18-page bibliography.

**Journal of Conflict Resolution.** Nearly every issue of the journal has at least one article related to interpersonal conflict.

**Gerald R. Miller** and **Herbert W. Simons.** *Perspectives on Communication in Social Conflict.* Englewood Cliffs, New Jersey: Prentice-Hall, 1974. Several of the eight articles are relevant to interpersonal conflict. This book also provides an excellent bibliography.

**Chapter Nine:
Interpersonal Influence:
Power and Persuasion**

Burning brightly within each of us is the need to believe that we matter, that we have some control over our own destiny and some influence on our environment and on the people around us. In this chapter, we will explore the sources of influence and the means of exerting influence *ethically*—we will explore power and persuasion.

In this unit we have sought to explore problem areas. Why is this chapter on power and persuasion in a unit with barriers and conflict? Because power and persuasion are often improperly applied and as such further inflame a conflict or become a barrier. Whether any person should attempt to influence others seems to be a moot point—people do attempt influence. So, our goal is not to challenge the right to influence but to offer an analysis that will enable you to influence others within the bounds of interpersonal ethics.

## Power

If a person is powerless, it means that he or she is unable to bring about change. Nothing is more frustrating than to be in a position of knowing that change must occur but without the power to bring it about. What is this "power" that is so necessary in the execution of change within interpersonal settings and relationships? Power is most often defined as

a *potential;* it is the potential for changing attitudes, beliefs, and behaviors of others. The presence of power does not insure change— but the absence of power makes it nearly impossible for a person to exert any influence.

Everyone has some power at some times and under some circumstances. To determine whether or not you have power and under what circumstances, we want to examine the sources of social power. Several social psychologists have offered analyses of social power. Our analysis is based upon that of Raven and French.[1] They discuss five categories: coercive power, reward power, legitimate power, expert power, and referent power. Let us examine each. In our examina-

[1]John R. P. French, Jr., and Bertram Raven, "The Bases of Social Power," reprinted *in* Dorwin Cartwright and Alvin Zander (Eds.), *Group Dynamics,* 3rd ed. (New York: Harper & Row, 1968), pp. 259–270.

*Coercive power can be the threat of force.*

tion, we will consider definition, use of the power, and effectiveness as a potential for exerting influence.

### Coercive Power

Coercive power derives from the potential to punish. Coercive power can be either physical or psychological; it can be actual or threatened force. The elements of coercion are size, strength, and possession of weapons. If we remember the definition of power as the *potential* for change, we can see that coercive power can be present without a person ever attempting to exercise it. The old vaudeville routine, with the question "Where does a gorilla sit when he comes into a room?" and the answer, "Anywhere he wants to," illustrates the effect of this potential.

How do people use their coercive power? Most often coercive power is used as a threat. You may attempt to coerce your little brother into acting in a specified way by threatening to hit him if he does not. A robber attempts to coerce his victim to hand over money by threatening to harm with a gun, a knife, or a club. A foreman may attempt to coerce an employee by threatening an undesirable assignment or even involuntary termination. Each of these represents the exercising of coercion by threatened punishment. Coercion works when the person being coerced perceives the demanded action as less harmful to him than the threatened punishment; coer-

cion fails as a means of exerting influence if the person perceives the demanded action as more painful than the threatened punishment. Jack Benny, who built his comic image on miserliness, evoked one of the longest sustaining laughs in entertainment history when he responded to the threat "Your money or your life" with a long pause, then "Just a minute, I'm thinking." If your little brother decides that getting hit is less painful to him than taking a bath, he just may take the punishment, if he cannot run faster than you can.

How effective is coercion as a means of exerting influence in an interpersonal setting? If by "effective" we mean getting the desired result, coercion can be very effective. If, however, we mean getting the desired result in a way that is likely to improve the interpersonal relationship, coercion is likely to be quite ineffective. It is human nature, for those of us who are not masochists, to resent the threat of punishment. Some individuals become so resentful at the threat of even mild punishment that they will subject themselves to brutal hardships rather than submit to the implied threat of force. Others who comply because of their distaste for the threatened punishment are likely to manifest their resentment in revenge behavior; a person may look for any way possible to strike back. Coercion often has overtones of brute force—and most of us believe that if a person's only way of exerting influence is through force, then he is unworthy of our compliance in change in belief, attitude, or action.

### Reward Power

Reward power derives from the potential that one person can bestow "rewards" upon another. The elements of reward power are the bestowing of monetary, physical, or psychological benefits to another person.

How do people use their reward power? Most often reward power is used as a motivator for change in attitude, belief, or action. You may offer to reward your little brother if he will take a bath. Your instructor can reward you for good work in this course by a good grade. Your girl friend or boy friend may attempt to motivate you to do something by promising you a special gift for your birthday, Christmas, or Valentine's Day.

Reward power works as a means of exerting influence if the person sees the reward as large enough or important enough to compensate for the pain of the action called for and if he or she believes the one who promises has the power to give that reward. Let us illustrate both parts of this statement. If you offer to reward your little brother with an ice cream bar for taking a bath, he may well decide that the treat is too small a reward for enduring the pain of such an extensive cleanup. If you offered him all the ice cream bars he could eat, he may well doubt your financial resources to do what you say you will do. Your instructor offers to reward good work with an A grade in the course. If you believe that the time and effort involved is more than you care to expend, the A grade might not arouse enough motivation in you; or, if you regard grades as unimportant, you are unlikely to make the effort to do the work.

How effective is reward as a means of exerting influence in the interpersonal setting? In comparison with coercion, reward is much a superior motivator. Most of us are more likely to be motivated to work by promise of reward than by threat of punishment. In this context, the reward is seen as a positive element. Ballplayers work hard to have a good season in hopes of a reward of higher pay; students do work hard in classes in hopes of a reward of high grades. Just remember that, to be effective, the reward must be large enough.

Under some circumstances, reward power is regarded negatively. If for some reason you do not believe a person has a legitimate motive for offering a reward or if the person is offering a reward for actions that are objectionable to you or if you do not respect the person offering the reward, you may reject the offer, reject the reward, or seek to bring down the person or agency misusing the reward power. Reward power is least effective when it is seen as bribery by one who chooses not to be bribed. Bribery by definition is a reward offered for questionable motives to do questionable deeds. For most of us, if we believe the offer to reward is made as bribery, we are likely to resent it.

### Legitimate Power

Legitimate power derives from the potential for influence gained through the process of election, selection, or position. The ra-

Chapter Nine:
Interpersonal
Influence:
Power and
Persuasion

175

tionale for bestowing legitimate power is the belief that a person in certain positions has the responsibility of attempting to exert influence. The President, senators, and congressmen gain legitimate power through the ballot; your teachers, cabinet members, and committee chairmen gain legitimate power through appointment; and in families the father and mother, the oldest child, or the oldest male child may have legitimate power through tradition or cultural norms.

If a person is perceived to hold power legitimately, we are likely to cooperate with attempts to exercise that power. It is OK for the chairman of a meeting to ask you to quit talking in order to aid the group effort; it may not be OK for one of the other members to ask you. It is OK for the coach of the team to pressure a player to change his style of play; it may not be OK for another player to do so. It may be OK for the oldest child to give the other children chore assignments; it may not be OK for the second oldest to do so.

The extent to which a person will be influenced by the exercise of legitimate power is likely to depend upon factors other than the legitimate power itself. For instance, if the leader is perceived as "powerless" to enforce demands, a member of the rank-and-file may ignore the call to act. In this instance, the rank-and-file member may doubt reward or coercive power potential accompanying the leader's legitimate power. Or a citizen may not do what the President or a senator or a congressman asks because the citizen has no respect for these persons in power.

Probably the most important benefit accruing to one who has legitimate power is the right to exercise other means of influence that are not perceived as OK when exercised by a person who does not hold legitimate power. You are likely to "take" more from your instructor because he or she has the legitimate power to conduct procedures in your particular class. As a result of this legitimate right, then, you give to your instructor more leeway in, for example, critical behavioral response to you and others than you would permit to a person without the legitimate right.

### Expert Power

Expert power derives from the potential to influence based upon superior knowledge in a certain field. Expert power is present when you grant that another person holds information in a particular field that you perceive yourself needing. Your instructor has the potential for expert power in your class because he or she has knowledge and expertise that you need to have; a coach has potential for expert power because he or she has knowledge and expertise that players seek. You, likewise, have the potential for expert power in several areas such as cooking, playing tennis, or repairing automobiles.

How do people use expert power? They attempt to influence others through the promise of revealing information. A coach influences his players when he reveals information about a sport that the players perceive as useful in their efforts to master that sport. A professor influences his students by revealing information about a subject that the students perceive as useful in their education. Expert power fails to influence when a person does not believe that the information is useful to him, when he does not believe that the alleged expert does in fact have the relevant information, when he does not believe that the expert is able to disseminate that information in a usable manner, or when he believes that he has gained parity of information with the expert. An important element of expert power is that its potential exists only within the limited area of expertise. The tennis coach may hold expert power over his players on the subject of tennis, but not on the subject of calculus.

How effective is expert power? It seems to be quite effective within its limited scope. However, because information can be exchanged, once a person believes that he or she has received all the information there is to give, the expert loses the effect of his or her power. Moreover, expert power must be real to be effective. For example, if one of your friends works as an auto mechanic in a dealer's garage, he or she has the potential to influence your choice of sparkplugs. If on the basis of the mechanic's opinion that XYZ sparkplugs are superior, you purchase them for your car only to discover two months later that they have burned out, you are not likely to accept your mechanic friend's advice again. He or she has lost his or her expert power, as far as you are concerned.

Sometimes people use their expert power as a weapon. A person may purposely withhold information in order to maintain control over others. If a person believes that another is manipulating him with use of expert power that may be grounds for loss of that power.

## Referent Power

Referent power derives from the potential to influence others simply because they identify with the one who influences them. Many persons have power simply because of qualities that cause others to love and trust them. "Charisma" is one word used to label this power. Whatever you wish to call it, people do acknowledge and yield to power residing in certain persons for no apparent reason beyond belief in the individual.

How effective is referent power? Not only does referent power stand on its own as a potential for influence, but also referent power underlies the value of the other bases of power we have considered. Expert power, legitimate power, reward power, even coercive power have greater potential for influence if the powerful person is also perceived as having referent power; moreover, if one doubts the referent power he is less likely to be influenced by any of the other types of power.

Because of the great importance of the elements of referent power we will consider them in considerable detail later in this chapter in the discussion of personal credibility.

Chapter Nine:
Interpersonal
Influence:
Power and
Persuasion

**177**

## Communication Session

*Reflection*

1. Consider at least three people that you hold power over some or most of the time. What is the principal source of that power? What power or combinations of power are you likely to use? Under what circumstances do you use or resort to coercion or bribery?

2. Consider at least three people who hold power over you. How do they exercise that power?

*Actualization*

1. For each of the statements below decide whether it is an attempt to influence based on reward power (R), coercive power (C), legitimate power (L), referent power (Rf), or expert power (E).

____1. You will wear your hair the way I tell you to wear your hair because I'm your mother.

____2. After studying the effects of radiation for eight years I have concluded that . . .

____3. As long as you do what I say, no one will get hurt.

____4. Sara, I'd be so proud of you if you made the Dean's list.

____5. If you'll drop my books at the library, I'll clean the room.

____6. Trust me—I can do it.

2. Work in groups of six. Your instructor will give you goal cards. One member of each group will pick a goal. He or she must then try to influence another member of the group toward that goal. The other group members will observe from what power bases the people work.

*Discussion*

What power bases do you most resent? Why?

**Answers:** 1. L; 2. E; 3. C; 4. R; 5. R; 6. Rf.

## Persuasion

When you do in fact hold power over another person there are several ways in which you can act to exert influence. Influence is the act of changing attitude, belief, value, or behavior. Whereas power is the *potential* for inducing change, influence is the *act* of inducing change. In other words, influence is the actualization of power. In our discussion of the bases of social power, we considered the direct use of the various bases of power to influence. Assuming that Bill has power with regard to Jack, Bill could influence Jack to work harder on his bowling. If the nature of Bill's power was physical he might force Jack to practice. If he had the capacity for reward, Bill might offer Jack a monetary reward for bowling a 200 game in tomorrow's tournament. However, in addition to being able to directly actualize power, through coercion and reward, Bill can persuade. Persuasion is the conscious act of influencing—it is the conscious verbal attempt to change attitude or behavior *without an overt display of power.* Persuasion is more easily achieved if a person has some power over another—but attempts to persuade are not characterized by blatant power plays.

We think persuasion is an especially appropriate means of interpersonal influence. It is appropriate because it allows freedom of choice. The persuader implies no extraneous inducements nor does he or she control the other person's actions. Cartwright and Zander point out that because of the belief in the importance of freedom of choice in a democratic society, persuasion is a very positive means of exerting influence.[2] We see a knowledge of means of persuasion as vital in maintaining what Keller and Brown described as the interpersonal ethic, requiring that you meet the need to influence by allowing others freedom of choice.[3]

Whereas an individual's power exists irrespective of his or her attempt to use it or exploit it, persuasion is a conscious, usually verbal attempt of one individual to affect the

attitudes or behaviors of others. Like power, persuasion also can be discussed in terms of categories. These categories or "means of persuasion" have been developed as a result of more than two thousand years of study of the persuasive process. The persuasive process is a product of reasoning, motivation through emotional appeal, and credibility. These means may be utilized individually or in concert to achieve the desired result.

### Logical Reasoning

Most of you want some justification for changing your attitudes or modifying your behavior. You want to know why you should

---

[2]Cartwright and Zander, *Group Dynamics*, p. 221.

[3]Paul W. Keller and Charles T. Brown, "An Interpersonal Ethic for Communication," *Journal of Communication*, Vol. 18 (1968), p. 79.

*Persuasion allows freedom of choice.*

Chapter Nine:
Interpersonal
Influence:
Power and
Persuasion

179

respond a particular way. One means of persuasion is providing the logical reasons for the desired attitude or behavior. The persuader need not give complete proof of the proposition—in fact, complete proof may be impossible to give. More likely the persuader need only provide enough substantiation of justification to satisfy the receiver's need. Statements that provide substantiation or justification are called *reasons*. If your friend wants you to go to a particular movie with him, he may be able to persuade you by giving you the reasons that (1) it has an exciting plot, (2) it has several excellent actors and actresses playing major roles, and (3) it has been nominated for an Academy award. These three reasons do not necessarily *prove* the worth of the movie, but they do nevertheless supply necessary substantiation. If the dinner club is unsure where they want to go for this month's gourmet meal, you may be able to persuade them by offering the reasons for considering the Chateau Bleu. If from your experience and your reading you have discovered that (1) the chef has won numerous awards for gourmet cooking, (2) the atmosphere is elegant, and (3) the prices are comparable with several other less renowned restaurants in town, these reasons alone may be enough to persuade.

Of course, reasons will need to be supported with evidence. It is unlikely that bare statement of reasons alone will be persuasive, but when you couple the statement of reasons with examples, documented facts, opinions of experts, the reasons take on added power.

We could perhaps conclude our discussion of logical reasoning right here with a summary statement that ethical interpersonal influence is achieved by the source presenting reasons and support for the proposition he or she advocates. Such an analysis falls short on one important ground—it does not provide a basis for either the source or the receiver to determine the strength or validity of the reasons presented. To make this determination, a person must have knowledge of some system of analysis that goes beyond intuitive judgment. Our goal in the next several pages is to offer you the rudiments of a system of analysis of logical argument. Knowledge of these rudiments will enable you to make reasonably accurate judgments of the soundness of reasoning. You may well wish to go more deeply into the subject. To that end, we have listed sources at the end of this chapter that you should find particularly valuable.

Reasoning is the process of drawing inferences. Thus, if you are given the facts that today's temperature is 38 degrees, the wind is blowing, and rain is falling, you may infer (reason or conclude) that "It's a miserable day." To explain the reasoning process we need to examine the three basic requirements of the process. These requirements are called the data, the conclusion, and the warrant.[4] Your understanding of these words will en-

---

[4]This analysis is based upon the ideas set forth by Stephen Toulmin, *The Uses of Argument* (Cambridge, England: Cambridge University Press, 1958).

able you to construct and analyze the simplest or the most complex forms of reasoning.

*Data* are the evidence, assumptions, or assertions that provide the basis for a conclusion—in our example, the data are the 38-degree temperature, the blowing wind, and the falling rain. The *conclusion* is the product of the reasoning, the inference—in our example, the conclusion is "It's a miserable day." The *warrant* is a statement denoting the substantive relationship between data and conclusion—it is the key that provides the essential test of the reasoning, and the only one of the essentials that is usually not included in the statement of the reasoning. Since in our example no warrant is provided, we must frame one. One way of stating a warrant for the example is "low temperature, wind, and rain are three major criteria or characteristics of a 'miserable day.'" Using (D) for data, stated or observed; (C) for conclusion; (W) for warrant; and an arrow to show the direction of the reasoning, our example could be laid out schematically as follows:

(D) Temperature 38°.   ⟶   (C) It's a miserable
Wind blowing.                 day.
Rain falling.

       (W) (Low temperature, wind,
       and rain are three major char-
       acteristics of a miserable day.)

The warrant is written in parentheses because it is implied rather than actually stated. The warrant, then, indicates how we drew the conclusion, the inference, from the data supplied.

So far you have seen how you can lay out a unit of reasoning. Now we need to show how you can test the essentials in order to judge the validity of the reasoning.

There are two tests applied to reasoning: test of data and test of warrant. For a logical conclusion to follow, the data must be sufficient in quantity and quality. If either no data or insufficient data are presented, you must supply more; if the data are inaccurate, biased, or from a questionable source, the conclusion will be suspect. If you are satisfied that "temperature 38 degrees," "wind blowing," and "rain falling" are accurate, you can examine the logic of the warrant. The warrant is tested by casting it as a "yes" or "no" question: "Is it true that low temperature, wind, and rain are the major characteristics of a miserable day?" If the answer is "yes," the reasoning is sound; if the answer is "no," the reasoning process is fallacious.

Schematic analysis of reasoning in the framework of data, conclusion, and warrant does not ensure the infallibility of the logic. However, if you take the time to write the process out in this manner and ask whether the warrant is supported by research, the chances of discovering illogical reasoning are increased considerably.

Although warrants could be phrased in many ways for any given unit of reasoning and literally hundreds of variations are possible in the kinds of reasoning, most methods

Chapter Nine:
Interpersonal
Influence:
Power and
Persuasion

181

of reasoning will fall into one of five categories: *generalization, causation, analogy, sign,* and *definition.* Since these categories do supply so many warrants, you should familiarize yourself with them. In the following discussion of five kinds of reasoning, the tests after the warrants indicate under what circumstances the warrants are reasonable.

Our goal here is not to explain, exemplify, and provide tests for every kind of reasoning link that can be established. What we want to consider here are the major forms that will work for you in the great majority of circumstances.

1. *Reasoning by generalization:* You are reasoning by generalization when your conclusion states that what is true in some instances is true in all instances. Generalization links are the basis for polls and predictions. Take, for example, the *data:* "Tom, Jack, and Bill studied and got A's" and the *conclusion* based on it: "Anyone who studies will get an A." The reasoning link *(warrant)* can be stated: "What is true in these representative instances will be true in all instances." To test this kind of argument you should ask: "Were enough instances cited? Were the instances typical? Were the instances representative?" (If the answer to any of these questions is "no," the reasoning is not sound.)

2. *Reasoning by causation:* You are reasoning by causation when your conclusion is based on a single circumstance or set of circumstances. Causation links are one of the most prevalent types of arguments you will discover. An example would be: *Data:* "We've had a very dry spring"; *conclusion:* "The wheat crop will be lower than usual." The reasoning link *(warrant)* can be stated: "The lack of sufficient rain *causes* a poor crop to result." To test this kind of argument you should ask: "Are the data (is the evidence) alone important enough to bring about the particular conclusion? If we eliminate the data, would we eliminate the effect?" (If not, the reasoning is unsound.) "Do some other data that accompany the cited data cause the effect?" (If so, the reasoning is not sound.) In real life, one set of circumstances rarely *causes* another. So be careful when using or hearing this type of argument.

3. *Reasoning by sign:* You are reasoning by sign when your conclusion is based upon the presence of observable data that usually or always accompanies other unobservable data. If, for example, Martha breaks out in hives, the presence of that data (breaking out) might lead Emily to the conclusion that Martha is having an allergy reaction. The reasoning link (the warrant) can be stated: "When one variable (in this case breaking out in hives) is usually or always associated with another variable (an allergy reaction), we can predict the existence of the other unobserved variable." Signs are often confused with causes, but signs are indications, not causes. Hives is a sign of an allergy reaction. Hives occurs when a person

is having such a reaction, but the hives does not *cause* the reaction. To test this kind of argument, you would ask: "Do the data cited always or usually indicate the conclusion drawn? Are sufficient signs present? Are contradictory signs in evidence?" (If so, the reasoning is not sound.)

4. *Reasoning by analogy:* You are reasoning by analogy when your conclusion is the result of a comparison with a similar set of circumstances. Although reasoning by analogy is very popular, it is regarded as the weakest form of reasoning. The analogy link is often stated: "What is true or will work in one set of circumstances is true or will work in another comparable set of circumstances." An example would be: *Data:* "A state lottery has proved very effective in New Jersey"; *conclusion:* "A state lottery will prove effective in Ohio." The reasoning link *(warrant)* can be stated, "If something works in New Jersey it will work in Ohio, because Ohio and New Jersey are so similar." To test this kind of argument you should ask: "Are the subjects really capable of being compared? Are the subjects being compared really similar in all important ways?" (If the answer to these questions is "no," the reasoning is not sound.) "Are any of the ways that the subjects are dissimilar important to the conclusion?" (If so, then the reasoning is not sound.)

5. *Reasoning by definition:* You are reasoning by definition when your conclusion is a definition or a descriptive generalization that follows from agreed-upon criteria. Again,

this is a very popular form of reasoning. An example would be: *Data:* "She takes charge; she uses good judgment; her goals are in the best interests of the group"; *conclusion:* "She is a good leader." The reasoning link *(warrant)* could be stated: "Taking charge, showing good judgment, and considering the best interests of the group are the characteristics most often associated with good leadership." To this kind of argument you should ask: "Are the characteristics mentioned the most important ones in determining the definition? As those characteristics best labeled with the stated term?" (If the answer to any of these is "no," the reasoning is not sound.) "Is an important aspect of the definition omitted in the statement of the characteristics?" (If so, then the reasoning is not sound.)

Chapter Nine:
Interpersonal
Influence:
Power and
Persuasion

**183**

## Communication Session

*Reflection*
Do you really listen to the logic of someone's argument? What do you consider good reasons?

*Actualization*
1. Below are some typical arguments you are likely to encounter. Indicate which ones are based on reasoning from (C) causation, (G) generalization, (A) analogy, (D) definition, or (S) sign.

___1. The chess club held a raffle, and they made a lot of money. I think we should too.

___2. Tom is aggressive, personable, and highly motivated—he ought to make a good salesman.

___3. Three of my students last year got A's on this test, five the year before, and three the year before that. There certainly will be some A's this year.

___4. I saw Sally in a maternity outfit—she must be pregnant.

___5. Listen, I like the way Mike thinks, Paul is an excellent mathematician and Craig and Phil are two of my best students and all four are Alpha Alpha's. As far as I'm concerned, the Alpha's are the group on campus with academic strength.

___6. If George hadn't come barging in, I never would have spilled my iced tea.

___7. Maybe that's the way you see it, but to me when high city officials are caught with their hands in the till and when police close their eyes to the actions of people with money, that's corruption.

___8. Barb wears her hair that way and guys fall all over her—I'm getting myself a hairdo like that.

2. For each of the eight above, draw a schematic and fill it in. You will have to write appropriate warrants. As an aid, we have done one for you:

We're going to have a bad wheat crop this year— we've had near drought conditions this spring.

**(D)** Near drought        ⟶  **(C)** We'll have a
conditions this                    bad wheat crop.
spring

   **(W)** (Insufficient spring rain
   results in—causes—a poor
   wheat crop.)

*Discussion*
Working in groups of four to six, discuss the relative strengths of each argument above.

*Actualization*
3. Working in groups of six, each group should generate four examples of arguments—one in each category. Record these on paper provided by your instructor. When all groups have completed their work, post the papers at the front of the class.

*Discussion*
Discuss the nature of the arguments on the paper. Are they properly identified? Are they valid?

**Answers:** 1. A; 2. D; 3. G; 4. S; 5. G; 6. C; 7. D; 8. A.

## Motivation

Reasoning provides the soundness of a particular proposition; motivation provides the trigger for action. Motivation is arousal of the person to *act* on his convictions. Motivation is often brought about by statements that reach the emotions or feelings of the individual. Most of us surround ourselves with a defensive shell that protects us from acting foolishly, in haste, without thinking. For some of us, the shell is very thick and very difficult to penetrate—for others, the shell is very thin and easily penetrated. Motivational means are intended to penetrate the shell and touch the feelings of the individual. Consider an example: The slogan "Give to the March of Dimes, it is a worthy charity" provides one good reason for giving, but it has little if any emotional impact. In contrast, the statements "No one knows when birth defects will mar the life of a newborn child; your son or daughter could be affected. Don't wait to see before caring—that's too late. Give now to help us find the causes for birth defects. In the name of your prospective son or daughter—won't you please give?" say about the same thing, but in this second case the words touch the feelings. Whether you are actually affected by this wording, it stands a much greater chance of motivating you to act than the mere statement of the reason.

As you think back over causes for your actions you may hear yourself saying that something impelled you to act. It is as if something inside of you took control of you and

directed your actions. That something is often your emotional response to various stimuli. What is an emotion? Simply defined, emotions "are labels we give to bodily feelings."[5] You recognize the presence of such emotions as love, sadness, happiness, joy, anxiety, anger, fear, hate, pity, and guilt. You hear yourself and others say such things as "I'm feeling anxious about the test," "I feel anger toward him for slighting me," "I feel sad that he's no longer able to work." Many of these emotions you feel are triggered by physical happenings: a dog jumps from behind a tree and frightens you, a friend falls and sprains his ankle and you feel sad; that person puts his or her arm around you and you feel joy. Emotions are also triggered by words. Someone says, "You idiot, what did you do a dumb thing like that for?" and you feel angry. Someone says, "I'd love to go with you," and you feel happiness. A friend says, "Go ahead with the gang—I'll be all right alone," and you feel guilty. Use of emotion is the conscious effort to phrase ideas in ways that affect the receiver's feelings. In order to do this you must first discover what emotion is most likely to motivate your receiver to do what you want. Then you must phrase your message in a manner that will activate that emotion, since the more your receiver feels your words, the more likely that he or she will act.

---

[5]Robert E. Lana and Ralph L. Rosnow, *Contemporary Psychology* (New York: Holt, Rinehart and Winston, 1972), p. 301.

Chapter Nine:
Interpersonal
Influence:
Power and
Persuasion

185

Interpersonally, motivation is not un-ethical so long as it is coordinated with or is an outgrowth of logical reasons. Empty emotional appeal for the purpose of arous-ing—of giving heat without light—is inter-personally unethical.

## Communication Session

*Reflection*

Think of the last time you were persuaded to do something that you normally would not do. Was it a logical argument that swayed you? Was it an emotional appeal? Or was it a logical argument presented emotionally? If the base was emotional, what emotions were involved?

*Actualization*

Try to frame an emotional appeal for each of the following causes: (1) the Equal Rights Amend-ment, (2) hunger in America, (3) registering to vote, (4) welfare reform.

*Discussion*

In groups of six, brainstorm a list of advantages and disadvantages to the use of emotional appeal. Record on paper. At the end of the discussion post paper at the front of the classroom and com-pare the lists.

## Credibility

All evidence points to the conclusion that persuasion is more likely to be achieved when people like, trust, and have confidence in the persuader. The Greeks called this concept *ethos*. You may call it image, charismatic effect, or the word we prefer—credibility. From our earlier discussion, you may well see a relationship between credibility as a means of persuasion and perceived expert and referent power.

Why are we willing to take the word of someone else on various issues? Since it is impossible for us to know all there is to know about everything (and even if it were *possible,* few of us would be willing to spend the time and effort), we seek shortcuts in our decision making—we rely on the judgment of others. Our thinking often goes something like this: "Why take the time to learn about the new highway when someone we trust tells us it is in our best interest?" "Why take the time to try every restaurant or read the many books telling about restaurants when someone we are willing to rely on tells us that Barney's is the best?" "Why take the time to study the candidates when our best friend tells us to vote for Smith?" Each of us places such trust in some people in order to take shortcuts in our decision making.

How do you determine on whom you will rely? Is it blind faith? Probably not. The presence (or our perception of the presence) of certain qualities will make the possessor a high credibility source. Although the spe-cific number of aspects of credibility differs somewhat in various analyses of that quality, most analyses include the importance of competence, intention, character, and personality.

*Competence* is a quality that commands our respect. Perhaps you see your roommate as a competent mathematician. If you perceive him or her as understanding the mathematical principles and being able to apply them, you may be willing to rely on that person to do your income tax, to help you with math, to be in charge of the budget.

A second important aspect of credibility is *intention*. A person's intentions or motives are particularly important in determining whether a person will like him, trust him, have respect for him, and/or believe him. For instance, you know a clothing salesman is trying to sell you the suit he helps you try on, so when he says to you "that suit is perfect for you" you may well question his intentions. On the other hand, if a bystander looks over at you and exclaims "Wow, you really look good in that style!" you are likely to accept the statement at face value because the person has no reason to say anything—his intentions are likely to be good. The more positively you view the intentions of the person, the more credible his or her words will seem to you.

A third important aspect of credibility is *character*. Character is sometimes defined as what a person is made of. You may well believe in a person who has a past record of honesty, industry, and trustworthiness.

The fourth important aspect of credibility

Chapter Nine:
Interpersonal
Influence:
Power and
Persuasion

187

is *personality*. Sometimes people have a strong "gut reaction" about others based solely on a first impression. Some people may strike you as being friendly, warm, nice to be around. Personality or likability may be the most important aspect of credibility.

Although credibility takes time to build, how people perceive you can be changed. Personality and character are projections of what you are, but competence and intention can be affected by what you say and what you do. A competent person shows that he knows what he is doing and why he is doing it. Some perceived incompetence grows from a person's apparent bumbling attempts to do a job. Often perceived incompetence is nothing more than carelessness, trying to do too many tasks at the same time, or not double checking procedures. Likewise even when your intentions are good, people may perceive them as bad if you are not open in stating why you behave as you do. Remember, people are not mind readers. When you don't explain your behaviors, others may assume they know or may read into your behavior intentions that are incorrect. If people do not see you as a credible person, you may be able to change your image by working on improving your competence and sharing your intentions.

### Ethics

We cannot leave the subject of persuasion without some discussion of ethics. What are ethics? Ethics are the standards of moral conduct that determine behavior. Ethics include both how you act and how you expect others to act. When you believe strongly in the righteousness of your cause, you may well be faced with the temptation of bowing to the belief "that the end justifies the means"—or to put it into blunt English, that you can say or do anything to achieve your goals. As we observe the world around us, we are all too well aware of the many people who have ridden roughshod over any moral or ethical principles operating within our society.

Whether or not you punish those who fail to meet your standards says a great deal about the importance you ascribe to your ethics. Although ethical codes are personal, society has a code of ethics that operates on at least the verbal level in that society.

What is your code of ethics? The following two points reflect the standards of hundreds of students that we have seen in classes during the last few years. These are but a starting point of a code of interpersonal ethics. These are not rules someone made up—they are statements of attitudes held by large numbers of your peers in our society.

1. *Lying is unethical.* Of all the attitudes about ethics, this is the one most universally held. When people know they are being lied to, they will usually reject the ideas of the person lying to them. If they find out later, they often look for ways to get back at that person.

2. *Grossly exaggerating or distorting facts is unethical.* Although some people seem willing

to accept "a little exaggeration" as human nature and may even use gross exaggeration for dramatic effect, most people regard the use of exaggeration in attempts to influence as the same as lying. Because the line between "some" exaggeration and "gross" exaggeration or "distortion" is often so difficult to distinguish, many people see any exaggeration as unethical.

In interpersonal interaction where only the two persons are involved, some are not inclined to look at sender responsibility in quite the same way as they do in a public speech, but we believe that any message source has the same ethical responsibility regardless of the setting in which statements are made. Any attempts to influence others should follow some ethical guidelines. Justifying unethical behavior on the ground of "informal setting" is itself unethical and reprehensible.

## Communication Session

*Reflection*

**What are your ethical standards? How do you see them operating in the interpersonal setting?**

*Actualization*

**Try to define your ethical code. You might begin by making a series of statements that begin, "It is wrong to _____; if someone does this, I am likely to react by _____." When you are finished, divide into groups of six and share as much as you feel comfortable in sharing. Notice the similarities and differences between your code and others' codes.**

*Discussion*

*1.* **How do you develop an ethical code? Has your code changed much?**

*2.* **Why were the Watergate and CIA scandals so disturbing for the American public?**

*3.* **Who should be responsible for teaching ethics?**

Chapter Nine:
Interpersonal
Influence:
Power and
Persuasion

189

## Payoffs

If we have succeeded in influencing you, you should now be able to

1. Define power and discuss its sources.

2. Discuss the positive and negative consequences of power utilization.

3. Define influence through persuasion.

4. Discuss three means of persuasion.

5. Explain the relationship among data, warrant, and conclusion.

6. Discuss and give an example of five categories of reasoning.

7. Test the validity of each of the categories of reasoning.

8. Explain the function of motivation in the persuasion process.

9. Add motivational language to an argument.

10. Explain the sources of credibility.

11. Outline and defend your own ethical standard.

## Suggested Readings

**Winston L. Brembeck** and **William S. Howell.** *Persuasion: A Means of Social Influence,* 2nd ed. Englewood Cliffs, New Jersey: Prentice-Hall, 1976. A standard textbook, recently revised, offering an excellent coverage of persuasion.

**Dorwin Cartwright** and **Alvin Zander.** *Group Dynamics: Research and Theory,* 3rd ed. New York: Harper & Row, 1968. Contains the Raven and French article on Power, plus several other articles developing different theories of power. Also has a good explanation of the relationship between power and persuasion.

**Rudolph F. Verderber.** *The Challenge of Effective Speaking,* 3rd ed. Belmont, California: Wadsworth Publishing Company, 1976. Chapter 14 provides a more detailed analysis of the reasoning process than is given in this chapter.

**Part D: Application of Skills to Settings**

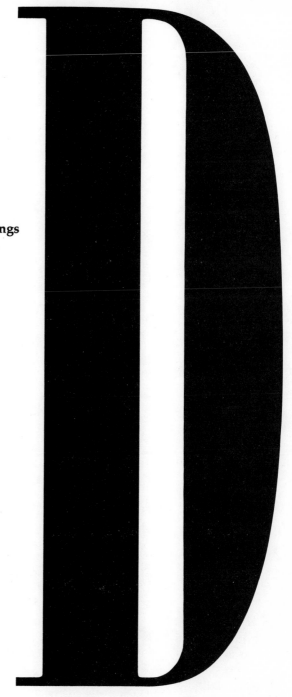

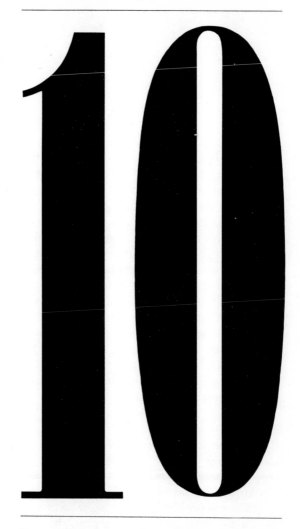

**Chapter Ten:**
**Small Group Communication**

Do you belong to a fraternal, governmental, or religious group? Have you ever worked on a committee of such a group? Has a professor ever divided your class into groups for some class project? Your answer to at least one of these questions is likely to be "yes." The fact is that some of our most important communication time occurs in groups.

In this chapter we would like to focus on those communication skills that are essential for the smooth functioning of a work group.

In our analysis, we are defining a work group as a small unit whose members interact face-to-face and who strive toward a common goal. The size recommended for an effective group varies, but many researchers set five to eight members as ideal. The type of goal for which a group strives also varies: a family may gather together to plan a vacation; a student committee handles details of a campus concert series; a board of directors sets policy for a major corporation. Yet for each of these groups to succeed, its members must not only utilize the skills we have discussed so far, but must also be able to understand and utilize the problem-solving method; there must be effective leadership; and participants must be able to fill necessary role functions.

## Preparation for Problem-solving Group Work

If a group is to be successful, it must be able to utilize the problem-solving method of stating the problem, analyzing the problem, suggesting solutions, and selecting the best solution.

### Stating the Problem

In many groups, much wheel-spinning takes place during the early stages of group discussion. Much of this results from members' questions about the function, purpose, or goal of the group. As soon as possible, the group should decide exactly what it is going to be doing. It is the responsibility of the person, agency, or parent group that forms a particular work group to give the group a specific charge. For example, a group may be formed for the purpose of "determining the nature of the spring social" or "preparing a guideline for hiring at a new plant." If the charge is not this clear, it is up to the group leader or representative to find out exactly why the group was formed and what its goals are. If stating the problem is up to the group, then the group should move immediately to get wordings down on paper; until everyone agrees what the problem is, they will never agree on how to solve it.

Problems may be stated as questions of fact, questions of value, and questions of policy.

1. *Questions of fact:* These consider the truth or falsity of an assertion. Implied in the question is the theoretical possibility of verifying the answer. For instance, "Does cigarette smoking cause cancer?" is a question of fact because the relationship between smoking and cancer can be measured. "Is Smith guilty of robbery?" is also a question of fact; Smith either committed the crime or he did not.

2. *Questions of value:* These consider relative goodness or badness. They are characterized by the inclusion of some evaluative word such as "good," "cool," "reliable," "effective," "worthy." The purpose of the question of value is to compare a subject with one or more

members of the same class. "Who is the best lecturer on campus?" is a question of value. Although you can set up criteria for "best" and measure your choice against those criteria, there is no way of verifying your findings. The answer is still a matter of judgment, not a matter of fact. "Is John Denver's music superior to Bob Dylan's?" "Is a small-college education better than a large-college education?" are both questions of value.

3. *Questions of policy:* These questions call for decisions as to whether future actions should be taken. The question is phrased to arrive at a solution or to test a tentative solution to a problem or a felt need. "What should we do to lower the crime rate?" seeks a solution that would best solve the problem of the increase

in crime. "Should the university give equal amounts of money to men's and to women's athletics?" provides a tentative solution to the problem of how we can achieve equity in financial support of athletics. The inclusion of the word "should" in all questions of policy makes them the easiest to recognize and the easiest to phrase of all problems.

### Analyzing the Problem

Once the group is in agreement about exactly what the problem is, it should move on to the next step, analyzing the problem. Analysis means determining the nature of the problem: its size, its causes, the forces that create or sustain it, and the criteria for eval-

*Before you can shape a plan, you must decide what obstacles
the solution must overcome.*

uating solutions. Sometimes analysis takes only a few minutes; at other times it may take longer. Both in preparation for problem solving and in the discussion itself, analysis is too often minimized or completely overlooked; it is the tendency of most groups to want to move directly to possible solutions. For instance, if your problem is to determine what should be done to solve the campus parking problem, you may be inclined to start by listing possible solutions immediately. Because this procedure sounds as if it is the logical beginning, the tendency is then to pursue these prematurely offered solutions. However, a solution or a plan can work only if it solves the problem at hand. Before you can shape a plan, you must decide what obstacles the solution must overcome, what symptoms the solution must eliminate, and with what other criteria your plan must deal. Before you even begin to suggest a solution, you should check to make sure that the following questions about the problem have been answered:

I. What is its size and scope?

   A. What are its symptoms? (What can we identify that shows that something is wrong or needs to be changed?)

   B. What are its causes? (What forces created it, sustain it, or otherwise keep it from being solved?)

II. What criteria should be used to test the solutions? Specifically, what checklist must the solution meet to best solve this problem? Must the plan eliminate the symptoms, be implemented within present resources, and so on?

## Suggesting Possible Solutions

For most problems, there are many possible solutions. Although you need not identify every one of the possibilities, you should not be content with your work until you have considered a wide variety of solutions. If you are considering a problem that needs only a single "yes" or "no" solution, your procedure may be altered. Should support for women's sports be increased? This question has only two possible answers. Still, you may need to suggest other solutions for comparison.

How do you come up with solutions? One way is to use brainstorming. Brainstorming is a method of generating ideas. The key idea of brainstorming is to list as many ideas as possible without attempting to evaluate any until the list is complete. The procedure for brainstorming is to free-associate, that is, to state ideas as they come to your mind in random order until you have compiled a long list. In a good ten- to fifteen-minute brainstorming session, you may think of ten to twenty solutions by yourself. Depending upon the nature of the topic, a group may come up with a list of a hundred possibilities in a relatively short period of time. Of course, some possible solutions will come through your reading, your interviews with authorities, or from your observation.

## Determining the Best Solution

During actual discussion, if the group has analyzed the problem carefully and has suggested enough possible solutions, then the final step involves only matching each proposed solution against the criteria. For instance, if you have determined that hiring more patrols, putting in closed-circuit TV, and locking outside doors after 9 P.M. are three possible solutions to the problem of reducing crime on campus, then you begin to measure each against the criteria. The one meeting the most criteria or that meets several criteria most effectively would then be selected.

Now let us put these all together with a sample (and somewhat abbreviated) outline that would help the group proceed logically. The group is being convened to discuss "meeting the needs of women on campus."

1. State the Problem—Suggested Wordings:

   What should be done to improve the plight of women on campus?

   What should be done to increase opportunities for women on campus?

   *What should be done to equalize social, athletic, and political opportunities for women on campus?

2. Analyze the Problem of Meeting the Needs of Women

   I. What is the size and scope of the problem?
      A. How many women are there on campus?
      B. What is the ratio of females to males on campus?

   C. What opportunities are currently available to women?
      1. What social organizations are there? What is the ratio of women to men who belong?
      2. Are women involved in political organizations on campus? To what extent?
      3. What athletic opportunities are open to women? Intramural? Intercollegiate?

   II. What are the causes of the problem?
      A. Do women feel discriminated against?
      B. Does the institution discriminate?
      C. Do societal norms inhibit women's participation?
      D. Do certain groups discriminate against women?

   III. What criteria should be used to test solutions?
      A. Will women favor solution?
      B. Will it cope with discrimination if discrimination does exist?
      C. Will it be enforceable?
      D. Will it comply with Chapter IX?

3. State Possible Solutions
   (The list can only be started at this point—other possible solutions will be revealed as the discussion progresses.)

   A women's center should be initiated?

   A special interest seat on all major committees should be given to women?

   Women's and men's athletic teams should be combined?

   (Others to be added.)

4. Determine Best Solution
   (To be completed during discussion.)

---

*Since the outline is made before the actual discussion, there is no guarantee that the remainder of the outline will relate entirely to the agreed-upon wording of the problem. As is illustrated by this example, however, outlining may anticipate group directions or at least serve as a valuable point of departure for the remainder of the discussion.

## Communication Session

*Reflection*

**Think of the last group with which you worked. Did the group follow the problem-solving method? If not, what steps were left out? What effect did leaving out steps have on the discussion? on the quality of the solution?**

*Actualization*

1. **Label the following questions fact (F), value (V), or policy (P).**

___1. **Is Ohio State the largest single-campus university in the United States?**

___2. **Should the United States support any government that seeks to remain free of Communism?**

___3. **Which computer costs the least to own and operate?**

___4. **Is Sparky Anderson the best manager in the National League?**

___5. **Should tuition be increased at Miller University next year?**

2. **Take one of the questions listed above. Outline the problem-solving method you would use to deal with this question.**

*Discussion*

**In your group of four to six people, discuss a plan for solving this problem: changing the foreign language requirements for graduation. Be sure to follow all the problem-solving steps.**

Answers: 1. F; 2. P; 3. F; 4. V; 5. P.

## Leadership in Problem-solving Discussion

A problem-solving group will not work well without effective leadership. Ordinarily, we think of an appointed or elected individual acting as leader and all others in the group acting as contributors of content. Although this is often the situation, it need not be. A group can be so organized that everyone shares the burden of leadership. Thus, a group can have leadership whether or not it has a designated leader. In order to decide whether your group should vest leadership responsibilities in one person, you must understand the advantages and disadvantages of each kind of situation.

When someone is appointed or elected leader, the group looks to that person for leadership. If he or she is a good leader, the group will benefit. Each participant can concentrate on considering the issues being raised, confident that the leader will guide the group justly. Disadvantages are related to inadequacy of the leader. When the leader is unsure, the group may ramble about aimlessly; when the leader dominates, participants do not feel free to contribute spontaneously and the discussion follows a path predetermined by the leader; when the leader is unskilled, the group can become frustrated and short-tempered. Good leadership is a necessity. When the appointed leader cannot provide it, the group suffers.

When the group is leaderless, everyone has the right and the obligation to show leadership. Ordinarily, leadership will emerge from one, two, or perhaps three members of the group. Since no one has been given the mantle of leadership, everyone is on equal footing, and the discussion can be more spontaneous. Disadvantages become evident in situations in which either no one assumes leadership or a few compete for leadership. In such situations, the discussion becomes "leadershipless." Depending upon the qualities of the participants, discussion by a leaderless group can arrive at good group solutions or it can degenerate into a rambling, meaningless collage of fact and opinion.

Because of its importance to group effectiveness, let us consider the question of leadership in greater detail by examining traits necessary for leadership, methods of gaining leadership, and styles of leadership.

## Leadership Traits

There have been numerous research efforts to discover those particular leadership traits that would enable us to predict leadership ability and account for leadership success. Modern researchers have largely abandoned the task for the simple reason that although some leadership traits have been identified, they are traits that are found in *all* people to varying degrees. Despite the conclusion that the trait approach to predicting leadership is futile, it may still be useful for us to examine those traits that are thought to be indicative of leadership.

Marvin Shaw, a leading authority in group research, found some correlation between individual traits and leadership measures.[1] The three traits cited are ability, sociability, and motivation. In group studies, he found that relative to ability, leaders exceed average group members in intelligence, scholarship, insight, and verbal facility. Relative to sociability, leaders exceed group members in regard to such things as dependability, activity, cooperativeness, and popularity. Relative to motivation, leaders exceed group members in initiative, persistence, and enthusiasm. This does not mean that a person with superior intelligence, or the one who is most liked, or the one with greatest enthusiasm will necessarily be the leader. We believe it does mean that a person is unlikely to be the leader if he does not exhibit at least some of these traits to a greater degree than do those he is attempting to lead.

Do you perceive yourself as having any or many of these traits? If you see these traits in yourself, then you are a potential leader. Since several individuals in almost any grouping of people have the potential for leadership, determination of the one who ends up actually leading others depends upon many things other than possession of these traits.

---

[1]Marvin E. Shaw, *Group Dynamics* (New York: McGraw-Hill Book Company, 1971), p. 269.

## Communication Session

*Reflection*

**What do you believe are your strongest leadership traits?**

*Discussion*

**In groups of three to six, discuss your opinions about the relative importance of various leadership traits.**

## Who Will Attempt to Lead?

In a group or societal setting, a normal model of leadership is one in which a person is appointed or elected to act as leader. In an interpersonal setting, however, the struggle for leadership proceeds without benefit of election or appointment. In fact, those involved may not perceive that a struggle takes place. In situations in which one individual has high needs to control and the other has high needs to be controlled, leadership will be established with no struggle at all. In most interpersonal settings, however, leadership is shared, switches back and forth, or develops into power struggles in which each party exercises his or her need or desire to lead.

To some extent, whether you will be permitted to lead again may well depend upon how you lead when you have the opportunity. Since leadership involves exerting influence, then how you lead may well depend upon whether this influence is a product of power, persuasion, or some combination. In effect, who will lead may well be a matter of style.

## Leadership Styles

The collection of a person's behaviors is called style. In a pioneer study White and Lippitt trained leaders to interact in one of three leadership styles: democratic, authoritarian, and laissez-faire.[2] The democratic leader may suggest specific policy, procedure, tasks, and/or roles for members, but this style of leadership allows the group to make the decisions. Group discussion is encouraged and is assisted by the leader. Everyone is free to participate in appraisal of group efforts.

The authoritarian style calls for the leader to be the sole determinant of policy, procedure, task, and/or roles of members. The leader makes personal praise or criticism of individual contributions.

The leader who adopts the laissez-faire style does nothing but supply information and material when asked. He does not take part in or direct decisions of the group. The group has complete freedom in determining policy, procedures, tasks and/or roles of group members, and appraisal. Laissez-faire procedure is essentially nonleadership.

In summary, as you can see, democratic leadership involves participants in decision making, authoritarian leadership is largely dictatorial, and laissez-faire provides no leadership.

After training these leaders, White and Lippitt subjected several groups to these various styles and then analyzed the results. The following analysis considers White and Lippitt's conclusions, but also includes other research to verify, supplement, and occasionally modify their conclusions.[3]

1. *More work is done under a democratic leader than in a laissez-faire setting.* For all practical purposes, laissez-faire leadership means no leadership at all. Whether you are seeking to lead another person or a group of people, laissez-faire style is least effective under all circumstances.

2. *More work is done under an authoritarian leader than under a democratic leader.* Whether this is true most of the time or only some of the time is open to some question. According to Shaw,[4] either the authoritarian group is more productive or there is no significant difference. This means that if the sole criterion is getting a job done, the democratic group is never more effective and is usually less so.

3. *Work motivation and originality are better under a democratic leader.* Evidence for this conclusion is quite consistent. In a democratic group, the members "have a piece of the action," they feel as if they have been active in the decision-making process. As a result, under democratic leadership individual members are more likely to blossom. Not only is individual growth potential the greatest, but

[2]Ralph White and Ronald Lippitt, "Leader Behavior and Member Reactions in Three Social Climates," reprinted *in* Dorwin Cartwright and Alvin Zander (Eds.), *Group Dynamics*, 3rd ed. (New York: Harper & Row, 1968), pp. 318–335.

[3]White and Lippitt, "Leader Behavior," p. 334.
[4]Shaw, *Group Dynamics*, p. 274.

also individuals feel better about the group process.

4. *Authoritarianism seems to create aggression and discontent.* However, the discontent may not appear on the surface. Again, research continues to substantiate this point. Notice that under an authoritarian leader members may not be very vocal with their discontent during the group process—in fact an authoritarian group often gives the impression of complete harmony. However, below-the-surface discontent usually manifests itself in other ways. It may be in grousing after the meeting about what took place in discussions; it may be in foot dragging in implementation stages of the proposal; it may be in abandonment of the decision if the going gets rough during implementation; it may be in just an indifference or hostility about taking time to work with the group.

5. *There is more dependence and less individuality in authoritarian groups.* Whereas democratic leadership may help the individual to blossom, authoritarian leadership seems to stifle the individual. Because the authoritarian leader has power and is quick to exercise it, everyone looks to the leader to see what to do, how to do it. There is very little chance for individuals to take initiative. Moreover, if the leader is absent, the authoritarian group tends to flounder.

6. *There is more group-mindedness and more friendliness under a democratic leader.* Putting it another way, people enjoy the group process more when they work under a democratic

*Authoritarianism creates aggression.*

leader. They often look forward to meetings, get caught up in the group action and become oblivious to time, and look back on the group activity as a positive experience.

This analysis of the literature indicates that most researchers favor democratic leadership. True. However, there are times when the democratic style is inappropriate and may lead to chaos. Participatory democracy has its limits. For instance, during a closely contested basketball game, the coach who calls a time-out has one minute to help his players handle a particular defensive alignment the other team is using. He will not use his minute in democratic processes—asking his players if they have any ideas or suggesting a plan and giving the players the opportunity to evaluate it. He will tell the players how to proceed, make a substitution if he needs to, and give the players encouragement to do what he tells them. When the accomplishment of the task is or appears to be more important than the feelings of members, then authoritarianism may be appropriate. (This is not to say that a basketball coach or any other leader who adopts the authoritarian style for the moment can disregard group feeling.) As studies have shown, a job gets done as fast or faster and often with fewer errors under an authoritarian leader. Authoritarian leadership also seems to work well when the authority really is much superior in knowledge and skill to the participants. Again, the basketball example bears this out. The coach is the coach because of what he knows—as long as the players re-

spect his superior knowledge, they will work under the authoritarian style.

There is at least one other advantage of the authoritarian form of leadership—it is easier. Learning to be a good democratic leader sometimes ends in the frustrations of laissez-faire nonleadership. In other words, some people confuse being a democratic leader with not leading at all. Since there is little ambiguity in authoritarian leadership—the leader gives directions and the group follows them—it is far easier to understand and administer.

If authoritarian leadership is your thing—and many authoritarian leaders do exist, are effective, and even win the approval of their groups—perhaps it would be well to consider one other point. The best authoritarian model seems to be "benevolent dictatorship." If the authority arises out of the need to control—and perhaps to even crush dissent—authority leads to tyranny. Even an authoritarian can be likable.

Our advice is that you examine your own style very closely. What is your natural inclination? How has it worked in the past? Would it be useful to blend some of the characteristics of another style with what comes naturally to you? Remember, these categories are not necessarily hard and fast. Still, the style you adopt is yours. If you have determined your approach, now you must consider your leadership behavior.

## Communication Session

*Reflection*

1. What is your leadership style? What are the strengths and weaknesses of that style?

2. Under which leadership style do you work best? Why?

*Actualization*

Break into three groups. One person from each group should be elected leader. These three will report to the instructor to get further direction on what the group is to discuss and how it is to proceed.

*Discussion*

Discuss your group's functioning. How did the leader help or hinder your group's success?

## Responsibilities of Leader

Regardless of whether a leader is appointed or whether several members of the group share leadership, there are certain leadership responsibilities that must be met. In this next section, let us assume that you have or wish to assume the responsibilities of leadership.

### Establishment of a Climate

As leader, your first job is to set up a comfortable physical setting that will encourage interaction. The leader is in charge of such physical matters as heat, light, and seating. Make sure the room is at a good comfortable temperature. Make sure that there is enough lighting, and, most important, make sure the seating arrangements are conducive to spirited interaction.

Too often, seating is too formal or too informal for the best discussion. By "too formal," we mean board-of-directors style. Imagine the long polished oak table with the chairman at the head, leading lieutenants at right and left, and the rest of the people down the line. Since seating may be an indication of status, how the seating is arranged can facilitate or hamper real interaction. In the board-of-directors style, a boss-and-subordinates pattern emerges. People are less likely to speak until they are asked to do so. Moreover, no one has a really good view of all the people present. However, an excessively informal seating may also inhibit interaction—especially if people sit together in small groups or behind one another.

The ideal is the circle. Here, everyone can see everyone else. At least physically, everyone has equal status. If the meeting place does not have a round table, you may be better off with either no table at all or a setting of tables that make a square at which the members can come close to the circle arrangement.

## Planning the Agenda

A second responsibility of the leader is to plan the agenda. You should do this alone or in consultation with the group. When possible, the agenda should be in the hands of the group several days before the meeting. How much preparation any individual member will make is based upon many factors, but unless the group has an agenda beforehand, members will not have an opportunity for careful preparation. Too often, when no agenda is planned, the group discussion is a haphazard affair, often frustrating and usually unsatisfying.

What goes in the agenda? Usually a sketch of some of the things that need to be accomplished. In a problem-solving discussion, the agenda should include a suggested procedure for handling the problem. In essence, it is an outline form of the steps of problem solving discussed earlier in this chapter. So if you are leading a group concerned with integrating the campus commuter into the social, political, and extracurricular aspects of student life, the following would be a satisfactory agenda:

1. *What is the size and the scope of the commuter problem?*

2. *What are the causes for commuters not being involved in social, political, and extracurricular activities?*

3. *What criteria should be used to test possible solutions to the problem?*

4. *What are some of the possible solutions to the problem?*

5. *What one solution or combination of solutions will work best to solve the problem?*

## Directing the Flow of Discussion

The leader is responsible for directing the flow of discussion. It is in this area that leadership skill is most tested. Let us examine carefully several of the most important elements of this responsibility.

**Discussants Should Have Equal Opportunity to Speak** Conclusions are valid only when they represent the thinking of the entire group. However, in discussions, some people are more likely or more willing to express themselves than others. For instance, if a typical eight-person group is left to its own devices, two or three people may tend to speak as much as the other five or six together; furthermore, one or two members may contribute little if anything. At the beginning of a discussion, you must operate under the assumption that every member of the group has something to contribute. To insure opportunity for equal participation, those who tend to dominate must be held somewhat in check, and those who are content to observe must be brought into the discussion more.

Accomplishing this ideal balance is a real test of leadership. If an ordinarily reluctant talker is embarrassed by another member of the group, he or she may become even more reluctant to participate. Likewise, if a talkative yet valuable member of the group is constantly restrained, he or she may lose value.

Let us first consider the handling of the shy or reluctant speaker. Often, apparently reluctant speakers want to talk but cannot get the floor. As leader you may solve this problem by clearing the road for that speaker. For instance, Mary may give visual and verbal clues of her desire to speak; she may come up on the edge of her seat, she may look as if she wants to talk, or she may even start to say something. Because the reluctant speaker in this posture may often relinquish the opportunity if another more aggressive person competes to be heard, you can help considerably with a comment such as "Just a second, Jim, I think Mary has something she wants to say here." Of course, the moment that Mary is sitting back in her chair with a somewhat vacant look is not the time for such a statement. A second method of drawing out the reluctant speaker is to phrase a question that is sure to elicit some answer and then perhaps some discussion. The most appropriate kind of question is one requiring an opinion rather than a fact. For instance, "Mary, what do you think of the validity of this approach to com-

bating crime?" is much better than "Mary, do you have anything to say here?" Not only is it specific, but also it requires more than a "yes" or "no" answer. Furthermore, such an opinion question will not embarrass Mary if she has no factual material to contribute. Tactful handling of the shy or reluctant person can pay big dividends. You may get some information that could not have been brought out in any other way; moreover, when Mary contributes a few times, it builds up her confidence, which in turn makes it easier for her to respond later when she has more to say. Of course, there are times when some members do not have anything worth saying, because they just are not prepared. Under such circumstances, it is best for you to leave them alone.

As a leader, you must also use tact with the overzealous speaker. Remember that Jim, the talkative person, may be talkative because he has done his homework—he may have more information than any other member of the group. If you turn him off, the group may suffer immensely. After he has finished talking, try statements such as: "Jim, that's a very valuable bit of material; let's see whether we can get some reactions from the other members of the group on this issue." Notice that a statement of this kind does not stop him; it suggests that he should hold off for a while. A difficult kind of participant to deal with is the one who must be heard regardless of whether he or she has anything to say or not. If subtle reminders are ineffective with this individual, you may have to say, "Jim,

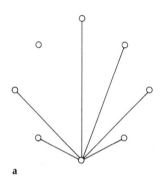 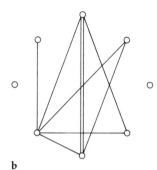 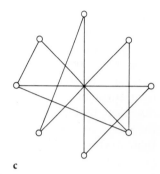

a                                    b                                    c

**Figure 10.1**

I know you want to talk, but you're just not giving anyone else a chance. Would you wait until we've heard everyone else on this point?" Of course, the person who may be the most difficult of all to control is the leader. Leaders often engage in little dialogues with each member of the group. They sometimes exercise so much control that participants believe that they can talk only in response to the leader.

There are three common patterns of group communication (see Figure 10.1, in which the lines represent the flow of discussion among the eight participants). Discussion *a* represents a leader-dominated group. The lack of interaction often leads to a rigid, formal, and usually poor discussion. Discussion *b* represents a more spontaneous group. Since three people dominate and a few are not heard, however, conclusions will not represent group thinking. Discussion *c* represents something close to the ideal pattern. It illustrates a great deal of spontaneity, a total group representa-

tion, and theoretically at least the greatest possibility for reliable conclusions.

**Keep the Discussion on the Topic** Not only must the leader see to it that the key ideas are discussed, but also he or she needs to get maximum value out of each point that is made. The skill that best helps here is appropriate questioning.

Although the members of any group bring a variety of skills, information, and degrees of motivation to the group, they do not always operate at peak efficiency without help from the leader. Perhaps one of the most effective tools of effective leadership is the ability to question appropriately. This skill involves knowing when to ask questions and knowing what kinds of questions to ask.

By and large, the leader should refrain from questions that can be answered "yes" or "no." To ask a group member whether he or she is satisfied with a point that was just made will not lead very far, for after the "yes" or "no" answer you must ask another question to draw the person out or you must change the subject. The two most effective types of questions are those that call for supporting information or the completely open-ended question that gives the member complete freedom of response. For instance, rather than asking John whether he has had any professors who were particularly good lecturers, you could say, "John, what are some of the characteristics that made your favorite lecturers particularly effective?"

When to ask questions is particularly important. Although we could list fifteen to twenty circumstances, let us focus on four purposes of questioning:

1. *To focus the discussion:* Individual statements usually have a point; the statements themselves relate to a larger point being made; and the general discussion relates to an issue or to an agenda item. You can use questions to determine a speaker's point or to determine the relationship of the point to the issue or agenda item; for instance: "Are you saying that the instances of marijuana leading to hard-drug use don't indicate a direct causal relationship?" Or, to what has just been said: "How does that information relate to the point that Mary just made?" Or, to ask about an issue or an agenda item: "In what way does this information relate to whether or not marijuana is a problem?"

2. *To probe for information:* Many statements need to be developed, supported, or in some way dealt with. Yet often members of a group apparently ignore or accept a point without probing it. When the point seems important, the leader should do something with it. For instance, on a question of source, you can say: "Where did you get that information, Jack?" Or, to develop a point: "That seems pretty important, what do we have that corroborates the point?" Or, to test the strength of a point: "Does that statement represent the thinking of the group?" Or, to generate discussion: "That point sounds rather controversial—should we accept the point as stated?"

3. *To initiate discussion:* During a discussion, there are times when lines of development are apparently ignored, when the group seems ready to agree before sufficient testing has taken place. At these times, it is up to the leader to suggest a starting point for further discussion; for instance: "OK, we seem to have a pretty good grasp of the nature of the problem, but we haven't looked at any causes yet. What are some of the causes?"

4. *To deal with interpersonal problems that develop:* Sometimes the leader can help a member ventilate very personal feelings; for instance: "Ted, I've heard you make some strong statements on this point. Would you care to share them with us?" At times, a group may attack a person instead of the information that is being presented. Here you can say: "I know Charley presented the point, but let's look at the merits of the information presented. Do we have any information that goes counter to this point?"

Questions by themselves are not going to make a discussion. In fact, some questions can hurt the discussion that is taking place. The effective leader uses questions sparingly but decisively.

**Summarize Frequently** Often a group talks for a considerable period, then takes a vote on how they feel about the subject. A good problem-solving discussion group should move in an orderly manner toward intermediate conclusions represented by summary statements seeking group consensus. For instance, on the question "What should be done to lower the crime rate on campus?" the group would have to reach consensus on each of the following questions:

1. *What is the problem?*

2. *What are the symptoms of the problem? (Draw intermediate conclusion; ask whether group agrees.)*

3. *What are the causes? (Draw intermediate conclusion on each cause separately or after all causes have been considered; ask whether group agrees.)*

4. *What criteria should be used to test the solutions?*

5. *What is one criterion? (Draw conclusions about each criterion.)*

6. *What are some of the possible conclusions? (Determine whether all possible solutions have been brought up.)*

7. *What is the best solution?*

8. *How do each of the solutions meet the criteria? (Discuss each and draw conclusions about each; ask whether group agrees.)*

9. *Which solution best meets the criteria? (The con-*

*clusion to this final question concludes the discussion; ask whether all agree.)*

During the discussion the group might draw six, eight, ten, or even fifteen conclusions before it is able to arrive at the answer to the topic question. The point is that the group should not arrive at the final conclusion until each of the subordinate questions is answered to the satisfaction of the entire group.

It is up to the leader to point up these conclusions by summarizing what has been said and seeking consensus on a conclusion. Everyone in the group should realize when the group has really arrived at some decision. If left to its own devices, a group will discuss a point for a while, then move on to another before a conclusion is drawn. The leader must sense when enough has been said to reach a consensus. Then he must phrase the conclusion, subject it to testing, and move on to another area. You should become familiar with phrases that can be used during the discussion:

*"I think most of us are stating the same points. Are we really in agreement that . . ."* (State the conclusion.)

*"We've been discussing this for a while and I think I sense an agreement. Let me state it, and then we'll see whether it does summarize group feeling."* (State the conclusion.)

*"Now we're getting on to another area. Let's make sure that we are really agreed on the point we've just finished."* (State the conclusion.)

*"Are we ready to summarize our feelings on this point?"* (State the conclusion.)

**Maintain Necessary Control** A leader must maintain control of the discussion. Remember, absence of leadership leads to chaos. Group members need to feel that someone is in charge. If the group has a set of formal rules, be sure that the rules are followed (at times bending is necessary, but total breaking does not help the group). As leader, remember that some members will be playing negative roles in the discussion; do not let them spoil the outcome. You are in charge. You are responsible. You have authority. You will need to exercise it on occasion for the benefit of the group. If John is about to talk for the fortieth time, it is up to you to harness him. If Jack and Mary are constantly sparring with each other, it is up to you to harmonize their differences. If something internal or external threatens the work of the group, it is up to you to deal with it. Also, when the group has solved its problem, end the discussion smoothly. Some discussion groups meet by time instead of by problem. Just because you are scheduled to discuss for an hour does not mean that you cannot stop in forty-five minutes if you have the job done.

## Responsibilities of Group Members

Even the most successful leader will fail if the members of the group do not fulfill their responsibilities. Good discussion is characterized by responsible contribution, objectivity, and accomplishment of various task and maintenance functions.

### Members Should Contribute Responsibly

One of the greatest differences between a work group and an informal social group is in the quality of the developmental material included. Responsible decision making is characterized by documented factual material, careful analysis of every item of information, and sound conclusions and evaluations about and from the factual material. Let us examine each of these characteristics. Since you need documented factual material, your preparation should be extensive. The more material you have sampled, the better knowledge you will have on the subject and the more valuable your contributions will be. Since, of course, you cannot predict all of the ideas that will be covered in the discussion you cannot prepare your actual contributions ahead of time. Nevertheless, you should be familiar enough with the material that you can find any item you need when you need it. Usually, you will bring your sources with you to the meeting.

A second characteristic of responsible contribution—careful analysis of every item of information—is shown by raising questions about and probing into contributions of others. Your obligation does not end with the reading into the record of items of information. Once an item of data has been submitted, it is the obligation of the membership to determine whether the item is accurate, typical, consistent, and otherwise valid. Suppose that in a discussion on reducing crime, a person mentioned that, according to *U.S. News & World Report*, crime had risen 33 percent in the past five years. The group should not leave this statement until they have explored it fully. What was the specific source of the data? On what were the data based? What years are being referred to? Is this consistent with other material? Is any counter-material available? Now, the purpose of these questions is not to debate the data, but to test them. If these data are partly true, questionable, or relevant only to certain kinds of crime, a different conclusion or set of conclusions would be appropriate.

Sound conclusions about and from the factual material, a third characteristic of responsible contribution, refers to the real goal of the group. Participants must pool information to provide a basis for conclusions about the question. You can still offer opinions, but unlike social sessions in which opinions substitute for data, in problem-solving groups opinions are based upon the previously tested materials.

## Members Should Be Objective

Let us focus on two recommendations for insuring objectivity of approach. First, report data, do not associate yourself with them. If you reported that crime has risen 33 percent in the past five years, do not feel that because you presented the data you must defend them. An excellent way of presenting data with a degree of disassociation is illustrated by the following: "According to *U.S. News & World Report*, crime has risen 33 percent in the past five years. That seems like a startling statistic. I wonder whether anyone else found either any substantiating or any contradictory data?" Presenting data in this way tells the group that you want discussion of the data and that, whether they are substantiated or disproven, you have no personal relationship with them. Contrast that disassociative approach with the following statement: "I think crime is going up at a fantastic rate. Why, I found that crime has gone up 33 percent in the past five years, and we just can't put up with that kind of thing." This member is taking a position with these data. Since anyone who questions the data or the conclusions is going to have to contend with the speaker, there is a good chance that the discussion that follows will not be the most objective.

A second recommendation for insuring objectivity is to solicit all viewpoints on every major issue. Suppose you were discussing the question "Should financial support of women's sports be raised?" Suppose that after extensive reading you believed that it should. If in the discussion you spoke only to support your position and you took issue with every bit of contrary material, you would not be responding objectively. Although there is nothing wrong with formulating tentative opinions based upon your research, in the discussion you should present material objectively whether it supports or opposes your tentative claims. If the group draws a conclusion that corresponds to your tentative conclusion, fine. At least all views have had the opportunity to be presented. If the group draws the opposite conclusion, you are not put in a defensive position. By being objective, you may find that during the discussion your views will change many times. Remember, if the best answer to the question could be found without discussion, the discussion would not be necessary.

### Members Should Fill Positive Roles

Everyone in the group has a responsibility for certain functions within the group. These functions are served as members carry out various roles. A role is a style of behavior that you determine for yourself or that is determined for you by expectations of the group. Sometimes a person plays one role and only one role in the group. At other times a given person may play several roles simultaneously or alternately, and, of course, more than one person can play a given role. In a successful group, all the positive roles are usually played sometime during the interaction; an unsuccessful group may be one in which no one plays the positive roles or one in which negative role-playing predominates. Let us ex-

amine the most common and most essential positive roles.

Group roles perform both task and maintenance functions. Task functions are those behaviors that are designed to "get the work done," while maintenance functions are behaviors whose purpose is to assure harmony and good feeling among group members. In a successful group, both functions are usually satisfied. Thus, when we analyze a group interaction, we look first to see how and whether they solved the problem; second, we look to see how well the group worked together, whether members like, respect, and understand other members of the group.

**Task Roles** In most groups there are at least four major task roles that can be identified.

1. The *information or opinion giver* provides content for the interaction. Actual information provides about 50 percent of what is done in a group. Without information and well-considered opinions, the group will not have the material upon which to base its decisions. Probably everyone in the group plays this role during the discussion. Nevertheless, usually one or more persons have really done their homework. Either as a result of past experience with this or a related problem, long conversations with persons who have worked with similar problems, or a great deal of study, these group members are relied upon

or called upon to provide the facts. In some groups, there is a designated resource person or consultant called in solely to fulfill the information-giving role. In most groups, one or more persons take it upon themselves to be especially well prepared. The information giver identifies himself by such statements as: "Well, when Jones Corporation considered this problem, they found . . ." Or, "That's a good point you made—just the other day I ran across these figures that substantiate your point." Or, "According to Professor Smith, it doesn't necessarily work that way. He says . . ."

2. The *information seeker*, the opposite of the information giver, is a role played by the member of the group who sees that at a given point the group will need data in order to function. Again, in most groups more than one person will take this role during the discussion, yet one or more are especially perceptive in seeing where more information is needed. The information seeker may be identified by such questions as "What did we say the base numbers were?" Or, "Have we decided how many people this really affects?" Or, "Well, what functions does this person serve?" Or, "Have we got anything to give us some background on this subject?"

3. The *expediter* is the individual who perceives when the group is going astray. Whether the group is meeting once or is an ongoing group, almost invariably some remarks will tend to sidetrack the group from the central point or issue before them. Sometimes apparent digressions are necessary to get background, to enlarge the scope, or even to give a person an opportunity to get something off his or her chest. Often in a group these momentary digressions lead to tangents that take the group far afield from their assignment. Because tangents are sometimes more fun than the task itself, a tangent often is not realized for what it is, and the group discusses it as if it were important to the group decision. The expediter is the person who helps the group stick to its agenda; he or she helps the group stay with the problem at hand. When the group has strayed, the expediter helps lead it back to the main stream. This role is revealed by such statements as: "Say, I'm enjoying this, but I can't quite see what it has to do with whether permissiveness is really a cause." Or, "Let's see, aren't we still trying to find out whether these are the only criteria that we should be considering?" Or, "I've got the feeling that this is important to the point we're on now, but I can't quite get hold of the relationship—am I off base?" Or, "Say, time is getting away from us and we've only considered two possible solutions. Aren't there some more?"

4. The *analyzer* is the person who is the master of technique. This person knows the problem-solving method inside out. The analyzer knows when the group has skipped a

point, has passed over a point too lightly, or has not taken a look at matters they need to. More than just *expediting,* the analyzer helps the group penetrate to the core of the problem they are working on. In addition, the analyzer examines the reasoning of various members. The analyzer may be recognized from such statements as: "Tom, you're generalizing from only one instance. Can you give us some others?" Or, "Wait a minute, after symptoms, we have to take a look at causes." Or, "I think we're passing over Jones too lightly. There are still criteria we haven't used to measure him by."

**Maintenance Roles** In most discussion groups there are at least two major maintenance roles that facilitate good working relationships.

1. The *harmonizer* is essential. It is a rare group that can expect to accomplish its task without some minor if not major conflicts. Even when people get along well, they are likely to get angry over some inconsequential points in heated discussion. Most groups experience some classic interpersonal conflicts caused by different personality types. The harmonizer is responsible for reducing and reconciling misunderstanding, disagreements, and conflicts. Good at pouring oil on troubled waters, he or she encourages objectivity and is especially good as a mediator for hostile, aggressively competing sides. A group cannot avoid some conflict, but if there is no one present to harmonize, participation can become an uncom-

fortable experience. The harmonizer may be recognized by such statements as: "Bill, I don't think you're giving Mary a chance to make her point." Or, "Tom, Jack, hold it a second. I know you're on opposite sides of this, but let's see where you might have some agreement." Or, "Sue, I get the feeling that something Todd said really bugged you, is that right?" Or, "Hold it, everybody, we're really coming up with some good stuff; let's not lose our momentum by getting into a name-calling thing."

2. The *gatekeeper* is the person who helps to keep communication channels open. If a group has seven people in it, the assumption is that all seven have something to contribute. However, if all are to feel comfortable in contributing, those who tend to dominate need to be held in check and those who tend to be reticent need to be encouraged. The gatekeeper is the one who sees that Jane is on the edge of her chair, ready to talk, but just cannot seem to get in, or that Don is rambling a bit and needs to be directed, or that Tom's need to talk so frequently is making Cesar withdraw from the conversation, or that Betty has just lost the thread of discussion. As we said earlier, a characteristic of good group work is interaction. The gatekeeper assumes the responsibility for facilitating interaction. The gatekeeper may be recognized by such statements as: "Joan, I see you've got something to say here . . ." Or, "You've made a really good point, Todd; I wonder whether we could get some reaction on it . . ." Or, "Bill

and Marge, it sounds like you're getting into a dialogue here; let's see what other ideas we have."

## Discussants Should Avoid Negative Roles

The following are the four most common negative roles that group discussants should try to avoid.

1. The *aggressor* is the person who works for his or her own status by criticizing almost everything or blaming others when things get rough. This person's main purpose seems to be to deflate the ego or status of others. One way of dealing with the aggressor is confrontation. Ask this person whether he or she is aware of what he or she is doing and what effect it is having on the group.

2. The *joker's* behavior is characterized by clowning, mimicking, or generally disrupting by making a joke of everything. Usually trying to call attention to self, the joker must be the center of attention. A little bit of a joker goes a long way. The group needs to get the joker to consider the problem seriously, or the joker will be a constant irritant to other members. One way to proceed is to encourage this individual when tensions need to be released but to ignore him or her when there is serious work to be done.

3. The *withdrawer* refuses to be a part of the group. Withdrawers are mental dropouts. Sometimes he or she is withdrawing from something that was said; sometimes withdrawal is just showing his or her indifference. Try to draw this person out with questions. Find out at what he or she is especially good and rely on him or her to do it. Sometimes a compliment will bring out the withdrawer.

4. The *monopolizer* needs to talk all the time. Usually this person is trying to impress the group that he or she is well read, knowledgable, and of value to the group. Encourage this person when his or her comments are helpful. But when the monopolizer is talking too much or when the comments are not helpful, the leader needs to interrupt the steady flow and/or draw others into the discussion.

## Evaluating Group Communication

Now that we have considered the criteria for group effectiveness, we can consider instruments for analyzing the group decision, individual participation, and the group process.

### The Decision

The first instrument (Figure 10-2) to be considered gives you an opportunity to look at the group *decision*. The rationale behind the use of this instrument is that since the group's goal is to arrive at a decision, a decision-based critical instrument will consider the end product of group communication. This instrument calls for you to discuss four major questions:

Figure 10-2

## Decision Analysis

**1.**

Did the group arrive at a decision?

**2.**

What action is taken as a result of the discussion?

**3.**

Was the group consensus a good one?

**4.**

Is there evidence that the product of the discussion is something different from what would have resulted from an immediate combination of individual beliefs and reactions?

1. *Did the group arrive at a decision?* Just because a group meets to discuss does not necessarily mean that it will arrive at a decision. As foolish as it may seem, some groups do thrash away for hours only to adjourn without having arrived at a decision. Of course, some groups discuss such serious problems that a decision cannot be reached without several meetings, but we are not talking about a group that plans to meet later to consider the issue further—we mean the group that "finishes" without arriving at some decision. Not arriving at a decision results in total frustration and disillusionment.

2. *What action is taken as a result of the group interaction?* Problem-solving discussion implies implementation. If the group has "finished" without considering means for putting the decision into action, then there is reason to question the practicability of the decision.

3. *Was the group consensus a good one?* This may be the most difficult question to answer. Whether a decision is good or not is of course a value judgment made by the evaluator. We suggest applying six criteria for such an evaluation: (1) Was quality information presented to serve as a base or foundation for the decision? (2) Were the data discussed fully? (3) Did interim conclusions relate to information presented or were they stated as opinions that had no relationship to content? (4) Did a given conclusion seem to be the product of group consideration, or was it determined by the persuasive or authoritarian power of the leader? (5) Was the final decision measured

against some set of criteria or objectives? (6) Did the group agree to support the decision?

4. *Is there evidence that the product of the group interaction is something different from what would have resulted from an immediate combination of individual beliefs and reactions?* Discussion is or should be a process. If the end product is indistinguishable from what could have been concluded at the beginning, then discussion was not the factor that brought about the decision.

## Individual Members

Although a group will have difficulty without good leadership, it may not be able to function at all without members who are willing and able to meet the task and maintenance functions of the group. The next critical instrument in group analysis (Figure 10-3) incorporates each of the elements considered earlier in the chapter and provides a relatively easy-to-use check list that can be kept for each individual.

## Leadership

Although some group discussions are leaderless, no discussion should be leadershipless. An important element of the evaluation process is to consider the nature of the leadership. If there is an appointed leader, and most groups have one, you can focus on that individual. If the group is truly leader-

**Individual Member Analysis:** For each of the following questions, rate the participant on a 1 to 5 basis: 1, high; 2, good; 3, average; 4, fair; 5, poor.

| Content: | 1 | 2 | 3 | 4 | 5 |
|---|---|---|---|---|---|
| Seems to be well prepared? | | | | | |
| Interacts? | | | | | |
| Maintains objectivity? | | | | | |
| Analyzes material as presented? | | | | | |
| Draws conclusions? | | | | | |
| | | | | | |

| Organization: | 1 | 2 | 3 | 4 | 5 |
|---|---|---|---|---|---|
| Is aware of the problem? | | | | | |
| Analyzes the problem? | | | | | |
| Suggests possible solutions? | | | | | |
| Tests each solution? | | | | | |
| | | | | | |

| Carrying Out Roles: | 1 | 2 | 3 | 4 | 5 |
|---|---|---|---|---|---|
| As information or opinion giver? | | | | | |
| As information or opinion seeker? | | | | | |
| As expediter? | | | | | |
| As analyzer? | | | | | |
| As harmonizer? | | | | | |
| As gatekeeper? | | | | | |

| **Carrying Out Negative Roles:**<br>(For this category a 1, high, would show that the person<br>was not playing that negative role) | 1 | 2 | 3 | 4 | 5 |
|---|---|---|---|---|---|
| As aggressor? | | | | | |
| As joker? | | | | | |
| As withdrawer? | | | | | |
| As monopolizer? | | | | | |

**Analysis:** Write a short profile of this person's contribution to the group based upon the above check list. Consider his relative effectiveness in helping (or hindering) the group in achieving its goal.

less, then you must consider attempts at leadership by the various members or focus on the apparent leader who emerges from the group.

The next check list (Figure 10-4) provides an easy-to-use instrument for evaluating group leadership.

## Communication Session

*Reflection*
**What role do you usually take in groups? Are you effective in that role?**

*Actualization*
1. **Each classroom group is given or selects a task that requires some research. Each group should be given approximately thirty to forty minutes for discussion. While group A is discussing, members of group B should observe and after the discussion give feedback during the remainder of the class period. For practice in using the various instruments, one observer could be asked to do a decision analysis, one could be asked to do an individual member analysis, and one could be asked to do a leadership analysis. In the next class period, group B would discuss and group A would observe and critique. Sample questions:**

> **What should be done to improve parking (advising, registration) on campus?**

> **What should be done to increase the participation of minorities in college or university teaching (governance, administration)?**

2. **Each classroom group has ten to fifteen minutes to arrive at a solution to the following dilemma: Five people are boating: the father, a 55-year-old heart specialist reputed to be the best in the state; his 36-year-old wife, a dermatologist; their 8-year-old child; their neighbor, a 43-year-old industrial salesman for a major corporation; and his wife, a 35-year-old former model who appears in frequent local television commercials. If some tragedy ensued and only one of the five could be saved, who should it be? One observer will be appointed for each group. The observer will use one of the three evaluation instruments discussed.**

**Figure 10-4**                                                                221

**Leadership Analysis:** For each of the following questions, rate the leadership on a 1 to 5 basis: 1, high; 2, good; 3, average; 4, fair; 5, poor.

| Leadership Traits: | 1 | 2 | 3 | 4 | 5 |
|---|---|---|---|---|---|
| Has sufficient understanding? | | | | | |
| Stimulates group? | | | | | |
| Has the respect of the group? | | | | | |
| | | | | | |

| Leadership Methods: | 1 | 2 | 3 | 4 | 5 |
|---|---|---|---|---|---|
| Establishes a good working climate? | | | | | |
| Has an agenda? | | | | | |
| Promotes systematic problem solving? | | | | | |
| Directs the flow of discussion? | | | | | |
| Encourages balanced participation? | | | | | |
| Asks good questions? | | | | | |
| Clarifies and crystallizes ideas? | | | | | |
| Summarizes frequently? | | | | | |
| Maintains necessary control? | | | | | |
| Brings the discussion to a satisfactory close? | | | | | |

**Analysis:** Write a short profile of this person's leadership, based upon the above check list. Consider his relative effectiveness in helping the group in achieving its goal.

*Discussion*

**After the exercise, the group should determine (1) what roles were operating in the group during the discussion, (2) who were performing those roles, and (3) what factors helped or hurt the problem-solving process.**

## Payoffs

Now that you have read and discussed this chapter, you should be able to

1. Differentiate between questions of fact, value, and policy.

2. Analyze a problem.

3. Brainstorm for solutions.

4. Discuss how to choose from among possible solutions.

5. Solve a problem using the problem-solving method.

6. Differentiate among authoritarian, democratic, and laissez-faire leadership.

7. Discuss the assets and liabilities of each leadership style.

8. Plan an agenda.

9. Apply the leadership skills of directing the flow of discussion, questioning, and summarizing.

10. Discuss the characteristics of responsible contribution.

11. Explain how you can insure objectivity of approach.

12. Identify and explain the task roles.

13. Identify and explain the maintenance roles.

14. Help someone who is fulfilling negative roles to start fulfilling positive ones.

**15.** Practice positive task and maintenance roles in group problem solving.

**16.** Evaluate group participation and leadership.

## Suggested Readings

**Ernest G. Bormann.** *Discussion and Group Methods: Theory and Practice,* 2nd ed. New York: Harper & Row, 1975. This is a comprehensive textbook on the subject of group discussion.

**Dorwin Cartwright** and **Alvin Zander.** *Group Dynamics: Research and Theory,* 3rd ed. New York: Harper & Row, 1968. This book is basic to any library of group research. It contains a wealth of information on all facets of group process.

**David Potter** and **Martin P. Andersen.** *Discussion in Small Groups: A Guide to Effective Practice,* 3rd ed. Belmont, California: Wadsworth Publishing Company, 1976. Although this is a much shorter book than Bormann, it is still quite comprehensive. Contains a practical approach to group discussion.

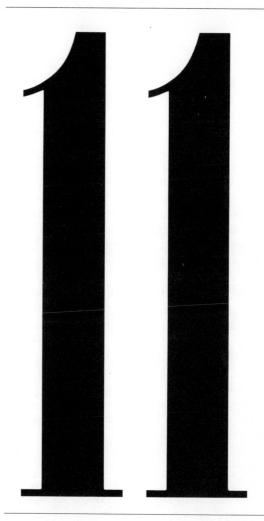

**Chapter Eleven:
Interviewing**

Although only a relatively small percentage of your future interpersonal interaction will involve interviewing, the time you spend in interview situations may be very important. Interviewing is a form of interpersonal interaction that is based primarily upon the asking and answering of questions. Unlike most of your interpersonal communication, interviewing can be planned ahead and is usually focused on one content area.

An interview may be for appraisal (making value judgments that may lead to promotion, reward, or firing), for counseling (helping a person to examine and perhaps solve his or her problems), or even for persuasion (influencing a person to buy a product). We believe that the two most important types of interviewing skills students need to study are those for gaining information and for job interviewing.

In this chapter we will consider methods of interviews, the phrasing of questions, and procedures for participating in information-getting and job interviews.

## Methods of Interviews

The two major methods of interviewing are directive and nondirective. A *directive interview* is one in which the interviewer is in control. He or she knows what is to be accomplished and has a well-conceived plan for achieving goals of the interview. The advantages of the directive interview are that its techniques are easy to learn and it takes less time than the nondirective interview, provides quantifiable data, and can be used to supplement other methods of data collecting. Its disadvantages are that it is inflexible, is limited in variety and depth of subject matter, and is narrow in scope.

The *nondirective interview* is one in which the interviewee is in control. It provides an opportunity to deal in depth with a wide range of subject matters, allows interviewer flexibility, and provides an opportunity to establish an ongoing relationship between interviewer and interviewee. However, it is time-consuming, requires acute psychological insight and sensitivity, and generates nonquantifiable data.

Some interviewers prefer the directive interview, some the nondirective, and some like a blend of the two. Since we believe you must learn to be in control before you can allow the other party to take control and still achieve the purpose of the interview, most of the suggestions in this chapter will relate to the directive interview. Moreover, the directive method is more common in the information-getting and job interviews. Before moving to the specifics of these two kinds of interviews, we need to discuss the one element common to all interviewing—questioning.

## Questions in Interviewing

An interview differs from other forms of interpersonal communication in its reliance upon the asking and answering of questions. Although we deal here specifically with questions in the interview situation, a knowledge of good question construction can be applied to any interpersonal encounter. Questions may be phrased as open or closed, primary or secondary, direct or neutral.

## Open versus Closed Questions

A first issue is the contrast between open and closed questions. Open questions are broad based—often specifying only the topic to be covered. They allow considerable freedom to the interviewee. Closed questions are those that can be answered "yes" or "no" or with only a few words.

Open questions range from those with virtually no restrictions like "Tell me about your life" to those that give some direction like "Tell me about your experiences with the speech department." Why do interviewers use open questions? Mostly to encourage the other person to talk, allowing the interviewer maximum opportunity to listen and to observe. As a result of this type of question, the interviewer discovers what the person perceives as important to him or her. Through open questions the interviewer is likely to elicit information that would not be forthcoming in response to closed questions. For instance, through his answer to an open question, a person may reveal prejudices, peculiarities, and other personal perceptions. Open questions take more time to answer, and the interviewer can lose control of the interview if he or she does not know how to work with the answers that come.

Closed questions range from those requiring only "yes" and "no" answers ("Do you like avocados?") to the short-answer variety ("How many years have you worked here?"; "What kinds of beer do you buy most frequently?"). The obvious advantage to the closed question is that the interviewer can maintain necessary control of the interview. Moreover, he or she can get a great amount of usable information in a short period of time. When you add that a closed schedule can be well planned in advance and that the interview itself requires less time and less effort on the part of the interviewee you begin to see why closed questions are popular with interviewers. The obvious disadvantages are that as an interviewer you will very seldom know why the person responded the way he or she did. The closed question gives little room for talking about ideas and feelings that fall between the "yes" and "no" extremes. Moreover, since the respondent has little opportunity to talk, he or she is less likely to volunteer useful information.

Which type of question is superior? A great deal depends upon what kinds of material you are seeking and how much time you have at your disposal. We will consider the possibility of blending the two types of questions as we talk about specific interviewing procedures.

## Communication Session

*Reflection*

Have you ever interviewed or been interviewed by anyone? If so, what type of interview was it? What method of interviewing was used? Were the questions mostly open or closed? How did the type of questions affect the interview?

*Actualization*

1. Indicate which of the following are (O) open questions and which are (C) closed questions:

___1. What makes you think Fox's chances are good in the upcoming election?

___2. Have you ever thought of running for City Council?

___3. How many persons are involved in the process of developing a new product?

___4. What is your opinion of the company's vacation policy?

___5. How do you think the student affairs office should be organized?

___6. Do you agree with Mr. Sheldon's position on attendance?

2. Select a subject for an interview. Determine what information you should like to know about that subject. Frame five open questions and five closed questions that attempt to yield the same information.

*Discussion*

In groups of four to six share your open and closed questions. Discuss the advantages and disadvantages for the list of open questions and the list of closed questions.

Answers: 1. O; 2. C; 3. C; 4. O; 5. O; 6. C.

### Primary versus Secondary Questions

A second useful distinction is the one between primary and secondary questions. Primary questions introduce topics; secondary questions follow up on the answers to primary questions. Some people refer to the secondary question as the "probing" question for it asks the interviewee to go more deeply into ideas and feelings behind his answers. A good list of primary questions can be made before the interview; good secondary questions call for you as an interviewer to listen carefully and be sensitive to both the content and the intent of the respondent's statements. Skill at use of secondary questions comes with interviewing experience.

Some secondary questions are just supportive statements designed to encourage the respondent to continue but in greater depth. Such priming questions as "And then?" "Is there more?" and "What happened next?" give the respondent reason to continue with his comments.

A second-level secondary question is a more specific probe such as "What did you do after . . . ?" "I'm not sure I fully understand what you were thinking at the time—can you tell me?" and "What do you mean by 'frequently'?" Questions of this kind encourage continuation, but along a specific line that you as the interviewer determine.

A third-level probe is one that plumbs the feelings of the respondent. Such questions as "How did you feel when you were cut from the squad?" "How did you react when you got such a beautiful gift?'' and ''What words best describe exactly what you were feeling when it happened?'' encourage the person to reveal emotions and moods.

One of the major reasons for a secondary or probing question is to motivate the respondent to enlarge upon an answer the interviewer believes is inadequate. Such follow-ups are necessary because the respondent may be purposely trying to be evasive, incomplete, or vague, or because the interviewee may not really understand how much detail you are looking for. Your follow-up questions show the person how much leeway you will give him in giving answers.

Keep in mind that the effectiveness of the follow-up questions may well depend upon your interpersonal skill in asking them. Since probing questions can alienate the interviewee (especially when the questions are perceived as threatening), such in-depth probes work best after you have gained the confidence of the respondent and when the questions are asked within the atmosphere of a positive interpersonal climate.

### Directed versus Neutral Questions

A third essential distinction to make is between the neutral and the directed question. A neutral question is one in which the respondent is free to give an answer without direction from the interviewer. In contrast, a directed question is one in which the interviewer suggests the answer he or she expects

*Skill at questioning comes with experience.*

or desires. Notice the difference in wording in the following pairs of questions:

**Neutral:** *How do you feel about working with Roger?*

**Directed:** *Working with Roger makes you feel uncomfortable, doesn't it?*

**Neutral:** *How would you compare a Volkswagen with other subcompact cars?*

**Directed:** *Wouldn't you like to own a Volkswagen?*

**Neutral:** *Tell me about the ways you respond to pressure?*

**Directed:** *When was the last time you went drinking to cope with the pressures you faced?*

Notice that the neutral question leaves it to the respondent to determine how he will answer. In the directed question, the person feels some pressure to answer a particular way.

Directed questions are called "leading" or "loaded" questions, depending upon the nature of the directive within them. Directed questions are frequently used by a person who conducts a persuasive interview with intention to control the attitude or behavior of the respondent. Since your interviewing experience is more likely to come through information and selection interviews, you should probably avoid the use of directed questions, which tend to elicit biased responses rather than usable information.

## Communication Session

*Actualization*

**Change each of the following directed questions to a neutral question:**

**Doesn't it depress you to see so many patients who will never get well?**

**After what Angelina did I bet you are really out to get her, aren't you?**

**Aren't you really excited about your new promotion?**

**Wouldn't you be upset about going to Philadelphia if you were traded?**

*Discussion*

**Under what circumstances if any are directed questions preferable to neutral questions?**

## Information-seeking Interview

Interviewing can be a valuable method for getting information on nearly any topic. Students can use the interview to get information for papers, lawyers interview witnesses to get facts to build their cases, doctors interview patients to get medical history before making diagnoses, and reporters interview sources to get facts for their stories. A good interviewing plan involves selecting the best person to interview, determining a procedure, conducting the interview itself, and interpreting the results.

### Selecting the Best Person

Somewhere on campus or in the larger community, there are people who have expertise in the problem areas you want to research. Your first step should be to find out who they are so you can arrange to talk with them. Suppose you are interested in published textbooks of faculty members. Whom should you interview? To find out, you would try to locate a list of publications written by faculty members and determine prospective interviewees yourself. Or, you could call the office of the provost or the dean and ask for names of faculty members who have written textbooks. After you had made a list of names, you would make an appointment with one or more persons on the list. Making an appointment is very important—you cannot just go walking into an office and expect the prospective interviewee to drop everything on the

spur of the moment. You are not going to get very much valuable information if the person is not willing to cooperate with you. To get an appointment you must know (1) why you need to interview this particular person (why the person should take time to talk with you) and (2) what information you hope to get from the interview.

Before going into the interview, you should do some research on the person you will be interviewing. If you are going to interview a faculty member who has written college textbooks, you should already have reviewed some material about publishing and you should know something about the faculty member. Not only will evidence of your preliminary research encourage the person to talk more openly with you (few people will either respect or talk in detail with a person who obviously knows nothing about the subject or the person), but also this familiarity with material will enable you to frame more penetrating questions.

In addition, you should be forthright in your reasons for seeking the interview. If you are interviewing the person as part of a class project, if you are writing a newspaper article on campus authors, or if you have some other reason, say so.

### Determining a Procedure

Good interviewing results from careful planning. The plan includes overall method and preparation of specific questions.

You must determine the kind of interview that is most likely to achieve your goals. As we mentioned earlier, interviews may be directive or nondirective, but we recommend the directive method—especially for the information-getting interview. You should write down the subject areas you want information on. Then write down all the questions you can think of, revise them until you have worded them clearly and concisely, and then put them in the order that seems most appropriate. On your written question schedule, you should leave enough space between questions so that you can fill in answers as completely as possible. Moreover, you should leave enough space for answers to secondary questions that you ask that are related to the primary questions you have prepared. Some interviewers try to play the entire interview by ear. Even the most skilled interviewer needs to have some preplanned questions to insure his covering important areas. The order and type of questions depend somewhat upon what you are hoping to achieve in the interview. Let us look at the interview opening, the body, and the closing.

**Initial Stages—the Interview Opening**    You should of course start by thanking the person for taking time to talk with you. In this initial stage, you are trying to develop a good rapport between you and your respondent. Start by asking some of your questions that can be answered easily and that will show your respect for the person you are interviewing. For

instance, in an interview with your professor on textbooks he has written, you might start with such questions as "I know writing is a big project—how long does it take to write a book?" or "Do you find you work better in the office or at home or some other place?" Such questions will set the interviewee at ease and get him talking freely. Since the most important consideration of this initial stage is to create a positive communication climate, keep the questions easy to answer, nonthreatening, and encouraging.

**The Body of the Interview**    The body of the interview includes the major questions you have prepared to ask. After the initial stages, you can move into the planned schedule. The following example gives you an idea of the method of setting up an interview question schedule. Notice that the questions are grouped and notice that the hard hitting questions that require careful thinking are placed later in the schedule. For instance, the question "Should a school use a book written by a professor teaching at that school?" is the final question on the list.

If you were planning to interview one or more teachers about textbook publishing experiences, you might prepare the following questions schedule:

I.  About Textbook Publishing in General
    1.  How do you go about getting a company to to publish your work?
    2.  Is there a difference between getting a textbook published and getting a novel published?

3. Does a textbook author need to have an agent?
4. How does an author apply for a copyright?

II. Experience of This Author
1. How many books have you written?
2. What company publishes your book(s)?
3. Besides monetary reward, what motivated you to write a textbook?
4. How long did it take you to write this book?
5. What are the most difficult aspects of writing a book for you?
6. Do you have to write many drafts?
7. How is a book edited?
8. Do you do the illustrations, pictures, and other visuals? If not, how are they done?

III. Opinions of This Author
1. How would you react if a teacher at another school photocopied a chapter from your book to hand out to his students?
2. Do most textbooks need to be revised or brought out in new editions as often as some are?
3. Do you think a school should use a book written by a professor at that school? Please explain.

You may or may not ask all of these questions in the actual interview. Before you begin, however, you must be satisfied that you have enough questions to yield the kind of information you want. As you get into your questions, you must be particularly sensitive to both content and intent of the respondent's answers so that you can frame secondary questions that will yield additional information.

**Closing the Interview** As you draw to the end of your planned questions, thank the person for taking time to talk with you. If you are going to publish the substance of the interview, it is courtesy to offer to let the person see a draft of your reporting of the interview before it goes into print. Although this practice is not followed by many interviewers, it helps to build and maintain your own credibility.

## Conducting the Interview

The best plan in the world will not result in a good interview unless you practice good interpersonal communication skills in conducting the interview. Let us focus on a few of the particularly important elements of good interviewing. Perhaps more than anything else, you should be courteous during the interview. Listen carefully—your job is not to debate or to give your opinion, but to get information from a person who has it. Whether you like the person or not or whether you agree with the person or not, you must respect his or her opinions—after all, you are the one who asked for the interview.

Put into practice your best receiver skills. If the person has given a rather long answer to a question, you should paraphrase what he has said to make sure your interpretation is correct. Also, keep the interview moving. You do not want to rush the person, but he or she is probably very busy with a full schedule of activities. It is usually a good idea to ask for a given amount of time when you first make the appointment. "I'd like to talk with you for about half an hour" is a statement that lets the person know how much time you have in mind. Sometimes the interviewee will want to extend the time. Ordinarily, however, when the time is up, you should call attention to that fact and be prepared to conclude.

Last, but certainly not least, you should be very much aware of the impression you make nonverbally. You should consider your clothes—you want to be dressed appropriately for the occasion. Since you are taking the person's time, you should show an interest in the person and what he or she has to say. How you look and act may well determine whether or not the person will warm up to you and give you the kind of interview you want.

### Interpreting and Evaluating the Results

The interview serves no useful purpose until you do something with the material you have uncovered, but you should not do anything with it until you have reviewed the material carefully. Especially if you took notes, it is important to write out complete answers carefully while information is still fresh in your mind. After you have processed the material from the interview, you may want to show the interviewee a copy of the data you are going to use. You do not want to be guilty of misquoting your source.

You may also find it necessary to check out the facts you have been given. If what the person has told you differs from material from other sources, you had better double check the accuracy of the material.

The most difficult part is making interpretations and drawing inferences from the information. Facts by themselves are not nearly so important as the conclusions that may be drawn from the facts. Be careful to see that you check and double check your thinking before you present the substance of the interview in a speech or for publication.

## Communication Session

*Reflection*

Have you ever conducted an interview? Did you utilize the steps outlined above? What was the result?

*Actualization*

Working in groups of four to six, determine a topic on which you might wish to conduct an information-getting interview.

1. Who would be the best person or persons to interview on this topic?

2. As a group, devise a list of questions for this information-seeking interview. Remember to frame open as well as closed questions. Make sure that you have appropriate secondary questions to use as follow-ups. Check to make sure that most questions are neutral rather than directed. Group the questions under major headings. Make sure you have some questions that are appropriate for opening the interview. Write the finished product on paper for posting.

*Discussion*

The class should compare the various interview plans. Look for poorly worded questions; make sure the organization of questions is logical.

*Actualization*

3. Conduct an in-class interview with a classmate in an area of his or her expertise.

4. Conduct an interview outside of class and submit a written report.

## Employment Interview

Although there is some question about the interview as a really valid tool for personnel selection, nearly every major position in nearly any field of endeavor requires that the applicant go through an interview. At its worst, an interview can be a waste of time for all parties involved; at its best, an interview can be an integral part of the process of selection and placement. Some of the common criteria for evaluating applicants for most positions are specific abilities, ambition, energy, ability to communicate, knowledge and intelligence, and integrity. A skillfully conducted interview can help the interviewer determine the applicant's strengths in several of these areas; likewise a skillfully conducted interview can help the interviewee reveal his or her strengths in many of these same areas.

Assuming then that the interview can be a valid instrument in the selection process, let us consider some of the procedures and methods that are most likely to be beneficial to the interviewer in conducting an interview and to the interviewee in taking part in one.

### Responsibilities of Interviewer

As an interviewer, you are the link between a job applicant and the company. Much of the applicant's impression of the company will be made on the basis of his or her impression of you. You should know what kinds of information applicants want to know about your company. In addition to the obvious desire for salary information, applicants also seek such information as opportunity for advancement, influence of personal ideas on company policy, company attitudes toward personal life and life style (political activities, marital status, "volunteer" work), and so forth. Moreover, you have nearly the sole responsibility of determining whether this person will be considered for the position available or whether this person will be kept in the running for possible company employment.

### Procedure

For the interview itself, a plan for a highly to moderately structured interview is most likely to elicit the most valid data. In the unstructured interview, the interviewers tend to talk more and tend to make decisions based upon less valid data than in structured interviews.[1] Especially if you are screening a large number of applicants, you want to make sure that all have been asked the same questions and that the questions cover a variety of subject areas.

Before the interview starts, you should be familiar with all available data about the applicant—application form, résumé, letters of recommendation, test scores if any are available. These written data will help determine

some of the questions you will want to ask under the various headings.

### The Interview

We will consider three aspects of the interview itself: the opening, the body, and the closing.

**The Opening of the Interview**  Obviously you should greet the applicant warmly. Call him or her by name and introduce yourself so that he or she can use your name. A warm handshake is also beneficial to getting things off to a good start. Be open with the applicant. If you are either going to take notes or record the interview let the applicant know why you are doing so.

Should you start with some ice-breaker questions to help establish a rapport? Or should you move right into the question schedule? A good interviewer senses the nature of the situation and tries to use a method that is most likely to encourage the applicant to talk and thus provide adequate answers to questions the company wants answered. Although "warm-up" questions may help some applicants, most of them are psychologically ready for the interview. As a result, many "warm-up" questions may be misinterpreted. The applicant may wonder about the motivation for such strange questions and they may make him or her even more nervous. Unless you have good reason for proceeding differ-

---

[1]P. B. Sheatsley, "Closed Questions Are Sometimes More Valid than Open End," *Public Opinion Quarterly*, Vol. 12 (1948), p. 12.

ently, the best advice seems to be to move into the question schedule expeditiously in as warm and friendly a manner as you can.

**The Body of the Interview**   The body of the interview consists of the question period. Let us begin with some guidelines for presenting yourself and your questions:

1. *Be careful of your own presentation.* Talk loudly enough to be heard. Try to be spontaneous. The interviewee is not going to respond well to obviously memorized questions fired in machine-gun fashion. Be sensitive to your own nonverbal communication. The interviewee is going to be looking for signs of disapproval—any inadvertent looks or unusual changes in quality or rhythm may convey a false impression. Remember that you can "load" a question by giving it a particular tone of voice, so be especially careful.

2. *Do not waste time.* You have available a wide variety of information about the candidate. Ask questions about information you already know only if you seek some special insights into the information. For instance, if an applicant indicates employment with a particular organization but does not give any detailed account of responsibilities, questions relating to that employment period would be appropriate.

3. *Avoid trick or loaded questions.* Applicants are always leery of dealing with questions that may be designed to make them look bad.

Moreover, if a candidate believes that you are trying to trick him or her, the suspicion may provoke a competitive rather than a positive atmosphere. Anything that serves to limit the applicant's responsiveness will be detrimental to the interview.

4. *Avoid questions that violate fair employment practice legislation.* Questions directed to a woman about her plans for marriage or, if she is married, about her plans to have children are not only irrelevant, but also illegal.

5. *Give the applicant an opportunity to ask questions.* Usually, near the end of the interview, you will want to take the time to see whether the applicant has any questions.

Now let's look at some of the specific questions that interviewers usually ask. This list is a combination of questions from a variety of sources and is only representative, not exhaustive. It imposes no limitations on your own creativity, but is intended to be suggestive of the kinds of questions you may wish to ask. You might use this as a starter list or as a check list for your own wording of questions. Notice that some questions are open-ended and some are closed, but none are "yes" or "no" questions.

1. *How did you select the school you attended?*

2. *What are your hobbies?*

3. *How did you determine your major?*

4. *What kind of position are you looking for?*

5. *Why do you think you would like to work for us?*

6. *What do you hope to accomplish?*

7. *What qualifications do you have that make you feel you would be beneficial to us?*

8. *What extracurricular activities did you engage in in school?*

9. *How do you feel about traveling?*

10. *What part of the country would you like to settle down in?*

11. *What kind of people do you enjoy interacting with?*

12. *What do you regard as an equitable salary for a person with your qualifications?*

13. *Is your transcript reflective of your ability? If not, why not?*

14. *What new skills would you like to learn?*

15. *Did you work your way through college?*

16. *At what age did you begin supporting yourself?*

17. *What causes you to lose your temper?*

18. *What are your major strengths? weaknesses?*

19. *What do you do to stay in good physical condition?*

20. *What are your professional goals for the future?*

21. *What kind of reading do you like to do?*

22. *Who has had the greatest influence on your life?*

23. *What have you done that shows your creativity?*

24. *How would you proceed if you were in charge of hiring?*

25. *What are your most important criteria for determining whether you will accept a position?*

**The Closing of the Interview**   Toward the end of the interview, you should always tell the applicant what will happen next. Tell him or her about the procedures for making the decision. Who has the authority? When will the decision be made? How will the applicant be notified? These are some of the questions you certainly should answer. Then close the interview in a courteous, neutral manner. You should neither build false hopes nor seem to discourage the applicant.

### Responsibilities of Job Applicant

Interviews are part—and an important part—of the process of seeking employment. Even for part-time and temporary jobs, you will benefit if you approach the interviewing process seriously and systematically. There really is no payoff in applying for positions that are obviously outside your area of expertise. It may seem a good idea to get interviewing experience, but you are wasting your time and the interviewer's time if you apply for a position you have no intention of taking or a position for which you are not qualified.

When you are granted an employment interview, remember that all you have to sell is yourself and your qualifications. You want to show yourself in the very best possible light. Therefore, you should be concerned about your appearance; if you really want a particular job, you will dress in a way that will be acceptable to the person or organization that may—or may not—hire you. You should be fully prepared for the interview, and two important responsibilities that you must meet before the interview itself are the résumé and the cover letter.

**The Résumé** Before most employers will even talk with you, they will want to see your résumé. A survey of the recruitment and employment policies and practices of the 500 largest U.S. corporations revealed the following information:[2]

A. Almost all preferred both a cover letter and a résumé (98 percent)

B. Most wanted the cover letter typewritten (67 percent)

C. More than 75 percent wanted the following information included in the résumé:

1. Personal information—date of birth, phone, address, marital status, number of dependents (92 percent)
2. Listing of special interests such as accounting, statistics, sales, finance, economics (91 percent)
3. Specific educational qualifications like major, minors, degrees, and the like (87 percent)
4. Willingness to relocate (86 percent)
5. List of scholarships, awards, and honors (86 percent)
6. Previous work experience including jobs, dates of employment, company addresses, reasons for leaving (82 percent)
7. Statement on physical or health status (80 percent)
8. Social data like fraternities, sororities, athletics, clubs, including offices held (76 percent)

D. More than 33 percent wanted the following information included in the résumé:

---

[2]"As You Were Saying—The Cover Letter and Résumé," *Personnel Journal,* Vol. 48 (September 1969), pp. 732–733. This article is a summary of information provided by Harold D. Janes, Professor of Management, University of Alabama.

*Remember that you have to sell yourself.*

1. Salary requirements (57 percent)
2. Source of applicant's college financing (57 percent)
3. Name of high school, class rank, and date of graduation (48 percent)
4. List of grades in major and minor college subjects (46 percent)
5. Special skills such as typing, fluency in a foreign language, operating computers (41 percent)
6. A list of references (33 percent)

E. Although more preferred one-page to two-page résumés (35 percent) a significant number preferred only one page (30 percent)

F. The cover letter should be short, contain specific areas of interest and availability; it should explain or amplify elements of the résumé; and it should be creative; and it should be clear, neat, and well typed.

**Getting Ready for the Interview** It is a good idea to give yourself a practice session. Try to anticipate some of the questions you will be asked and think carefully about your answers. You need not write out and practice answers; but, before the actual interview, you should have anticipated key questions, and you should have thought about such subjects as salary expectations, possible contribution to the company, special skills, and so forth.

**The Interview** Perhaps the best way of suggesting interviewing procedure is to list some of the common complaints that interviewers have about applicants. Although this list was compiled more than twenty years ago, it still

contains cautions that any applicant for employment will find valuable to consider.[3]

*The undesirable applicant:*

1. *Is caught lying*

2. *Shows lack of interest*

3. *Is belligerent, rude, or impolite*

4. *Lacks sincerity*

5. *Is evasive*

6. *Is concerned only about salary*

7. *Is unable to concentrate*

8. *Is indecisive*

9. *Is late*

10. *Is unable to express himself clearly*

11. *Wants to start in an executive position*

12. *Oversells case*

In light of these negative points, let us consider some positive approaches that will help you give the best possible impression.

1. *Be prompt.* The interview is the company's only clue to your work behavior. If you are late to the interview the interviewer may conclude that you are likely to be late for work. We suggest that you give yourself at least fifteen

---

[3]Selected from Charles S. Goetzinger, "An Analysis of Irritating Factors in Initial Employment Interviews of Male College Graduates," unpublished Ph.D. dissertation, Purdue University, 1954. Reported *in* Charles J. Stewart and William B. Cash, *Interviewing: Principles and Practices*, Dubuque, Iowa: Wm. C. Brown Company, 1974, pp. 162–163.

minutes' leeway to cover any possible traffic problems, and so forth.

2. *Look at the interviewer.* Remember that your nonverbal communication tells a lot about you. Company representatives are likely to consider eye contact a clue to your self-confidence.

3. *Determine if this is a directive or nondirective interview.* If it is directive, be sure to answer questions completely. Your responses will be compared with those of others who answer the same questions. If the interview appears to be nondirective, open up and talk. The interviewer will be trying to get to know you, and he can do that only if you cooperate.

4. *Give yourself time to think.* If the interviewer asks you a question that you had not anticipated, give yourself time to think before you answer. It is better to pause and think than to give a hasty answer that may cost you the job. If you do not understand the question, paraphrase it before you attempt to answer.

5. *Don't talk salary.* Talking salary during an interview can only have negative consequences for you. If you mention a salary that is too high, you can price yourself out of a job that you really wanted; if you mention a figure that is much lower than what the company was willing to pay, the company may lower its offer or reevaluate their impression of a person who has such a low opinion of his worth. One way of handling a salary question is to ask the interviewer, "What do you normally pay someone with my experi-

ence and education for this level position?" Such a question allows you to get an idea of what the salary will be without committing yourself to a figure.

6. *Don't talk benefits.* A company is usually interested in people who want to work, not in people who are interested only in reward. Benefits questions are appropriate after the company has made you an offer.

7. *If this is a starting position, do not badger the interviewer with questions concerning upward mobility.* The interviewer may view these types of questions as personally threatening. You should, however, quickly inquire if this position is a career opportunity. If it is, you can be sure that promotions are available for industrious workers.

8. *Ask questions about the type of work you will be doing.* The interview is your chance to find out if you would enjoy working for this company. You might ask for the interviewer to describe a typical work day for the person who will get this job. If the interview is conducted at the company offices, you might ask to see where you would be working.

9. *Do your homework.* Do not go for an interview knowing nothing about the company. Knowing about the company shows interest in the company. Know what the company produces or what services it renders; know whether the company is privately or publicly owned. Be aware of its financial health.

## Communication Session

*Reflection*

**What do you see as your major interviewing strengths? weaknesses?**

*Actualization*

*1.* **Prepare a résumé for a position such as you might apply for after graduation.**

*2.* **Working in pairs, each partner will interview the other for the particular job for which the résumé was prepared.**

## Payoffs

Now that you have read the material on interviewing, you should be able to

1.  Contrast the methods of interviewing.

2.  Be able to identify and phrase open and closed questions, primary and secondary questions, and neutral and directed questions.

3.  Know the steps in planning for an information-getting interview.

4.  Develop a schedule of questions for an information interview.

5.  Conduct an information interview.

6.  Explain the procedure used by job interviewers.

7.  Write a résumé.

8.  Participate in a job interview.

## Suggested Readings

The following two books are especially valuable:

**Robert L. Kahn** and **Charles F. Cannell.** *The Dynamics of Interviewing.* New York: John Wiley & Sons, 1957.

**Charles J. Stewart** and **William B. Cash.** *Interviewing: Principles and Practices.* Dubuque, Iowa: Wm. C. Brown Company, 1974. This newer book appears to be the best single source available on the subject.

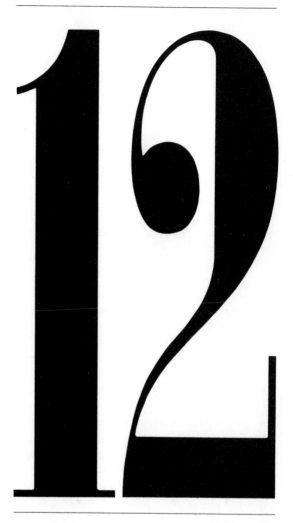

**Chapter Twelve:
Person-to-Person Communication:
Developing Relationships**

Virtually every skill we have considered in this textbook relates to your effectiveness as a communicator in the informal person-to-person communication setting. In this last chapter, we want to focus on the fundamental elements of the person-to-person setting that will give you further insight into building and developing social relationships. We see this chapter as a logical culmination of all that has preceded.

In this chapter, we will examine the levels of communication relationships, the role of communication in displaying interpersonal needs, and the basic criteria of sound interpersonal relationships. Then we want to provide you with three critical instruments that you can use to analyze various interpersonal communication encounters.

## Communication Relationships

You have different levels of social relationships with the various persons you know. The question to ask yourself is whether the kinds of relationships you have are really meeting your individual needs. In order to make such an assessment, you need to understand the nature of the various levels of communication. You could classify the kinds of communication relationships you have in four categories: the phatic level, the gossip level, the idea-exchange level, and the sharing-feelings level.

### The Phatic Level

On the phatic communication level, you acknowledge or recognize another person and you are willing to verbalize this recognition. It is identified by such statements as "How you doing?" "What do you say?" and "Great day, huh?" With none of these is more than a perfunctory reply expected. If in response to "How you doing?" the other person would stop and disclose in detail his or her current state of health, it is likely that you would be taken aback by the behavior. Phatic communication is not intended for sharing information; it is used to acknowledge recognition and it leaves the door open for exploration of higher levels of communication at some other time or in some other place. In terms of the communication functions we discussed in the very first chapter of this textbook, the phatic level serves an important function of meeting certain social expectations.

### Gossip Level

On the gossip level, two or more persons communicate by discussing other persons. Such statements as "Have you seen Bill lately—I hear he has a really great job" "Would you believe that Mary and Tom are going together? They never seemed to hit it off too well in the past" and "Irene is really working hard at losing weight. I saw her the other day talking with Suzie about the diet she's on" are typical of conversations on the gossip level.

The gossip level is considered a "safe" level of communication, for you can "gossip" for a long time with another person without really saying anything about yourself or without really learning anything about the other person. Gossip is a pleasant way to pass the time of day with people whom you know, but with whom you have no desire or need for a deeper relationship. Sometimes gossip is malicious; more often than not, however, gos-

Chapter Twelve:
Person-to-Person
Communication:
Developing
Relationships

245

sip is a way of interacting amicably with others without getting involved personally. You may notice that party conversation is largely on the gossip level.

## The Idea-exchange Level

On the idea-exchange level, persons share facts, opinions, beliefs, and values. This level of communication is common with friends and acquaintances. At the office, Zeb may talk with Hal about sports, Martha may talk with Ann about sewing, or Pete may talk with Jack about new cars. In more serious circumstances, Bart may talk with Al about the U.S. role in the Far East and Phyllis may talk with Myra about the Equal Rights Amendment. Although the discussions of foreign policy and women's rights may be "deeper" than chatter about sports or cars, both sets of conversations are on the idea-exchange level. On this level, you learn what the other person is thinking; through such conversations you can determine what you have in common, if anything, and you can decide whether or not you would like to have the relationship grow.

Remember the exercise you did on self-disclosure when you had to label disclosures as high-risk, moderate-risk, or low-risk? Most idea-exchange statements are disclosures of the low-risk or moderate-risk level. You can tell what you think about an idea or an action without revealing very much of the "real you." You may discover that many relationships seldom go beyond this level.

## Sharing-feelings Level

On the sharing-feelings level, persons not only reveal what they are thinking, but also how they feel about the ideas, actions, and behaviors of themselves and others. Although we have discussed the skill of describing feelings as an important part of the sending process on any communication level, the sharing of deep feelings is usually reserved for those whom you regard as close personal friends or intimate friends in an ongoing relationship.

Some achieve this level of communication with only one other person at any one time; many are on this level with members of the immediate family as well as with one or a few others; unfortunately, some seldom if ever achieve this level with anybody. We say "unfortunately" because it is on this level that you come to know and to really understand another person. Although it is unrealistic and may be undesirable to have such a relationship with many others, the presence of a sharing-feelings level of communication with at least some persons is regarded as a highly beneficial communication goal.

## Communication Session

*Reflection*
1. **Of all the persons you know, with what percentage do you relate on the phatic level, gossip level, idea-sharing level, feelings-sharing level?**

2. **On what basis do you determine on what level you will communicate with another person? When is this decision conscious or subconscious?**

*Discussion*
**In groups of four to six, discuss how each person determines the level on which he or she communicates with others.**

## Communicating Interpersonal Needs

What are the elements that operate to determine the nature of a communication relationship? Whether or not a relationship can be started, built, or maintained may well depend upon how well each person meets the interpersonal needs of the other. William Schutz provides an analysis of needs that we believe is very useful in helping people to determine whether their interpersonal communication is geared to meeting the interpersonal needs of others. Schutz discusses three interpersonal needs: for affection, for inclusion, and for control.[1]

### Affection

The need for affection is the need to express and to receive love. The "personal" individual is one who can express and receive affection effortlessly. He or she gets a joy out of relationships with others and his or her communication reflects that joy. People you know probably run the affection gamut. At one end of the spectrum are the "underpersonal" individuals. You have met them: they avoid close ties; they seldom show strong feelings toward others; and they shy away from those who show or who want to show affection. At the other end of the spectrum are the "overpersonal" individuals. You have

[1]William C. Schutz, *The Interpersonal Underworld* (Palo Alto, California: Science and Behavior Books, 1966), pp. 18–20.

Chapter Twelve:
Person-to-Person
Communication:
Developing
Relationships

247

probably encountered them, too—they thrive on establishing "close" relationships with everyone; they think of all others as their close friends and they are free with use of terms of personal endearment; they confide in persons they have met for the first time; and they want all others to think of them as friends and to be interpersonally "open" with them.

## Inclusion

The need for inclusion involves the need to be in the company of others. Everyone has some need to be social. Yet again, because people are individuals their inclusion behavior varies widely. At one extreme is the "undersocial" person who wants to be left alone.

*Some people are happy to be left alone.*

Although this person may occasionally seek company or may enjoy being included with some others if he or she is specifically invited, being around people is not the normal behavior. Whether this person finds the company of others threatening, whether he or she treasures solitude, or whether he or she has some other reason, much time is spent alone. At the other extreme is the "oversocial" person who needs constant companionship and dislikes or even fears being alone. If there is a party, he or she is there; if there is no party, then he or she starts one. The door is always open—everyone is welcome, and he or she expects others to welcome him or her. The ideal, of course, is to be comfortable alone or with others. The social person does not need constant company to feel fulfilled. His behavior is a cross between the loner and the social butterfly.

## Control

The need for control involves the need to feel that one is a responsible person successfully coming to grips with his environment. Again, how you respond to this need may vary somewhere between extremes. At one end is the person who shuns responsibility—he does not want to be in charge of anything. The "abdicrat," as he is called by Schutz, is extremely submissive and is afraid to make decisions or accept responsibility. At the other end is the person who likes to be—indeed who needs to be—in charge. The "autocrat"

must dominate others at all times. He usurps responsibility and makes every decision. The ideal could be called the "democrat." He is comfortable either leading or following. He can take charge when need be, but he can follow equally well. He stands behind his ideas, but he is not reluctant to submit when someone has a better idea.

On all three of these needs most of us fall somewhere along a continuum rather than at either of the extremes. Through our communication we display where we stand relative to each of these needs. As we interact with others we see whether their affection, inclusion, and control needs seem compatible with ours. As you see your relationships with others forming and breaking apart, you may well see your communication display of these needs determining or at least playing a part in the defining of the relationship.

## Communication Session

*Reflection*

Consider a person with whom you have a close interpersonal relationship. Does the above discussion help to explain the success of this interpersonal relationship? If so, how? If not, why not?

*Actualization*

1. On a 1 to 5 scale (1 low, 5 high), how would you rate yourself on the following:

   A. Need to express affection    1 2 3 4 5

   B. Need to receive affection from others    1 2 3 4 5

   C. Need to be included with other people in bull sessions, informal gatherings, and parties    1 2 3 4 5

   D. Willingness to include others with you to spend your leisure time    1 2 3 4 5

   E. Need to be in charge of situations in which you are involved    1 2 3 4 5

   F. Willingness to allow others to be in charge in situations in which you are involved    1 2 3 4 5

2. Ask a close friend to rate you on these same six criteria.

*Discussion*

With this close friend, discuss the similarities and differences in your perceptions of your behavior. What accounts for any differences that might exist?

## Criteria of a Sound Communication Relationship

At this point in your life, you may have a solid friendship or close personal relationship with at least one person and perhaps with several others. Once a mutually satisfying relationship has been achieved, however, it becomes all too easy to be complacent. Some people assume that, because of mutual love and respect, a particular relationship will go on indefinitely; they may discover, however, that various stresses and strains can weaken and perhaps destroy even the strongest relationships. What qualities are needed to help us withstand the inevitable stresses and strains on our relationships with others? In sorting out suggestions from philosophers, psychologists, and communications experts, we believe that you stand an excellent chance of maintaining a sound communication relationship if three qualities are present: openness in communication, sensitivity in placement of reasonable demands, and restraint relative to the need to control.

### Openness in Communication

In an earlier chapter, we defined openness as a willingness to self-disclose and a willingness to receive feedback. A communication relationship is strengthened by the existence of a mutually satisfying blend of self-disclosure and feedback between the two persons. How can you tell whether you and another are sharing enough to keep the relationship growing? The best method is to discuss it. As the basis for a worthwhile discussion, we suggest the drawing and analysis of Johari windows.

The Johari window (named after its two originators, Joe Luft and Harry Ingham)[2] is a tool that you can use to examine the relationship between disclosure and feedback. The window is divided into four sections or panes as shown in Figure 12-1.

The first quadrant is called the "open" pane of the window. The open pane is used to represent everything about a person that he or she knows and freely shares with others. It also shows others' observations of him or his behavior that he is aware of. For instance, most people are willing to discuss biographical data, the kind of car they drive, where they go to school, their favorite restaurant, and countless other items of information. Moreover, most people are aware of certain of their mannerisms that others observe. A person may be well aware that he gets red when he is embarrassed or that he walks with a slouch when he is tired. If you were preparing a Johari window that represented your relationship with another person, you would include in the open pane all the items of information that you would be free to share with that other person.

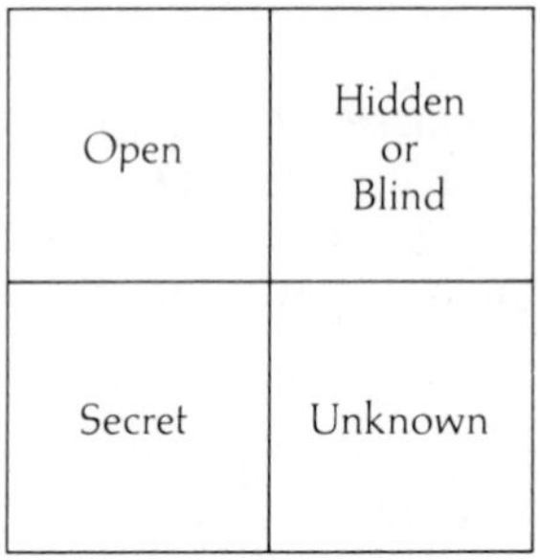


**Figure 12-1**

The second quadrant of the window is the "secret" pane of the window. The secret pane is used to represent all those things a person knows about himself or herself that he or she does not normally share with others. For instance, many people are less likely to share items of information that they regard as personal. This information may run the gamut from items like where Charley keeps his clean socks or why he does not care for squash to deep secrets that seem very threatening to him. If you were preparing a Johari window that represented your relationship with another person, you would include in the secret pane all the items of information that you are unwilling to share with that other person. Secret information moves into the open part of the window only when you change your attitude about revealing that specific information. If, for example, Kathy was engaged at one time but the information is something that she usually does not let people know, it

[2]Reprinted from *Group Processes: An Introduction to Group Dynamics* by Joseph Luft. By permission Mayfield Publishing Company (formerly National Press Books). Copyright © 1963, 1970 by Joseph Luft.

Chapter Twelve:
Person-to-Person
Communication:
Developing
Relationships

251

would be in the secret part of her window. If for some reason she decided to disclose this information to you, it would move into the open part of the Johari window that she drew to represent her relationship with you.

The third quadrant of the window is called the hidden or blind area. The hidden pane is used to represent information others know about a person that he or she is unaware of. Most people have blind spots—behaviors that are observable to others but for some reason are unknown to the person who does them. If Charley snores when he sleeps, if he always wrinkles up his nose when he does not like something, or if he gets a gleam in his eye when he sees a girl he would like to get to know, these may well be nonverbal behaviors that he is blind to. Information in the hidden area of the window moves to the open area through feedback from others. As discussed earlier, we are constantly getting feedback, but some of us are more receptive to that feedback than others. If you were preparing a Johari window that represented your relationship with another person, the size of the hidden or blind pane would depend upon how receptive you are to the verbal or nonverbal feedback of that person. For instance, if Ken draws Charley for a roommate at the dorm, he might announce to Charley that he snores or he might "feed back" information to Charley in a more subtle manner. If Charley does not choose to "hear" what Ken tells him, the blind spot continues. On the other hand, if Charley is receptive to such feedback, the blind or hidden pane gets smaller and the open pane enlarges.

The fourth and last quadrant of the window is called the "unknown." It represents information about a given person that is not known to anyone—not even the person himself. If no one is aware of this information, how do we know it exists? We know it exists because the unknown manifests itself on occasion. This manifestation might be called the "ah ha!" experience. For instance, let us suppose that you had never thought of yourself as a leader (therefore, your leadership capability is unknown to you) and let us say that your friend had never thought of you as a leader either. Now, let us further suppose that some emergency arises and you are forced to assume a leadership position. If your friend has an "ah ha!" experience and realizes how well you led the group, the information about your leadership abilities moves from the unknown part of the window to the hidden part of the window, where it is known to him but not to you. If your friend then shares this new-found perception of you with you by means of feedback, this information moves into the open part of your window, where it is known to both you and your friend. The second way the unknown becomes known is by means of your own unaided realization—after assuming this leadership position *you* might realize that you are a good leader. In such event, the information about your leadership ability moves into the secret part of the window, where it is known to you but not to your friend. Should you disclose this realization to your friend, it then moves into the open part of your window.

Thus as you can see, with each bit of self-disclosure or feedback, the sizes and shapes of the various panes of the window change. For each relationship you have with another person you can construct a window that represents the nature of that relationship in terms of the behaviors we have been discussing. Let us look at four different representations and consider what they mean.

Figure 12-2 shows a relationship in which the open area is very small. The person is not sharing much information about himself and is blind to what the other person knows or thinks about him. This window is typical of a relationship during the first stages of getting to know a person; it is also typical of a person who keeps to himself and does not want, desire, or need to interact on more than a superficial level with others.

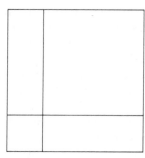

**Figure 12-3**

Figure 12-3 shows a relationship in which a person is willing to share his thoughts and feelings, but gets or is receptive to very little feedback from the other person. Such a person may perceive himself to be very open in his communication. Yet his communication is limited by his unwillingness or lack of interest in learning about what others observe.

Figure 12-4 shows a relationship in which a person seeks out and is very receptive to feedback but is quite reluctant to share much of himself. He wants to hear what others have

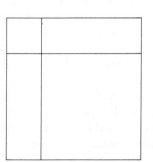

**Figure 12-2**

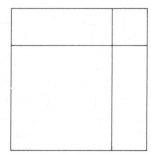

**Figure 12-4**

Chapter Twelve:
Person-to-Person
Communication:
Developing
Relationships

253

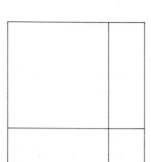

Figure 12-5

## Communication Session

*Reflection*
**Regarding the persons you communicate with on a more or less regular basis, does the open part of your window tend to be large or small? Explain?**

*Actualization*
**Working with an intimate or a close friend, each of you draw a window that represents your perception of your relationship with the other. Then each of you draw a window that represents what you perceive to be the other's relationship with you. Share the windows. How do they compare? If there are differences in the representations, talk with your friend about them.**

observed, but he is not willing or is afraid to disclose his observations or feelings.

Figure 12-5 shows a relationship in which a person both seeks out and is very receptive to feedback and is willing to share information and feelings he has. This is the kind of window we would expect to see depicting a close relationship of friends and/or intimates. Even though Figure 12-5 is the best model of communication for friends and intimates, the windows of Figures 12-2, 12-3, and 12-4 depict most of our communication relationships. Although no one need share every idea or feeling with others and no one need be receptive to every person's reaction to him, having a relatively large open pane is conducive to good interpersonal communication.

## Sensitive Placing of Realistic Demands

It is unlikely that two people can be close to each other for very long without one or both seeing in the other behaviors that he or she would like to see changed. In a good interpersonal relationship, participants may place demands upon each other, but the demands must be realistic and the demands must be sensitively communicated.

Realistic demands are those that each person is capable of fulfilling without harm to the individual. A woman may demand that her husband give up sports—a man may demand that his wife give up seeing her women friends. Neither of these demands is realistic. Although each of these demands may be capable of being fulfilled, neither is likely to be fulfilled without hurting the other individual. It may well be realistic, on the other hand, for the woman to demand that her husband limit the total hours he gives to sports or for the man to demand his wife limit the total hours she spends with women friends.

How such demands are placed is every bit as important as the nature of the demands

*Demands must be realistic.*

Chapter Twelve:
Person-to-Person
Communication:
Developing
Relationships

255

themselves. Descriptiveness (rather than judgment), provisionalism (rather than dogmatism), and equality (rather than superiority) are all communication skills that should be used in the phrasing of these demands. We have already seen that defensiveness is easily aroused when discussion centers on a subject one or both persons feel very deeply about.

## Restraint of the Need to Control

In each person, the control need varies from strong to weak. Yet even persons with relatively low control needs may attempt to exercise control when they perceive that the behavior of the other person is changing the nature of the communication relationship. All too often, unfortunately, when two people enter into a relationship they firmly believe that both (especially the other) will forever be as they were at the beginning of that relationship. Have you never heard comments like "She wasn't interested in going back to school when I first met her" or "He's a different person—he joined Kiwanis and now he wants to spend all his free time 'doing good'"? Sometimes changes in one person in a relationship are so great and in such a direction that the relationship cannot be maintained. Some deterioration in marriages may be attributed to such developments. When a person perceives himself or herself as threatened by changes in another, he or she may experience a strong desire to place controls on the other

person in order to halt or alter the perceived change.

We must recognize, however, that change is a part of growth. Just because two persons are joined in a relationship does not preclude the need or desirability of change. What are the alternatives to trying to control the other person? If the relationship is to continue, either the threatened person must change with the other or must adapt to the particular change. If the wife goes back to school to study for a degree, either the husband must involve himself in the subject matter she is studying or he must change his approach to his wife who is achieving a different education level. Either the wife must share her husband's interest in Kiwanis or she must adapt to his change in time priorities.

## Analyzing Interpersonal Communication

Of all the forms of communication, interpersonal communication is the most difficult to analyze and evaluate. Why? Because the greatest amount of our interpersonal communication is in informal settings with no "audience." Moreover, the flow is quick, speaker and receiver switch roles rapidly, a response may be as short as one or two words, and some or much of the meaning is sent and verified by nonverbal means.

Nevertheless, to say that personal communication is beyond analysis begs the question. Since you can improve your communication by analyzing what you are doing and how you are doing it, you need some objective system of analysis. To provide a working base for an evaluation instrument, let us take a look at criteria for communication effectiveness and see how these fit together into an interpersonal analysis profile.

The key to an analysis is determining effectiveness. Since communication involves sharing meaning with another, effectiveness depends upon communication of meaning. If each partner in a conversation really "understands" or "hears" what the other is saying, then communication has taken place. Of course, the analysis of effectiveness, or outcome, is complicated by the importance of the communication, the length of time involved, and the complexity. A one-hour encounter with your boy friend or girl friend on an important issue over which you are really at odds requires a considerably higher level of communication skill than a three-minute encounter with an old friend about getting together for lunch. Likewise, the analysis of each encounter would require differing degrees of skill.

All right, let us consider two sets of questions on which the evaluation instrument will be based:

1. *What was the apparent purpose of the encounter?* Was it for enjoyment? Fulfilling social expectations? Building a relationship? Negotiating with others? Exchanging information? Problem solving? Influencing?

2. *How were the elements of communication handled?* Did the sender himself or the receiver himself contribute to or detract from the effectiveness? Did the verbal or nonverbal message contribute to or detract from the communication? Were any communication barriers present? Were the barriers reduced or eliminated as the encounter continued? Did the barriers interfere with effectiveness?

Before presenting the evaluation instruments themselves, we need to consider who should analyze your interpersonal communication. Because there is seldom a third-party observer present during your conversations, you may have to make the analysis yourself after the fact. Such an analysis is difficult, but it can be done. After an encounter, you have feelings about whether it was satisfactory or not; and it is useful to take the time to "replay" it. You can determine whether your communication is effective and why. Of course, you should be an even more effective critic of encounters you are able to observe.

The first instrument we will consider is a descriptive-analytical, after-the-fact procedure (see Figure 12-6 on page 258). With this instrument, you can analyze why communication was or was not successful.

The second instrument we will consider enables you to evaluate the means (see Figure 12-7 on pages 259–260). This instrument calls for you to replay the confrontation noting the presence or absence of various skills.

Chapter Twelve:
Person-to-Person
Communication:
Developing
Relationships

257

## Communication Session

*Reflection*

**Are you able to be objective in self-analysis? Under what circumstances?**

*Actualization*

**Using either analysis form (Figure 12-6 or 12-7) as the instrument, analyze one of your communication encounters. Select one that occurred during the past day or two so that the dialogue is fresh in your mind.**

## Payoffs

In analyzing person-to-person communication, you should now be able to

1. Explain the communication levels and determine upon which level you communicate with others.

2. Define interpersonal needs.

3. Discuss the criteria of a sound communication relationship.

4. Draw a Johari window.

5. Analyze a communication encounter.

## Suggested Readings

**Sidney M. Jourard.** *Healthy Personality.* New York: Macmillan Publishing Co., 1974. Although the entire book is worth reading you should find Chapter 10, "Personal Relations and Healthy Personality" especially valuable.

**Joseph Luft.** *Group Process: An Introduction to Group Dynamics.* Palo Alto, California: Mayfield Publishing Company, 1970. Contains a complete explanation of the Johari window.

**William C. Schutz.** *The Interpersonal Underworld.* Palo Alto, California: Science and Behavior Books, 1966. It is in this book that Schutz explains in detail his research on the interpersonal needs of inclusion, affection, and control.

Figure 12-6

## Communication Analysis: Descriptive

### 1.

Participants:

### 2.

Apparent purpose of the encounter:

### 3.

Outcome – what was the result?

### 4.

Describe the entire encounter. Use dialogue wherever possible.

### 5.

List the reasons for success or failure of the communication:

Figure 12-7                                                                 259

## Communication Analysis: Skills

**Participants:**

**Apparent purpose of the encounter:**

**Outcome – what was the result?**

Play back the dialogue as you remember it. Indicate whether or not various skills were employed in the dialogue. Describe their use and consider their relative effectiveness:

**Climate skills:**

| ☐ Empathy | ☐ Equality |
|---|---|
| ☐ Descriptiveness | ☐ Openness to others – self-disclosure |
| ☐ Provisionalism | ☐ Openness to others – feedback |

**Receiver skills:**

| ☐ Listening | ☐ Questioning |
|---|---|
| ☐ Feedback | ☐ Interpreting |
| ☐ Paraphrasing | ☐ Evaluating |
| ☐ Supporting statements | ☐ Feedback on personal style |

**Sender skills:**

| | |
|---|---|
| ☐ Separating fact from inference | ☐ Using specific and concrete symbols |
| ☐ Dating | ☐ Fluency |
| ☐ Indexing | ☐ Crediting |
| ☐ Accuracy in symbol selection | ☐ Describing feelings |

**What barriers, if any, developed in the encounter?**
**How were they made apparent? How were they met?**

| | |
|---|---|
| ☐ Transfer stations | ☐ Inappropriate responses |
| ☐ Information overload | ☐ Defensiveness |
| ☐ Noise | ☐ Overaction |
| ☐ Suspicion | ☐ Hidden agenda |
| ☐ Gaps | |

Part E: Appendixes

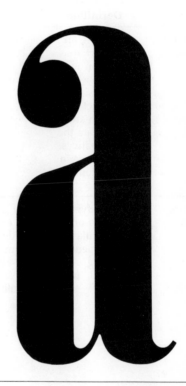

Appendix a:
Glossary of Basic Communication
Skills

| Skill | Definition | Use | Procedure | Example | Pages |
|-------|-----------|-----|-----------|---------|-------|
| **Accurate Symbol Selection** | Selecting words to represent thoughts and feelings that are recognized by others in our culture as symbolizing those thoughts and feelings. | To increase the probability of sender decoding message accurately. | **1.** Mentally phrase your idea. **2.** Do key words truly represent your meaning? **3.** If not, make appropriate substitutions. | ''Bill, would you go get my watch off the [thinks 'hutch' mentally corrects] buffet?'' | 86-87 |

| Skill | Definition | Use | Procedure | Example | Pages |
|---|---|---|---|---|---|
| **Arbitration, Seeking** | Finding an impartial person who, after hearing both sides of a conflict, will weigh and evaluate the alternatives and make a decision for you. | To resolve conflict when other methods have failed. | **1.** Agree on an arbitrator. **2.** Make sure arbitrator is competent to make decision. **3.** Make a verbal contract to abide by arbitrator's decision. | "I can see that we're dead-locked. How about asking Dr. Wright's opinion and going along with what she says?" | 166-167 |
| **Crediting Others** | Identifying the source of a particular statement or feeling. A verbal "foot-note." | To give credit to others in order to con-firm them and to avoid possible hard feelings. | When you are using ideas you got from others, include their names— give credit to them—when you state the ideas. | No credit: "We've got to make some changes in our course offer-ing. I think we should offer a course in attitude change." Crediting: "We've got to make some changes in our course offer-ings. Laura suggested we offer a course in attitude change, and I agree." | 92-94 |

Appendix a:
Glossary of
Basic
Communication
Skills

265

| Skill | Definition | Use | Procedure | Example | Pages |
|-------|-----------|-----|-----------|---------|-------|
| **Crediting Self—Making "I" Statements** | Identifying *yourself* as the source of a particular idea or feeling. | To transmit information accurately, to help receiver fully understand, to avoid creating defensiveness, to acknowledge personal responsibility, and to avoid allness. | When an idea, an opinion, a feeling is *yours*, say so. | Instead of saying "Maury's is the best restaurant in town," say "*I believe Maury's is the best restaurant in town.*" | 93-94 |
| **Dating** | Indicating *when* the data were true. | To avoid the pitfalls of language that allow you to speak of a dynamic world in static terms. | Verbally indicate the time period in which data were observed. | When Jake says "How good a hitter is Steve?" Mark replies by dating his evaluation: "*When I worked with him two years ago*, he couldn't hit the curve." | 83-84 |
| **Describing Behavior** | Accurately recounting specific observable actions of another without labeling the behavior as good or bad, right or wrong. | To create a supportive climate, to give helpful feedback, and to help support descriptions of feelings. | **1.** Observe the behavior. **2.** Report only what you observed. **3.** Refrain from judging the merit of the observation. | Instead of saying "She is such a snob," say "She has walked by us three times now without speaking." | 42-43 |

| Skill | Definition | Use | Procedure | Example | Pages |
|---|---|---|---|---|---|
| **Describing Feelings** | A sender statement that puts his or her emotional state into words. | For self-disclosure; to teach people how to treat you. | **1.** Get in touch with the feelings you are having. Identify them— hate? anger? joy? <br><br> **2.** Credit your feelings— make an "I" statement. <br><br> **3.** Make sure the statement contains an emotion. <br><br> **4.** Describe the specific cause of the feeling, if known. | "I'm depressed and discouraged because I didn't get the job." <br><br> "I'm feeling very warm and loving toward you right now." | 94-98 |
| **Descriptive-ness** (See Describing Behavior and Describing Feelings.) | | | | | |

Appendix a:
Glossary of
Basic
Communication
Skills

267

| Skill | Definition | Use | Procedure | Example | Pages |
|---|---|---|---|---|---|
| **Discussion** | Verbal weighing and considering of the pros and cons of the issues in conflict. | To resolve conflict. | **1.** Be cooperative, not competitive. **2.** Be objective in presentation. **3.** Be open in stating feelings and beliefs. **4.** Be open to possible solutions. **5.** Paraphrase others' statements. | "Now if I understand what you've been saying, you think we should get married in September because by then we will have both graduated. I guess that makes sense, but I'm afraid if we wait that long it will hurt our relationship . . ." | 160, 162-163 |
| **Empathizing** | Being able to detect and identify the the immediate affective state of another. Responding in an appropriate manner. | To create or to promote a supportive climate. | **1.** Listen actively to what the person is saying. **2.** Try to recall or to imagine what you would feel like under those same circumstances. **3.** Say something that indicates your sensitivity to those feelings. | When Jerry says "I really feel embarrassed about wearing braces in college," Mary empathizes and replies, "Yeah, I can understand that—I remember the things I had to put up with when I wore braces." | 38-40 |

| Skill | Definition | Use | Procedure | Example | Pages |
|---|---|---|---|---|---|
| **Equality** | Seeing others as worthwhile as self. | To create or promote a supportive climate. | **1.** Consider what you are about to say.<br><br>**2.** Does it contain words or phrases that indicate or imply that you as sender are in some way superior to the receiver?<br><br>**3.** If so, recast the sentence to alter the intent. | Instead of saying "As you gain maturity you'll learn how to cope with these situations," say "That was a difficult one. But handling difficult ones helps you gain the experience —and we all need experience to help us with special cases." | 45-46 |
| **Evaluating** | Placing a value judgment on what has been said or done. | Limited to when another person asks for evaluation. Unsolicited evaluation can and often does cause defensiveness. | **1.** Make sure the context calls for or allows evaluation to be given.<br><br>**2.** Precede a negative statement with a related positive one.<br><br>**3.** Focus on only one behavior at a time.<br><br>**4.** Include what the person can do to improve. | Instead of criticizing a speech by saying "That's a bad example, Joe" say, "Most of your supporting statements do the job, but that example doesn't develop the idea very clearly." | 72-73 |

Appendix a:
Glossary of
Basic
Communication
Skills

269

| Skill | Definition | Use | Procedure | Example | Pages |
|-------|-----------|-----|-----------|---------|-------|
| Feedback, Giving | Responses to a person that provide that person with information about himself. | To give people new information about themselves. To help them see themselves as others see them. | 1. Given only when the person indicates a readiness. 2. Should be positive as well as negative. 3. Should be specific rather than general. 4. Give the feedback at the earliest possible time. 5. Direct the feedback toward behavior a person can do something about. 6. Phrase feedback descriptively rather than evaluatively. | Carol says, "Bob, I've noticed something about your behavior with Jenny, would you like to hear it?" After Bob assures her that he would, she continues, "Well the last few times we've all been together, whenever Jenny starts to relate an experience, you interrupt her and finish telling the story." | 75-76 |

| Skill | Definition | Use | Procedure | Example | Pages |
|---|---|---|---|---|---|
| **Feedback, Receiving** | Creating a climate in which others feel comfortable giving you feedback. | To get information that will help you better understand yourself and your effect on others. | 1. Ask for feedback only when you are really willing to hear it—outline what you are willing to hear feedback on. 2. Avoid verbal-nonverbal contradictions. 3. Paraphrase what you hear. 4. Show others that you are appreciative of what they have told you. | Mary asks, "Tim, when I'm in a group do I talk too loud?" Tim replies, "Now that you mention it, Mary, you really do—and it's kind of embarrassing to me." "Thank you for being honest with me, Tim." | 53-55 |
| **Indexing** | Verbally accounting for individual differences. | To avoid allness in speaking. | When talking about an individual member of a group, acknowledge potential for individual differences. | **George:** "He's a politician, and I don't trust him." **Bill:** "Whether politicians are dishonest in general or not, we don't know Petrowski, and he may be honest." | 84-85 |

Appendix a:
Glossary of
Basic
Communication
Skills

271

| Skill | Definition | Use | Procedure | Example | Pages |
|---|---|---|---|---|---|
| **Interpreting** | Attempting to point out an alternative or hidden meaning to an event. | To help a person see the possible meanings of words, actions, and events. | **1.** Consider your motives for interpreting. **2.** Phrase an alternative to the sender's interpretation —one that is intended to help the sender see that other interpretations are available. | **Pam:** Sue must really be angry with me —Yesterday she walked right by me at the market and didn't even say 'hi.'" **Paula:** "Maybe she's not angry at all— maybe she just didn't see you." | 73-74 |
| **Intrapersonal Messages, Identifying** | Analysis of which kinds of statements are controlling behavior: critical-evaluative; emotional reaction; or rational analysis. | To determine how you develop self-fulfilling prophecies. | **1.** Record what was said. **2.** Label it appropriately. | "And in the midst of the discussion I said, 'I won't do it—you can't make me!' Wow, my emotions really con-trolled my behavior on that one." | 28-29 |
| **Listening** (See also Paraphrasing, Supporting, Questioning, Interpreting, Evaluating.) | Making sense out of what you hear. | To receive oral communica-tion. | **1.** Get ready to listen. **2.** Shift from speaker to listener completely. **3.** Listen actively. **4.** Withhold evaluation. | [Not applicable.] | 61-64 |

| Skill | Definition | Use | Procedure | Example | Pages |
|-------|-----------|-----|-----------|---------|-------|
| **Negotiating** | Resolving conflict through trade-offs. | To resolve conflict when people will not change their positions. | **1.** Determine whether activities in conflict cannot both be accomplished. **2.** Are negotiable elements of fairly equal importance? **3.** Suggest a compromise position or suggest that if one person's idea is followed now the other's will be followed next. | "You've got to get to the store, and I've got to get this paper done. I'll drive you to the store tonight and help you with the shopping if you'll help me by typing my paper tomorrow morning." | 166 |
| **Paraphrasing** | Restatement of the content or intent of the sender's verbal message. | To increase listening efficiency; to avoid message confusion; to discover sender's motivation. | **1.** Actively listen to the message. **2.** Decode the message. **3.** Reencode the message into your own symbols. **4.** Try making your statement either more general or more specific than original. | **Julia:** "I saw the best movie—you have to see it." **Tony:** (content paraphrase) "I take it that you really like the plot." (intent paraphrase) "Sounds like the movie really made you happy." | 65-67 |

Appendix a:
Glossary of
Basic
Communication
Skills

273

| Skill | Definition | Use | Procedure | Example | Pages |
|---|---|---|---|---|---|
| **Perception Checking** | A verbal statement that tests your understanding of how another person feels. | To clarify the meaning of nonverbal behavior. | **1.** Watch the behavior of another. **2.** Decode perception. **3.** Ask your-self: what does that behavior mean to me? **4.** Choose appropriate symbols for encoding. **5.** Make sure encoding is descriptive. | **Gary:** "I think we should rent costumes for the party." **Allan:** (Knits his brows and frowns as Gary talks.) **Gary:** "I get the feeling that you are not pleased with the idea of renting costumes." | 121-123 |
| **Problem-solving Method** | An organized procedure for solving problems. | To settle conflicts cooperatively; To help individuals and groups solve problems. | **1.** Identify the problem. **2.** Analyze the nature of the problem. **3.** Suggest possible solutions. **4.** Select the solution that best meets the needs. **5.** Implement the solution. | See detailed example on page 197. | 194-198 |

| Skill | Definition | Use | Procedure | Example | Pages |
|-------|-----------|-----|-----------|---------|-------|
| **Provision-alism** | A statement that reflects a tentative approach to a particular problem. | Allows you to express your opinion, but recognizes that others may have valid ideas; helps create or maintain a positive communication climate. | **1.** Consider what you are about to say. **2.** Determine whether it contains a wording that shows an attitude of finality, positiveness, or allness. **3.** If it does, add a qualifying statement that recognizes (a) that the statement is your opinion or (b) that the statement may not be entirely true or only true under these circumstances. | Instead of saying "That was a horrible movie," say "Others may have liked it, but I didn't care for it at all." | 43-45 |

Appendix a:
Glossary of
Basic
Communication
Skills

275

| Skill | Definition | Use | Procedure | Example | Pages |
|-------|-----------|-----|-----------|---------|-------|
| **Questioning** | Getting more information about a situation. | To help get a more complete picture before making other comments; to help a shy person open up; to clarify meaning. | **1.** Determine motives for questioning. **2.** Determine what kind of information you need to know. **3.** Phrase question(s) to achieve the goal. **4.** Make sure paralanguage is accurate. | **Mary:** "Well, we've dated a few times." **Sue:** "What do you mean by a few times?" | 70-71 |
| **Self-disclosure** | Sharing biographical data, personal ideas, and feelings that are unknown to the other person. | To create or maintain a positive communication climate. | **1.** Disclosure should be an acceptable risk. **2.** Should move to deeper levels. **3.** Should be part of an ongoing relationship. **4.** Should be reciprocal. **5.** Should consider receiver's ability to handle the disclosure. | May tells her current boy friend, "I've been engaged three times before." | 47-52 |

| Skill | Definition | Use | Procedure | Example | Pages |
|-------|-----------|-----|-----------|---------|-------|
| **Separating Fact from Inference** | Being able to differentiate between a verifiable statement and a conclusion drawn from or about the phenomenon observed. | To avoid embarrassment, minor inconvenience, or serious problems resulting from behavior based on inferences rather than facts. | **1.** Determine if you are inferring or if you are reporting observation. **2.** Recognize that inference may not be true. **3.** Do not act on inferences as though they are facts. | Ted observes a truck with "Ace Plumbing" on the door parked in the drive next door, and says, "Looks like the Joneses got a problem." He pauses, and says, "Well, at least I'm inferring that the truck indicates some problem." | 80-82 |
| **Speaking Fluently** | Speaking in smooth, uncluttered sentences. Avoiding such nonfluencies as vocal segregates, "you know," and empty expletives. | To avoid antagonizing the receiver; to decrease noise; to improve message reception. | **1.** Become aware of the nonfluencies you use. **2.** In practice sessions, see how long you can talk without using a nonfluency. **3.** In conversation, mentally note usages. | "Will you get me, uh, you know, a glass of water? Let me try that again—Will you get me a glass of water, please?" | 88-91 |

Appendix a:
Glossary of
Basic
Communication
Skills

277

| Skill | Definition | Use | Procedure | Example | Pages |
|---|---|---|---|---|---|
| **Specific, Concrete Symbols** | Using words that indicate a single item within a category or a single representation of an abstract value. | To help receiver picture a thought analogous to sender's. | Whenever you find yourself using a word that leaves possible ambiguity or that does not allow the receiver to "see" exactly what you mean, select a more specific or concrete term. | Instead of saying "Get that junk off the table" say "Get the toys off the table." Instead of saying "He drives a cool car," say "He drives a red Jaguar convertible." | 87-88 |
| **Supporting** | Saying something that soothes, reduces tension, or pacifies. | To help the sender to feel better about himself or what he has said or done. | 1. Actively listen to the message. 2. Try to empathize with the person's feelings. 3. Phrase a reply that confirms the person's right to these feelings. | "I'm so disappointed I didn't make the team." "I can understand that, you worked so hard." | 69-70 |

**Appendix b:**
**Glossary of Communication**
**Problems**

| Problem | Defined | Cost | Suggestions for Solving | Pages |
|---------|---------|------|-------------------------|-------|
| **Aggression** | Attempting to force another to accept your ideas through physical or psychological threats or actions. | Conflicts are created or escalated. | **1.** Resist the urge to threaten. **2.** Describe your feelings. | 159-160 |

| Problem | Defined | Cost | Suggestions for Solving | Pages |
|---|---|---|---|---|
| **Competitive Attitude** | Viewing conflict as a win-lose situation. | Creates or escalates conflict. Heightens competitive feelings in others. | 1. Approach situation cooperatively. 2. Demonstrate your desire to resolve perceived conflict in a mutually beneficial way. | 154-157 |
| **Defensiveness** | A negative feeling and/or behavior that results when a person feels threatened. | Interferes with open communication. | 1. Be descriptive rather than evaluative. 2. Be problem-solving rather than control oriented. 3. Be spontaneous rather than strategic. 4. Be empathic rather than neutral. 5. Be equal rather than superior. 6. Be tentative rather than dogmatic. | 141-142 |
| **Evaluative Responses** | Statements that judge a person's ideas, feelings, and behaviors. | Creates defensiveness. | Be descriptive rather than evaluative. | 140-141 |

| Problem | Defined | Cost | Suggestions for Solving | Pages |
|---------|---------|------|-------------------------|-------|
| Gaps | Communication distances between persons or groups of people. | Message distortion, stereotyping, prejudice. | 1. Recognize that communication becomes more difficult as differences between communicators are increased. 2. Build bridges between *individuals*. 3. Index statements carefully. | 136-138 |
| Hidden Agenda | A reason or motive for behavior that is undisclosed to the other participant(s). | It may destroy trust between individuals; it causes defensiveness; it is manipulative. | 1. A sender should self-disclose motives; 2. A receiver should describe behavior and perception check. | 144-146 |
| Inappropriate Responses | Responses that do not meet the expectation of the other person, or responses that disconfirm the other person. | Cause defensiveness. | Substitute paraphrasing, questioning, interpreting, or supporting. | 139-141 |

| Problem | Defined | Cost | Suggestions for Solving | Pages |
|---------|---------|------|-------------------------|-------|
| **Incongruous Responses** | Messages whose verbal cues conflict with the non-verbal cues. | Cause defensiveness. | **1.** A sender should be honest and describe his true feelings.<br><br>**2.** A receiver should perception check. | 140-141 |
| **Information Overload** | Receiving more information than you can process at that time; or sending more than the other person can process. | Loss of at least part of the message. Possible frustration. | **1.** A receiver should use selective perception and if possible paraphrase.<br><br>**2.** A sender should limit details, group ideas, and emphasize key points. | 132 |
| **Interrupting Response** | Breaking in before the sender has finished. | Creates climate of superiority. | Allow person to finish sentence or complete thought. | 139-140 |
| **Irrelevant Response** | One that bears no relationship to what has been said. | Tends to disconfirm, to make person question his own value. | Listen to what other person has to say; at least acknowledge that you heard. | 139 |

| Problem | Defined | Cost | Suggestions for Solving | Pages |
|---|---|---|---|---|
| **Noise, Physical** | External factors clogging the channels of communication. | Overrides or interferes with message reception. | **1.** Receiver can eliminate the noise or turn up powers of concentration.<br><br>**2.** Sender can compensate for the noise. | 132-133 |
| **Noise, Semantic** | Decoding with a different meaning than sender intends. | Distortion of meaning. | **1.** As sender, determine meanings, encode with care, analyze receivers to determine whether they are likely to understand language you have selected.<br><br>**2.** As receiver, listen actively and paraphrase if possible. | 133-134 |

| Problem | Defined | Cost | Suggestions for Solving | Pages |
|---|---|---|---|---|
| **Overreaction** | Reacting emotionally to a degree greater than the stimulus of the reaction—losing your head. | It short-circuits skills; disrupts communication. | **1.** If you feel yourself overreacting, try to disengage.<br><br>**2.** Try to describe feelings rather than overreacting.<br><br>**3.** Force yourself to go through steps of problem solving.<br><br>**4.** As a receiver, try not to act defensively; speak softly and carefully so as not to stimulate further overreaction. | 142-143 |
| **Surrender to Conflict** | Giving in to another for sole purpose of avoiding conflict. | Can become insufferable martyr. | **1.** Describe your feelings.<br>**2.** Credit your feelings. | 158 |

| Problem | Defined | Cost | Suggestions for Solving | Pages |
|---------|---------|------|------------------------|-------|
| **Suspicion** | An unhealthy fear of the unknown, the unusual, or people in authority. | Tremendous psychological pressure; prohibits open interaction. | 1. Build a climate of trust. 2. Practice placing responsibility in others. 3. Take note of benefits of trusting behavior. | 135-136 |
| **Tangential Response** | Statements that change the subject without truly responding appropriately. | Imply that sender's statement is not important enough to deal with. | Consider why a person makes a statement; then, before you change the subject, deal with the implications of the statement. | 140 |
| **Transfer Stations** | Chain-link communication that passes through several receivers before getting to destination. | Message distortion. Usually the greater the number of transfer stations, the greater the distortion. | 1. Create face-to-face settings whenever possible. 2. If message must be sent chain-link fashion, each individual receiver should paraphrase carefully. | 130-131 |

| Problem | Defined | Cost | Suggestions for Solving | Pages |
|---|---|---|---|---|
| **Withdrawal** | Removing one's self physically or psychologically from setting. | Conflicts are not resolved, only put off. | Resist urge to withdraw; describe feelings. | 157-158 |

**Index**